READINGS ON EQUAL EDUCATION
(Formerly *Educating the Disadvantaged*)

SERIES EDITOR

Edward P. St. John

ADVISORY PANEL

READINGS
ON EQUAL
EDUCATION

Volume 20

IMPROVING ACCESS AND COLLEGE
SUCCESS FOR DIVERSE STUDENTS

STUDIES OF THE GATES MILLENNIUM
SCHOLARS PROGRAM

Volume Editor
and Series Editor
Edward P. St. John

AMS PRESS, INC.
NEW YORK

READINGS ON EQUAL EDUCATION
VOLUME 20
Improving Access and College Success for Diverse Students
Studies of the Gates Millennium Scholars Program

ISSN 0270-1448
Set ISBN 0-404-10100-3
Volume 20 ISBN 0-404-10120-8
Library of Congress Catalog Card Number 77-83137

All AMS Books are printed on acid-free paper that meets the guidelines for performance and durability of the Committee on Production Guidelines for Book Longevity of the Council on Library Resources.

AMS PRESS, INC.
63 FLUSHING AVENUE – UNIT #221
BROOKLYN NAVY YARD, BLDG. 292, SUITE 417
BROOKLYN, NY 11205-1054, USA

Manufactured in the United States of America

FOREWORD

Deborah J. Wilds

Despite burgeoning college enrollments over the past two decades, persistent gaps exist in high school graduation and college-going for low-income students and youth of color. African-American and Hispanic students remain 30 percent less likely than White students to graduate from high school and less than half as likely to earn a college degree. The Advisory Committee on Student Financial Assistance estimates that approximately 400,000 college-qualified low-income students could not attend four-year colleges for financial reasons in 2001-02. Additionally, only 17 percent of low-income students earn bachelor's degrees by age 24 compared with 52 percent of students from upper-income families.

Given the educational demands of the twenty-first century and the wealth of this nation, the poor college preparation, attendance, and completion rates of students of color and low-income youth stand as one of the most outrageous and perilous forms of injustice in America today. As a nation, if we truly value our future, we must ensure that all young people complete high school with the knowledge and skills needed to be successful in college. However, that is only part of the equation. We must also ensure that they have the financial, academic, and social supports to access and successfully complete college.

Volume 20 of *Readings on Equal Education* presents research about one effort, the Gates Millennium Scholars (GMS), that is designed to increase financial access and degree completion for 20,000 high-achieving low-income students of color. GMS is a 20-

year, billion-dollar scholarship commitment for high-ability American Indian, Latino, African American and Asian Pacific American students by the Bill & Melinda Gates Foundation. The foundation is deeply committed to dramatically improving educational opportunities for the least advantaged in our nation. Its education program aims to significantly increase the number of students who graduate from high school prepared to succeed in college and work, and in our democracy as contributing and engaged citizens. Improving educational access through the creation of rigorous, relevant, and personalized high school environments and broadening financial access through targeted scholarships are strategies central to achieving these goals.

The foundation and its benefactors view GMS as an investment that will have multiple benefits by increasing undergraduate degree completion and broadening the pool of minority talent in graduate fields in which they are sorely underrepresented—science, math, engineering, computer science, education, and library science. Through GMS and its other scholarship programs, the foundation hopes to expand the diverse cadre of future leaders. The foundation is also committed to assessing the success of this initiative, while capturing knowledge about effective practice that can inform both policy and practice.

Shortly after the first scholarships were awarded in 2000, the foundation put a research program in place to evaluate the design, delivery, and impact of GMS, and, more generally, to better understand the key practices, experiences, and attributes that help prepare low-income minority youth for college and contribute to their sustained success in college and beyond. Some of the nation's best educational researchers were assembled through a Research Advisory Council (RAC) to guide and carry out the research. The foundation also contracted with The McKenzie Group (TMG) to evaluate the delivery of the GMS program, and with the National Opinion Research Center (NORC) at the University of Chicago to carry out a longitudinal survey of selected cohorts of GMS scholars and students who applied for the award but were not selected. The information collected in these studies serves as the initial research data for the program.

The studies presented in this volume are based on the initial survey and focus group findings on the first two GMS classes, which totaled over 5,000 scholars combined and more than 3,000 nonrecipients who serve as a comparison group. These initial research findings provide clear evidence that most GMS scholars overcame challenging circumstances, attended large urban high schools where they were often among a handful of students of color who were placed in rigorous college preparatory courses, and took advantage of those opportunities by excelling academically and by becoming leaders at their schools and in their communities. Initial research findings also indicate that most GMS scholars possess a sense of purpose, clear direction, and the kind of fortitude of character that motivates them to achieve. Having met some of the GMS scholars, I smile when I think of them because they are truly a phenomenal group of young people. These young people have survived against the odds, and they are succeeding in college at outstanding rates. Yet, despite all they have to offer to their campus communities, initial studies also show that they often find themselves battling to overcome stereotypes about who they are and what they can accomplish.

The researchers and writers of this volume of *Readings on Equal Education* share the foundation concern about the future of educational opportunities in the U.S. Through their research and analysis, they are seeking answers to critical questions about college access and success. They, as we at the foundation, are passionate about reforming our schools so that every school achieves consistently high outcomes for every child. They, as we, want to ensure that children from poor families have the same range of quality postsecondary opportunities available to them that are afforded to the sons and daughters of the affluent. I thank them for their dedication and commitment to these issues and to the young people whose lives they hope to impact through their scholarship. Special thanks to Edward St. John for the leadership he provided in the writing and editing of this volume.

The foundation and its administrative partners for GMS—the United Negro College Fund, the Hispanic Scholarship Fund, the American Indian Graduate Center, and the Organization of Chinese Americans, as well as the GMS Advisory Board are committed to the support and long-term success of each scholar. Much has been learned since the program's inception, and as the program matures we will learn even more. Because of the size and length of this scholarship commitment, coupled with the foundation's desire to track both scholars and nonrecipients, GMS is a natural experiment that provides a tremendous opportunity to improve the life outcomes of promising students and simultaneously document the impact of increased financial access and academic support on minority student success.

We hope that the studies contained within this volume will expand and enrich the knowledge base on how to improve educational access and degree attainment for students of color and other underserved students. We look forward to the contributions that GMS scholars will inevitability make to the nation. And, we await the future research that will document their accomplishments.

Deborah J. Wilds
Senior Program Officer
Bill & Melinda Gates Foundation
Seattle, WA

CONTENTS

VOLUME 20

WALTER R. ALLEN is Allan Murray Cartter Professor of Higher Education and Professor of Sociology, University of California, Los Angeles. His academic interests include diversity and equity in higher education and race, ethnicity and inequality. His most recent book is *African American Education: Race, Community, Inequality and Achievement—A Tribute to Edgar G. Epps* (co-edited with M. B. Spencer and C. O'Connor. London: JAI Press, Inc.). Dr. Allen holds a Ph.D. in sociology from the University of Chicago.

MARGUERITE BONOUS-HAMMARTH is director of Admissions and Relations with Schools at the University of California, Irvine. In her current position, she oversees implementation of system-wide and campus policies related to undergraduate admissions. Her current research and teaching interests focus on understanding factors that influence achievement and career success for ethnic minority students and for undergraduates in science and mathematics. She received her Ph.D. in education from the University of California, Los Angeles.

CHOONG-GEUN CHUNG is the senior statistician for the Indiana Project on Academic Success at Indiana University, Bloomington. His research interests are statistical models for school reform, access and persistence in higher education, and issues in minority representation in special education.

SUZANNE B. CLERY is a senior research associate at JBL Associates, Inc. Ms. Clery has her MBA from the University of Maryland and B.A. in Economics from Virginia Tech. She has been with JBL Associates for thirteen years. She has worked as an analyst on projects related to accreditation, educational outcomes, institutional characteristics and finance, and student characteristics and financial aid.

RASHNA GHADIALY is a research scientist at the National Opinion Research Center (NORC) at the University of Chicago. Her involvements include questionnaire development, monitoring data collection, preparing survey item data files and code books, and overall quality control. She is one of the coauthors of the GMS 2002 and 2003 Final Report. She serves as the research scientist for the Gates Millennium Scholars Tracking and Longitudinal Study.

YUQIN GONG is currently a graduate research assistant and a Ph.D. student in Educational Policy Studies at the University of Illinois at Urbana-Champaign. She previously held the position of lecturer at the Beijing Institute of Economics and Management.

SYLVIA HURTADO is professor and director of the Higher Education Research Institute at UCLA in the Graduate School of Education and Information Studies. Her recent co-authored books include *Enacting Diverse Learning Environments* (Jossey-Bass) and *Intergroup Dialogue: Deliberative Democracy in Schools, Colleges, Workplace, and Community* (University of Michigan Press). She was named among the top 15 influential faculty whose work has had an impact in the field by *Black Issues in Higher Education.*

THOMAS F. NELSON LAIRD received his Ph.D. in higher education from the University of Michigan and is currently a research analyst in the Center for Postsecondary Research at Indiana University. His research focuses on diversity-related programs and experiences that promote student success and preparation for effective citizenship in a pluralistic society.

JOHN B. LEE is currently the president of JBL Associates, Inc., an independent consulting firm that specializes in postsecondary education policy analysis. Previously, Dr. Lee worked for Abt Associates, the Education and Labor Committee of the U.S. House of Representatives, the Education Commission of the States, and Stanford Research International. He also spent time as an instructor, academic senate president, and president of the faculty union at Laney Community College in Oakland, California.

BRONWYN NICHOLS LODATO is a senior survey director at the National Opinion Research Center (NORC) at the University of Chicago in NORC's Education and Child Development Studies Department. She has 12 years of experience in project management on education studies at the elementary, secondary, and postsecondary levels. She serves as the project director for the Gates Millennium Scholars Tracking and Longitudinal Study.

RAYMOND M. LODATO is a survey director at the National Opinion Research Center (NORC) at the University of Chicago. He received his Ph.D. in political science from the University of Chicago in 1997 and is a lecturer in its undergraduate public policy program. He is the deputy project director of the Gates Millennium Scholars Tracking and Longitudinal Study.

DAVID R. MERKOWITZ, Ph.D., is president of Strategic Communications, a Washington, D.C. public affairs consulting firm. His experience encompasses education, politics, government, and journalism. Before starting his own company, he was Director of Public Affairs at the American Council on Education for nearly ten years. He has taught at four universities; been a newspaper reporter, editor, and syndicated columnist; and held senior staff positions in the U.S. Congress.

DAWN OWENS-NICHOLSON works as a data services professional and statistical consultant at the University of Illinois at Urbana-Champaign. She holds a master's degree in sociology and is interested in issues of racial and sexual equality in education and other areas of social interaction.

THOMAS E. PERORAZIO is a candidate for the Ph.D. at the University of Michigan Center for the Study of Higher and Postsecondary Education. His academic interests include the effects of globalization on research universities.

WILLIAM E. SEDLACEK is a professor of education and assistant director of the Counseling Center at the University of Maryland. His research interests include race, gender, and multicultural issues in higher education. He has specialized in developing alternative measures to tests and grades that predict student success. His most recent book is *Beyond the Big Test: Noncognitive Assessment in Higher Education* (Jossey-Bass, 2004).

HUNG-BIN SHEU is a doctoral student in counseling psychology at the University of Maryland. He is interested in multicultural issues and has conducted research on career development and subjective well-being of racial/ethnic minorities as well as multicultural counseling competency and training.

EDWARD P. ST. JOHN is a professor in the Department of Educational Leadership and Policy Studies at Indiana University. He will be Collegiate Professor of Education at the University of Michigan effective January 2005. He recently published *Refinancing the College Dream: Access, Equal Opportunity, and Justice for Taxpayers* (Johns Hopkins University Press, 2003) and co-edited *Incentive-Based Budgeting in Public Universities* (Edward Elgar, 2002) and *Reinterpreting Urban School Reform: Have Urban Schools Failed, or Has the Reform Movement Failed Urban Schools?* (SUNY Press, 2003). He holds an Ed.D. from Harvard and M.Ed. and B.S. degrees from the University of California, Davis.

SUSAN A. SUH (C. Phil., University of California, Los Angeles, 2001) is a doctoral candidate in the Department of Sociology at UCLA. Her research interests include race/ethnicity theory, sociology of higher education, workplace experiences, and race/class/gender perspectives. Ms. Suh is completing her dissertation work on the significance of race in the workplace experiences of Asian Pacific American academics in higher education. Prior to her interests in academia, she worked as an engineer after receiving a B.S. from Columbia University. She is the proud mother of Mina Min Delloro-Suh.

WILLIAM T. TRENT (Ph.D. in sociology, University of North Carolina, Chapel Hill) is professor of Educational Policy Studies and Sociology at the University of Illinois at Urbana-Champaign. He is a Fulbright Senior Scholar for 2003-2004. He is currently principal investigator for a three-year, IES-funded project examining pathways to careers in the academy for students of color.

MICHELE ZIMOWSKI is a senior methodologist at the National Opinion Research Center (NORC) at the University of Chicago. She received her Ph.D. in methodology from the University of Chicago and is the author of more than 40 publications and presentations in the statistical and methodological literature. Currently she is the statistician for the Gates Millennium Scholars Tracking and Longitudinal Study.

INTRODUCTION

IMPROVING ACCESS AND COLLEGE SUCCESS FOR DIVERSE STUDENTS: STUDIES OF THE GATES MILLENNIUM SCHOLARS PROGRAM

Edward P. St. John

Volume 20 of *Readings on Equal Education* initiates a new period in the history of the annual. I assume the role of series editor with an awareness of the critical challenges facing researchers, policymakers, and educators who are concerned about the future of equal educational opportunity in the United States. To understand how this volume contributes to a new agenda for research on equal education, it is important to briefly review the challenges facing those who are committed to promoting educational opportunity and ensuring academic success for an increasingly diverse population.

Facing Critical Challenges

While equal educational opportunity was central to education policy in the United States in the 1960s and 1970s, this emphasis has given way to policies that focus on educational excellence, privatization, and accountability. These shifts are global, affecting education policy not just in the U.S., but also worldwide. Rather than merely mourn the loss of the historic commitment to equity, it is important to consider the major arguments that underlie the current debates on education policy. In the current context we should consider the question of "equal education" from three vantage points.

The New Inequality

The nation's commitment to ensuring equal opportunity has declined since 1980. The percentage of students completing high school increased through the 1960s and the rates of college enrollment were nearly equal for African American and White high school graduates in the 1970s, but both of these equity indicators have worsened in the past two decades: there is now a substantial gap in college enrollment opportunities for African American and Hispanic high school graduates compared to their White peers, a new inequality (St. John, 2003). After a few decades of reductions in inequalities after *Brown*, the nation's commitment to equalizing educational opportunity vaporized.

Fifty years after *Brown v. Board of Education* (1954) there is greater racial isolation for African Americans in public schools than was true before the groundbreaking court decision (Fossey, 2003; Orfield & Eaton, 1996). State and federal policies on education and public finance can increase the inequalities in educational opportunity as well as reduce inequalities, depending on the effects of policies implemented at any point in time, compared to a prior period. For a brief period between 1954 and 1978, educational and public finance policies influenced a reduction in inequality, although it was never eliminated. As the socially progressive policies of the 1970s period gave way to new concerns about educational quality and taxpayer costs, new education and public finance policies were implemented that actually increased inequality once again—as measured by increases in high school drop-out rates, special education referrals, and inequalities in educational opportunity.

Some have argued that the 1970s were the aberration with respect to the federal commitment to higher education (Hearn & Holdsworth, 2003). If this turns out to be true, then researchers who are concerned about social equity must seek to find solutions that improve equity within the cost constraints imposed on these new conditions, possibly through restructuring current policies and programs (St. John, 2003). The commitment to social justice— including equal educational opportunity—is too important to give up.

Gaining Perspective on Equal Education

To understand why equal education has faded away from the forefront of educational and public finance policy, we need to consider the other claims that have replaced equal opportunity as a policy goal. In education policy, concerns about education quality predate the emphasis on equalizing educational opportunity. Before *Brown,* most education policy in the U.S. focused on expanding educational opportunity, adding to the generally accepted definition of education as a basic right. Efforts to provide, and even mandate, opportunity for K-12 education for all children, provide educational benefits to veterans after World War II, expand higher education, and provide mass higher education to the baby boom generation expanded the notion of the basic right to education.

Public concerns about the quality of education have periodically resurfaced, from the response to Russia's launching of the first satellite with passage of the *National Defense Education Act* (1958) to the excellence movement that emerged in response to the publication of *A Nation at Risk* (1983). Indeed, it can be argued that these concerns now dominate public policy on education, given the *No Child Left Behind Act* (2002). The recent efforts to refocus education policy on student achievement are appropriately characterized as a discourse about the right to a quality education, shifting the foci of education policies to raising standards of education for all, as a basic right, rather than equalizing the opportunity to attain an education.

In public finance policy on K-12 and higher education, it is critical to consider the underlying concern about improving efficiency. Both the movement to privatization of education and the shift to the use of loans as a means of financing higher education have an underlying intent of reducing costs to taxpayers. These policies have reduced the taxpayer cost of higher education in the U.S. by shifting a larger share of the cost to students and their families. Thus taxpayer costs are certainly an issue that needs to be openly and explicitly considered in the debates about education public policy.

However, concerns about costs need to be balanced with concerns about both quality and educational opportunity. Balancing quality gains with education costs can lead to a false image of efficiency unless equal education opportunity is brought into the merits used to judge education policy (St. John, 2003). While there have been gains in college enrollment rates for high school graduates, there is a great deal of evidence that a large number of qualified students have been left behind (Fitzgerald, in press; Lee, in press; St. John, 2003b; St. John, Chung, Musoba, Simmons, Wooden, & Mendez, 2004).

Forming a New Agenda

Fifty years after *Brown* and twenty years after initiating *Readings on Equal Education*, it is time to rethink roles of public education policy and public finance in educational opportunities. There are three major tasks in moving toward this goal.

Task 1: Assess the Impact of Interventions and Policies on Equal Educational Opportunity. It is critical to build an understanding of how educational policies influence equality in educational opportunity. It is essential to consider how reforms implemented with the intent of improving achievement-related outcomes actually influence educational opportunities for low-income students and minorities, as well as for others who have limited access to basic educational opportunities. All major reforms can have influence on educational opportunities whether or not those effects are intended.

Task 2: Examine Effects of Interventions and Policies on Excellence and Efficiency as well as Equity. It is also crucial to broaden the discourse about equal education to consider the concerns about quality and the efficient use of tax dollars, with an eye on the risk of creating false efficiencies. Therefore a challenge for those who advocate remedies that address educational inequalities is to consider both the costs of these reforms compared to the status quo as well as the impact of reform strategy on the education of the majority. The research on affirmative action conducted by its proponents (Bowen & Bok, 1998) provides an indication of the practice and political importance of making these linkages.

Task 3: Rethink the Role of Policy When Considering Implications of Policy Research. It is also important to rethink strategies, with an emphasis on illuminating workable changes in education and finance policies that encourage balance in educational outcomes. If research records the intended and unintended effects of current and alternative approaches to education policy, then it should be possible to think through new policy remedies. Thus, rather than merely endorsing and critiquing current policies, researchers can also engage in a process of thinking through alternatives to the status quo.

These tasks have more than merely political legitimacy. They are bold steps, rooted in the goal of finding balanced approaches to education and public finance policies. These tasks require sound research methods, informed by generally accepted theory. Given the limited consensus on education policy, using sound theory and methods to explore alternative policies represents a necessary step toward improving equality in educational opportunity.

About Volume 20

As a collective contribution to the research literature on equal education, volume 20 illustrates how the programs of philanthropists can provide natural experiments that test alternative approaches to public policy. The Gates Millennium Scholars (GMS) Program provides grants to high-achieving students of color with the intent of fostering a new generation of leadership in American society. The program has committed to funding about 1,000 new undergraduate students each year over a 20-year period, ensuring sufficient scholarship support to meet financial need through their undergraduate education and even through graduate school in selected fields. In addition to undertaking this 20-year commitment to student financial aid, the Bill and Melinda Gates Foundation collaborated with a team of research advisors to design a research program that could provide an honest evaluation of the effects of the program. In chapter 1, Merkowitz provides an overview of GMS and the research reported in this volume. He identifies the major themes that emerge from this initial round of research.

In the 2000-01 academic year, the GMS program not only funded the first freshman cohort, but also funded groups of continuing undergraduates and graduate students to fill the pipeline. In 2001-02 and subsequent years, about 1,000 new scholars received aid. As described by Nichols Lodato and her colleagues in chapter 2, the National Opinion Research Center (NORC) developed surveys of the 2000-01 and 2001-02 cohorts, sampling both recipients and nonrecipients. The students sampled as nonrecipients in these first two cohorts met the academic qualifications for GMS awards, but were not selected for financial or other reasons. While the sample populations surveyed include all qualified applicants, the GMS program is appropriately viewed as a natural experiment because noncognitive variables were used in selection (Sedlacek, 2004), rather than random assignment among qualified applicants.

Chapter 3 considers how the high schools of origin compare to the great majority of U.S. high schools. Trent, Gong, and Owens-Nicholson combine the files of the 2001 freshman cohort with a high school characteristics file. They examine how high schools that prepare high-achieving minority students compare to the typical high school.

As a second step in setting the context, in chapter 4, Allen, Bonous-Hammarth, and Suh examine the role of preparation for the survey population. Their study uses mixed methods. They analyze interviews with GMS students about their high school and early college experiences, illuminating the challenges students encounter in their adjustment to college. In addition, they use the 2001 cohort to examine the role of preparation in analyses of the college choice and adjustment processes. Thus, in combination with chapter 2, this chapter provides insights into the similarities between the recipients and nonrecipients. High-achieving students of color overcome many challenges on their journeys through college.

Chapter 5 presents the analysis of the impact of receiving GMS awards on financial access for recipients. Since awards were made somewhat more randomly in 2000 than in 2001, it was appropriate to start the analyses of the financial effects of the aid with the first freshman cohort. St. John and Chung examine the impact of the receipt of an award on college choice and persistence, controlling for other variables that might have influenced these choices.

In chapter 6, Hurtado, Laird, and Perorazio compare recipients and nonrecipients in the 2001 cohort, focusing on the college transition process. Their analyses examine the relationships between the receipt of GMS awards and concerns about living costs, work during college, and other indicators of involvement and engagement in college. They explore some of the ways the GMS awards enabled students to make the college transition.

Then in chapter 7, Sedlacek and Sheu further examine differences in the experiences of recipients and nonrecipients, focusing on indicators of academic success in college. They examine time spent studying, involvement in academic activities, difficulties managing time, attitudes toward persistence, and other indicators of academic success. In combination, chapters 6 and 7 provide a rich analysis of the ways the additional funding provided by GMS gave students the opportunity to more fully engage in academic life and benefit from this experience.

Since the comparison group in the NORC survey includes many academically qualified GMS applicants who did not qualify for Pell, it was necessary to ask: "How do college choices and persistence for GMS recipients compare to minority students who received Pell?" To address this question, in chapter 8, Lee compares GMS recipients to a national sample of high-achieving students of color who received Pell Grants. This comparison confirms that GMS did substantially change the aid packages for low-income students, a topic that could not be fully addressed with the NORC database.

In addition to promoting academic success during college, the GMS program aims to encourage more students of color to pursue graduate education in fields in which they are currently underrepresented: math/science, including computer science; engineering; education; and library and information sciences. While undergraduate students received the same amount of aid whether or not they chose majors in these fields, the promise of support through graduate school provided an additional incentive for funded students to choose majors that could lead to continuing funding. However, in addition to increasing grant aid, GMS reduced debt during college. In chapter 9, St. John and Chung tackle the complex set of questions related to the role of GMS scholarships and debt burden in major choice, an issue of substantial and direct policy relevance.

Another long-term goal of the GMS program is to encourage and foster a new generation of leaders of color. This goal extends substantially beyond the boundaries of colleges and includes civic and economic leadership after college and graduate school. While history will judge whether GMS achieved this long-term goal, it is possible to encourage leadership skills among students who receive aid. In fact, the GMS program provides leadership training during the first year of involvement in the program and encourages networking among recipients during college and afterwards. In chapter 10, Sedlacek and Sheu examine the correlates of leadership activity among GMS recipients, exploring ethnic differences in the role of leadership behavior, as well as examining the impact of aid on these behaviors.

In the concluding chapter, I look across these scholarly contributions, reflecting on the goals of the GMS program and the challenges facing advocates of equal opportunity. Consonant with the critical tasks identified above, I examine how this research might inform a reconstruction of policy on diversity in higher education as well as public finance policy in higher education.

References

Bowen, W. G., & Bok, D. (1998). *The shape of the river: Long-term consequences of considering race in college and university admissions.* Princeton, NJ: Princeton University Press.

Brown et al. v. Board of Education of Topeka et al., 347 U.S. 483 (1954).

Fitzgerald, B. (2004). Federal financial aid and college access. In E. P. St. John (Ed.), *Readings on equal education*: Vol. 19, *Public policy and college access: Investigating the federal and state roles in equalizing postsecondary opportunity* (pp. 1-28). New York: AMS Press, Inc.

Fossey, R. E. (2003). Desegregation is over in the inner cities: What do we do now? In L. F. Miron & E. P. St. John (Eds.),

Reinterpreting urban school reform: Have urban schools failed, or has the reform movement failed urban schools? Albany: State University of New York Press.

Hearn, J., & Holdsworth, J. (in press). Federal student aid: The shift from grants to loans. In M. D. Parsons & E. P. St. John (Eds.), *Public funding for higher education: Changing contexts and new rationales.* Baltimore: Johns Hopkins Press.

Lee, J. B. (2004). Access revisited: A preliminary reanalysis of NELS. In E. P. St. John (Ed.), *Readings on equal education*: Vol. 19, *Public policy and college access: Investigating the federal and state roles in equalizing postsecondary opportunity* (pp. 87-96). New York: AMS Press, Inc.

National Commission on Excellence in Education. (1983). *A nation at risk.* Washington, DC: Author.

National Defense Education Act, Pub. L. No. 85-864, 72 Stat. 1580 (1958).

No Child Left Behind Act, Pub. L. No. 107-110, 115 Stat. 1425 (2002).

Orfield, G., & Eaton, S. E. (1996). *Dismantling desegregation: The quiet reversal of Brown v. Board of Education.* New York: Free Press.

Sedlacek, W. E. (2004). *Beyond the big test: Noncognitive assessment in higher education.* San Francisco: Jossey-Bass.

Sedlacek, W. E. (2003). *Measurement and evaluation in counseling and development.* San Francisco: Jossey-Bass.

St. John, E. P. (2003). *Refinancing the college dream: Affordability in the new higher education market.* Baltimore: Johns Hopkins University Press.

St. John, E. P., Chung, C. G., Musoba, G. D., Simmons, A. B., Wooden, O. S., & Mendez, J. (2004). *Expanding college access: The impact of state finance strategies.* Indianapolis: The Lumina Foundation for Education.

CHAPTER 1

OPPORTUNITY ANSWERED: SUMMARY RESEARCH FINDINGS ON THE GATES MILLENNIUM SCHOLARS PROGRAM

David Merkowitz

By almost any measure, the Gates Millennium Scholars are accomplished, outstanding, high-performing students. The fact that the GMS program has been able to identify thousands of academically well-prepared and highly motivated low-income students of color, and that these students apparently are succeeding at many of the nation's most prestigious colleges and universities, challenges the conventional wisdom about the relationships among poverty, race, and educational attainment.

One unfortunate consequence of the sometimes bitter public debates of the past 20 years over K-12 school reform and affirmative action in higher education has been the stigmatization of low-income minority students as almost uniformly at risk of educational and social marginalization. However else they might differ, virtually all critics of public education agree that its core problems are found in schools that serve concentrations of low-income students of color. It is these schools, usually located in inner cities, older suburbs, and rural areas, that have been the target of the most stringent state reform efforts. Yet, the GMS program demonstrates that even the worst schools contain enormous reservoirs of talent, and that some of their students excel notwithstanding the forces arrayed against them.

In its first four years, despite its stringent standards, GMS has attracted far more qualified nominees than it could fund. Still others have been turned down because, though they fulfill the academic criteria, they fail to meet one or more of the other program requirements. Yet, most of these students attended high schools with inadequate resources, high dropout rates, and low test scores. Somehow, they managed to succeed where others failed.

Large numbers of GMS recipients are enrolled in highly selective colleges and universities. Overall, they receive high grades, are making normal academic progress, and expect to graduate on time. They are engaged in their education and in campus and civic activities. A substantial portion major in some of the most demanding disciplines and they expect to pursue graduate study, often in fields where they will continue to receive GMS support.

About the Program and the Research

The GMS program, established in September 1999 by the Bill & Melinda Gates Foundation, represents a 20-year, $1 billion commitment to provide financial assistance to high-achieving minority college students. Its goal is to increase access to higher education for outstanding African American, American Indian/Alaska Native, Asian Pacific Islander American, and Hispanic American students who have shown leadership promise but have demonstrated high financial need. Through targeted assistance for graduate study, it also seeks to increase the numbers of minorities in key fields where their ethnic and racial groups currently are underrepresented.

The program awards approximately 1,000 new scholarships each year, which recipients may use to attend the college of their choice. Scholarships are renewable annually for up to five years.

Undergraduates may major in any field, and recipients who choose to pursue advanced degrees in math, science (including computer science), engineering, education, and library science receive support for postgraduate studies for up to four years.

GMS is a "last dollar" scholarship, meaning that it is designed to meet all remaining financial need after federal, state, institutional, or other private grants or scholarships are deducted. Thus recipients are not required to take out loans or work while they pursue their degrees, though some choose to do so.

The GMS program is administered by the United Negro College Fund, along with three partner organizations: the American Indian Graduate Scholars, the Hispanic Scholarship Fund, and the Organization of Chinese Americans. The partners conduct outreach to students in their respective racial or ethnic group, help select recipients, and disburse scholarship funds. They also communicate with and provide support to recipients during and after the award process.

Complete information about the nomination process is available on the GMS Web site at http://www.gmsp.org.

To promote leadership among GMS recipients, the program each year brings incoming freshman Scholars to regional conferences where they meet with prominent speakers and panels of experts and engage in small-group community-building activities and community service projects.

To get the program up and running as quickly as possible and to "fill the pipeline," GMS provided scholarships to 1,430 entering freshmen, 2,406 continuing undergraduates, and 217 graduate students for the 2000-01 academic year. Since then, approximately 3,000 more entering freshmen have received awards.

As of June 2003, 924 Scholars had earned baccalaureate and/or advanced degrees. About 30 percent of those who completed their undergraduate studies enrolled in graduate schools with GMS support.

Of the 5,786 current Scholars, 997 are first-year students, 4,414 are continuing undergraduates, and 375 are graduate students. That total includes 2,085 African Americans, 1,869 Hispanic Americans, 1,193 Asian Pacific Islander Americans, and 639 American Indians/Alaska Natives. The average high school

GPA for entering freshmen ranges between 3.7 and 3.8; their overall average college GPA is 3.4.

GMS nominees must have a cumulative GPA of 3.3 on a 4.0 scale and meet the eligibility criteria for a federal Pell Grant. They also are evaluated on a set of "noncognitive" criteria, including their long-term goals, their leadership qualities, their ability to "navigate the system," and nontraditional ways in which they have acquired knowledge. This process allows the program to identify nominees who have overcome significant obstacles and possess outstanding abilities.

The foundation initiated a research effort with three priorities:

- to explore the effect of the GMS program on recipients, particularly from the perspectives of finances, academics, and leadership;
- to identify the precollegiate schooling and cocurricular experiences that best prepared students to receive a GMS award; and
- to analyze civic and social outcomes after college, the attitudes of recipients and nonrecipients, and the use of noncognitive factors in the GMS selection process.

At the core of the research project is a longitudinal study that will make GMS recipients possibly the most closely followed group of college students in history. During the first five years, the National Opinion Research Center (NORC) at the University of Chicago is collecting data on three student cohorts, each consisting of all GMS recipients and, for comparison purposes, a sample of nominees who did not receive awards. The data is gathered through a series of Web-based surveys, which thus far have been administered to the first two cohorts: GMS recipients and nonrecipients in the program's first and second years.

Several of the studies based on initial analyses of the survey data focus on entering freshmen and continuing undergraduates in the 2000-01 cohort; others use data on recipients and nonrecipients in the 2001-02 freshman class only. For his paper, Walter Allen conducted focus groups with Scholars at a GMS leadership conference. To examine the high school backgrounds of GMS nominees, William Trent and his colleagues merged data from the survey with variables from other databases maintained by the U.S. Department of Education, including the Common Core dataset and the Office for Civil Rights Year 2000 Elementary and Secondary dataset. Future analyses will make use of additional data to compare GMS recipients and nonrecipients with other students.

This chapter synthesizes the studies, rather than simply summarizing them; it teases out themes and weaves together strands in the research to present a more holistic picture of the GMS program, its participants, and the impact it is having on their lives. Although citations are not provided for every instance where passages are partially quoted or paraphrased, endnotes in each section indicate the studies from which they are derived. The chapter also draws upon focus groups with GMS recipients conducted by The McKenzie Group of Washington, DC as part of its GMS program evaluation, as well as drafts of several chapters from a book in progress by Edward P. St. John that makes use of the GMS database.

Major Findings

Given the relative youth of GMS and that the longitudinal study has tracked both the freshman recipients and nonrecipients only partway through their undergraduate careers, the first round of analyses covered by this chapter cannot reach firm conclusions about the academic and social outcomes of the program. Nonetheless, they furnish early indicators of the progress Scholars are making—markers that point toward their ultimate success.

At the same time, some of the data in the longitudinal study do lend themselves to definitive findings. Nothing in the background of these students will change: the schools they attended, the forces that influenced their development to date, their college choices and educational aspirations, their financial concerns. For this reason, these early findings offer important insights into the factors that distinguish GMS recipients from their peers that have propelled them forward in their academic careers, that continue to affect their progress, and that will shape their futures.

Opportunities and Inequities

Taken together, the NORC surveys, the other databases, and the focus groups on which these analyses draw demonstrate that talented, highly motivated, promising students of color in the United States continue to be systematically denied educational opportunities. These young people disproportionately attend K-12 schools with inferior educational resources; they lack access to college planning information; and they labor under the burden of racial and ethnic stereotypes that unfairly deny their potential while also depriving them of the tools they need to become full participants in our society and economy.

In the focus groups, GMS recipients recognized not only the inequities between high schools but also those within their own schools in terms of educational resources and experiences. They described how formal academic tracking and informal mechanisms prevented certain groups of students from accessing college preparatory tracks with rigorous coursework, and how informal interactions with counselors and teachers often were colored by negative racial and ethnic stereotypes.

Still, thousands of GMS nominees, both recipients and nonrecipients, have overcome these barriers. To an extent, this can be attributed to their internal motivation, which led them to work hard and take advantage of whatever opportunities presented themselves in their educational and social environments. But typically, their determination and resiliency can be traced to other factors—parental and family encouragement, the intervention of mentors and school personnel—that were unavailable to other students.

For many of the nominees, measures such as standardized test scores and the number of Advanced Placement (AP) courses taken proved inadequate indicators of academic potential. Some overcame extraordinary hardships or destructive behaviors—drugs, gangs, homelessness, etc.—to realize in time that they could live productive, fulfilling lives if they devoted themselves to their education.

More than two out of three GMS recipients are female, reflecting the disparate achievement levels of minority boys and girls and the higher dropout rates and social problems of minority males. For African Americans, the proportion is almost three out of four.

The typical GMS nominee attends a large, urban public high school with a heavy concentration of low-income students. About two thirds of the high schools attended by those in the 2001 freshman cohort ranked in the highest quartile (more than 1,123 students) nationally in terms of size. However, those schools still tend to be racially and/or ethnically mixed; less than one third of nominees indicated that most of their high school classes were with students from only their own group.

Large high schools ordinarily are more impersonal, less safe, and suffer from other deficiencies; however, because of their size, they may offer more AP courses. About 65 percent of the schools attended by GMS recipients offered four or more AP courses, compared with only 37 percent of all U.S. public high schools. Still, about one third of GMS nominees reported taking no AP exams; another third took four or more.

Overall, school factors were closely associated with the odds of students being selected for a scholarship. While the number of AP courses offered by their schools suggests that many recipients had an opportunity to learn at high levels, the data also show that a climate of fairness contributed in important ways. If the experience of GMS recipients is any indication, schools that have equitable rates of participation in gifted programs and parity in rates of representation in special education, expulsion, and suspension across racial groups provide a milieu more conducive to academic success by low-income minority students.

Attitudes and Expectations

Students' attitudes are critical to their success, a truism borne out by these analyses. But these attitudes do not emerge in a vacuum; they are linked closely to their personal backgrounds and the settings in which they grow up and go to school.[1]

GMS recipients tend to have a higher level of academic self-esteem—a measure of how they feel about their chances for success—than do nonrecipients. They also feel that they have greater control over their plans and their lives. As a consequence, they have higher educational expectations.

These positive attitudes appear to be linked closely to the attributes of the high schools they attended. For example, nominees who attended large schools, schools that offered more AP courses, and schools with a smaller student-teacher ratio have higher academic self-esteem, as do those who went to schools with greater parity in gifted program enrollment and lower minority representation in special education. Students' academic self-esteem also aligns with their mothers' educational level, as well as with a positive "locus of control"—that is, the degree to which they believe they control their own destiny. Male nominees have somewhat lower levels of academic self-esteem—and of educational expectations—than females.

Scholars in the focus groups testified to the importance of parental support in forming their college aspirations. In fact, they said their parents frequently treated college attendance as a requirement, not an option, reinforcing this goal implicitly as well as explicitly. The Scholars also portrayed college attendance as a way to rise above their current economic circumstances and attain a "better life"—often something that had been denied their parents because they lacked sufficient education. African American and Hispanic Scholars in particular credited mentors and supporters who provided critical assistance as they sought to overcome educational disadvantage, poverty, and hardship.

The Role of Finances

Public concern about the affordability of higher education has been a front-burner issue for policymakers and the media for two decades. How to pay for college for their children often tops the list of parents' worries about the future; many doubt they will be able to do so, a fear compounded recently by large tuition increases at public institutions prompted by cuts in state support.[2]

Federal officials—both members of Congress and successive administrations—have responded primarily by seeking to alleviate the anxieties of those most likely to vote: the middle class. Thus, they have regularly raised the limits on guaranteed student loans and enacted numerous tax credits and tax-sheltered saving programs, all of which favor middle-income students. On the other hand, the maximum Pell Grant award—the federal government's primary program of assistance for low-income students—has gone up only fitfully. By 2000, when the GMS program was implemented, the net cost of attending a public four-year college for low-income students had grown dramatically due to the decline in value of federal need-based grants and spiraling tuition charges. For example, whereas in 1975-76 the maximum Pell award covered 85 percent of the cost of attendance at four-year public institutions, and 69 percent in 1980-81, by 1999-2000 that proportion had dropped to 39 percent.

The shift in emphasis in federal aid from grants to loans and tax incentives has limited access to higher education for low-income students. Between 1980 and 1992, the overall share of high school graduates that enrolled in postsecondary institutions within two years grew dramatically, from 68 to 75 percent. But while the college-going rate of students from the highest-earning families surged from 80 to 90 percent, the proportion from the lowest-income quartile barely budged, rising from 57 to 60 percent. Even more notably, the gap between low-income and high-income students who went to four-year colleges grew in just 10 years from a 26-point differential to 37 percentage points.

Yet many state and federal officials consistently have attributed the lagging college enrollment rates of minority students to the failure of the public schools. The preponderance of official policy literature since 1980 simply overlooks the role of need-based aid in promoting access.

In this context, GMS offers an important test of the impact of financial aid—in the form of need-based grants—on educational opportunity. Even considering that GMS recipients are high-performing students with strong college aspirations, the findings are dramatic. Four out of five survey respondents indicated that finances were a very important factor in choosing the college they attended. And financial constraints often forced them to attend less selective—and less challenging—institutions.

Even after they had been enrolled for a year, many students continued to express concern about paying for college expenses. However, receiving a GMS award allayed that concern considerably. Only 41 percent of Scholars said that they still found it very difficult to meet their expenses, compared with 55 percent of nonrecipients.

These difficulties probably explain why, despite the last-dollar feature of GMS, many Scholars continue to borrow and work while enrolled. However, they do so at far lower rates. In the year of the survey, GMS recipients in the 2001 cohort borrowed an average of $1,288—less than half the $2,904 borrowed by nonrecipients. They worked for pay an average of just under 11 hours per week, compared with about 14 hours weekly for nonrecipients.

GMS awards were strongly associated with enrollment in four-year colleges. Although the vast majority of nominees attended four-year colleges (about 93% of the 2001 cohort), GMS recipients were less likely to enroll in two-year colleges (3.6%, compared with 7.7% for nonrecipients). Overall, nominees for whom costs are central in their choice of college destination are more likely to enroll in public institutions. However, the last-dollar feature of GMS may have expanded the choices enjoyed by recipients. In the 2000 cohort, they were about one third more likely to enroll in private colleges than in public institutions. In addition, GMS recipients in the 2001 cohort on average attended more selective institutions than did nonrecipients; the colleges attended by recipients had an average acceptance rate of 58.4 percent, compared with 63.1 percent for those attended by nonrecipients.

GMS also had a direct and indirect effect on persistence in college, as measured by the ability to maintain continuous enrollment. Most nominees in the 2000 cohort had enrolled continuously by the time they responded to the survey, but after other variables were considered, GMS recipients were more likely to maintain continuous enrollment than were nonrecipients. In other words, the last-dollar aid enabled them to stay in college when some of their similarly qualified peers had to stop out.

In the initial year of the program, some freshman GMS recipients did not receive notice of their awards until after the beginning of the fall term. However, the additional aid did not provide an incentive for them to change colleges. The only group with a high transfer rate was nominees who enrolled initially in two-year colleges; these students were five times more likely than others to change schools during their first two years.

For low-income minority students facing extensive unmet need, the best option was to enroll in a two-year community college. For many, this would be their final step on the educational ladder.

Choosing a Major

The impact of receiving a GMS award on students' choice of majors is important because of the program's explicit goal of increasing the number of minorities in the target disciplines. At this early stage, the evidence is inconclusive, but indications are that the scholarships may have had a direct effect on some educational choices. Analysis of the survey results also demonstrates that relieving their prospective debt burden may have influenced the major choice processes of recipients (St. John & Chung, chapter 9).

GMS awards appeared to enable some of the freshmen in the 2000 cohort to choose majors in engineering. In addition, receiving a scholarship also had a direct effect on decisions by continuing students to choose education majors. It appears that GMS enables some Scholars to pursue education majors in spite of the lower earnings associated with careers in this field. Quite possibly, this is an intrinsic choice—that is, GMS recipients chose education out of personal interests and commitment. It also is possible that they chose the major because of the potential for receiving aid during graduate school. In combination, these findings provide evidence that GMS is achieving one of its goals, enabling students to choose undergraduate majors in fields that are preferred by the program designers and that they believe to be in the public interest.

The amount of debt burden is negatively associated with some major choices, particularly education, math, and science. Prior research indicates that minorities are more likely to choose majors with linkages to employment. However, for the first time, the GMS survey provides evidence that debt burden inhibits major choices by high-achieving minority students. High debt is problematic in the field of education because salaries are lower than in business and many other applied fields. Thus, high debt discourages students from choosing education as a major and career, limiting the number of high-achieving students who enter teaching.

The finding that debt is negatively associated with the choice of majors in math and science is important because the representation of people of color among the nation's scientists remains an important social and policy issue. Advanced degrees are needed to gain opportunity for higher salaries in the sciences, but those earnings still are modest compared with the economic returns in law and medicine—fields that require similarly long years of study—and in business. The survey results also indicate that some minorities lack sufficient support from faculty to continue academically in math and science. Therefore, the prospects of facing high debt burden may add to the discouragement that minority students who seek opportunities in these fields already experience.

Finally, as detailed below, receiving a GMS award had an indirect effect on the educational choices made by recipients by giving them the opportunity to become engaged in student life and to work more directly with faculty. This serves as a validation for the design concept behind the GMS program.

Adjusting to College

Virtually all students face challenges in making the transition from high school to college. For low-income students of color, many of them the first in their families to attend college, those challenges can be especially daunting. And for GMS recipients, who generally enroll in academically demanding institutions, the transition can be more extreme (Hurtado, et al., chapter 6). The degree to which they successfully negotiate this transition is a critical marker for both them and the program, and ultimately will determine whether GMS will fulfill its lofty goals. It also speaks to strong disagreements among policymakers, advocates, and educators about the use of affirmative action in college admissions and the fairness of placing minority students whose academic credentials may not be as glittering as their peers' into the highly competitive milieu of selective institutions. Additionally, comparing the degree of adjustment and success of GMS recipients and nonrecipients can illuminate the difference financial aid can make in the lives and experience of talented, low-income students.

GMS applicants are a unique population: they aspire to a college degree, are seeking ways to fund their education, and have done their best to prepare themselves for college despite the many obstacles and additional challenges they have had to surmount. These low-income students must have the academic self-confidence to compete in a national scholarship program and may have received some counseling or advising to take advantage of such an opportunity.

Survey findings show that just over one third of all respondents reported some difficulty in their academic adjustment to college, that is, they had trouble keeping up with schoolwork and managing their time. The fact that most (approximately two thirds) recipients and nonrecipients encounter no problems with academic adjustment probably reflects the confidence they have in their abilities and their feeling that they are prepared to meet the academic challenge of college. Nor, on the surface, does either group encounter much difficulty with social adjustment.

As stated earlier, GMS recipients, particularly African Americans and Asian Pacific Islander Americans, find it less difficult than do nonrecipients to pay for their college expenses. This, of course, was not surprising given the amount of financial assistance they receive through the program.

However, more detailed analysis shows differences between the two groups that could have long-term consequences. For instance, Scholars are more likely to have overcome problems associated with low levels of parental education; on average, the mothers of nonrecipients have more formal education than do the mothers of recipients. Despite this disadvantage, recipients did not experience much more difficulty than nonrecipients did in academic or social adjustment.

In addition, as noted previously, Scholars are more likely to attend selective and private institutions, suggesting that they may be inclined to choose colleges where the competition, income, and academic preparation of peers are high. In other words, GMS recipients adjust about as well as nonrecipients who attend less demanding schools where the background differences between student peers may be less divergent.

In the first year of college, Scholars took out much lower student loans, worked fewer hours for pay, and were more likely to live on campus. Also, they were more likely to engage academically, rely on their racial group for support, report that a faculty member had taken interest in their development, and be committed to earning a degree. These findings confirm that because they had less concern about meeting college and living expenses, they could focus on engagement in college and other aspects of the transition experience. Thus, they were more likely than nonrecipients to exhibit behaviors and receive support that contributed to their adjustment to college and their long-term academic success.

Overall, nominees with high self-esteem—both personal and academic—adjusted to college best, as did those who selected their college based on its academic reputation. Interestingly, survey respondents who studied longer each week had greater problems with academic adjustment, as was true for those who spent more time working. It may be that the students who studied more than usual were more concerned about making the transition to college-level work. In the first year of college, it is not uncommon for students to work especially hard to compensate for inequalities in their high school preparation. Even the brightest students realize that they have to adjust to new levels of academic competition and the expectations of the faculty.

As might be expected, the amount of time students spend working is directly related to the level of their concern about paying for college. Ironically, this means that those most invested in their education—judging by the long hours they work to pay for it—are least likely to enjoy the benefits of academic and social engagement.

African Americans reported the greatest ease in social adjustment—for example, making friends and getting assistance from others—of all racial and ethnic groups. However, during the first year of college, the larger the campus, the less socially adjusted most survey respondents felt. This probably reflects the time it takes to find a niche and a welcoming community at large schools.

Thus, while participation in the GMS program does not appear to have a significant direct impact on academic and social adjustment, it would seem to have an effect by easing financial concerns, enhancing college choice, freeing up time, and influencing the behavior of recipients.

Academic Success

Because the GMS program relies heavily on noncognitive criteria in the selection process, it is critical to assess how well recipients do in college to see whether these variables are adequate predictors of success.[3] The high standards used to screen GMS nominees for eligibility—in particular the requirement of a 3.3 GPA—ensure that recipients have a relatively strong academic background. However, grading standards vary from one high school to another and the GPA has been devalued by grade inflation; thus, most colleges depend on standardized test scores to predict whether students will be successful. The GMS program does not, primarily because the scores minority students achieve on such tests often do not adequately reflect their potential or predict their future performance. In addition to their grades, nominees are judged on the academic rigor of their high school curriculum and their ability to write a good essay explaining their interest in becoming a Scholar. However, their answers to the noncognitive questions on the application form they fill out frequently determine who receives a scholarship and who doesn't.[4]

Because members of the 2001 cohort completed the survey after they had been in college for only a year, it is far too early to ascertain their ultimate success. However, the fact that GMS recipients in this group are earning good grades, even at highly competitive institutions, is evidence that the selection process is working.

The mean cumulative GPA of 2001 GMS recipients after a year in college was 3.25. Nearly all (95%) indicated that they were very unlikely to drop out and were strongly committed to earning a degree at their current institution. Most of the remainder answered that they were somewhat unlikely to drop out. Significantly, 90 percent or more of male recipients from each racial and ethnic group said they were very unlikely to drop out. Less than 2 percent responded that they were very or somewhat likely to leave school before earning a degree.

Nonrecipients also stated overwhelmingly that they were unlikely to drop out. This reflects the fact that they, too, are good students, but it should be remembered that on average they attend less selective—and presumably less demanding—institutions. Given that only about 50 percent of college students earn baccalaureate degrees within six years of enrollment, and that the highest rates of dropout are in the first two years, these findings bode well for the long-term persistence of both groups.

The determination of GMS recipients to complete degrees at their current institutions demonstrates their tenacity in interpreting the system and making it work for them—one of the noncognitive variables used in their selection. Higher education environments often are difficult for students of color to negotiate due to institutional barriers, prejudice, and racism, and transferring sometimes allows them to avoid issues that they must learn to handle to be successful.

The great majority of GMS recipients, about 90 percent, expect to complete an advanced degree. The expectations of nonrecipients are marginally lower, though still high. In addition, recipients were more academically engaged than nonrecipients—another sign of their likely success.

Leadership

Because leadership development is one of the fundamental aims of the GMS program, the surveys have sought to gauge the extent to which Scholars take on leadership roles on campus and what factors contribute to their doing so. The respondents whose answers were analyzed—in this case members of the 2000 freshman cohort—had completed only two years of college, so definitive conclusions about their leadership involvement could not be drawn. However, because the Scholars had attended conferences where they were encouraged to assume leadership roles, and because most students who engage in extracurricular activities or community service begin early in their college careers, it is reasonable to infer that the pattern of their undergraduate lives already had been set.[5]

The analysis shows that, overall, about half of GMS recipients and nonrecipients were engaged in campus leadership activities, but nonrecipients tended to hold such positions at a slightly higher rate. Scholars who did not hold a leadership position were more academically engaged than their nonrecipient peers. This may help to explain the seeming anomaly that students selected for a scholarship in part because of their history of leadership are less involved in such activities than their counterparts. The nonleader

Scholars reported that they frequently work with other students on class assignments, discuss ideas with other students and faculty, study hard, and work on creative projects—more so than nonrecipients who were not involved in leadership. In other words, they were spending time on activities that contributed to their academic success, time they otherwise might have spent pursuing leadership opportunities.

Racial and Ethnic Differences

To gauge the success of the GMS program, it is important to understand the backgrounds of the participants, the strengths and weaknesses of high-performing, low-income students of color, the particular challenges encountered by different groups, and how they respond. Too often, discussions about minority students lump all of them together into one general, presumably homogeneous category. And when separate racial and ethnic identities are acknowledged, they frequently are stereotyped in ways that ignore the sometimes stark distinctions among subgroups and individuals. Whatever its motivation, the failure or refusal to recognize racial and ethnic differences among minority students and between them and their White peers ultimately does more harm than good. Rather than reinforcing students' individuality, it denies it, by disregarding the social context in which they live, the specific circumstances with which they must contend, and the steps institutions can take to support and promote their development.[6]

The analyses of the GMS surveys reveal numerous such distinctions, and the data provide a rich vein for future research.

These early findings refute many common stereotypes of racial groups—for example, that African Americans and Latinos consistently have more academic and social difficulties. On the contrary, the data show that African American students are the least likely of all groups to believe that planning does not work out. They also have the least difficulty keeping up with their college homework. In addition, compared with the other groups, African Americans are more likely to aspire to advanced degrees and to be involved in campus leadership activities.

The circumstances of Asian Pacific Islander Americans are particularly worth exploring. The literature on educational choices by Asian Americans paints a picture of exceptional levels of attainment. Indeed, among members of the 2001 freshman cohort, Asian Pacific Islander Americans tend to hold the highest educational aspirations of all groups. They take more high school math and science classes as well as AP exams, and have the highest admissions test scores, yet they are no more likely to attend their first-choice college, even though they tend to enroll in institutions that are more selective. On measures of socioeconomic status, Asian Pacific Islander Americans and Latinos fall lower than other groups on the economic spectrum.

Asian Pacific Islander Americans most likely were in the racial minority in their high school classes and are the most likely to lack self-esteem or a sense of control over their lives. Although they spend the most time studying, they report the greatest difficulty of all groups with academic adjustment (such as keeping up with homework).

In general, Asian Pacific Islander American participants in the focus groups conducted by Walter Allen and The McKenzie Group felt obliged to live up to the "model minority" myth, to strive and achieve because of others' expectations. However, they also recognized the negative consequences of this stereotype. Often, they reported, they were steered away from assistance, tutoring, and other vital academic resources by student service personnel or faculty members who believed that they did not need or would not benefit from such help.

Asian Pacific Islander American Scholars also expressed the most inner conflict over the principles of community and care that were emphasized in the GMS leadership training. Because they were from such diverse cultures, they did not share the same concept of ethnic identity as other Scholars and experienced more isolation in focus groups composed solely of Asian Pacific Islanders than in cross-ethnic sessions. Nonetheless, the survey data show that Asian Pacific Islanders—whether or not they received GMS awards—are no less likely to assume leadership positions on campus than other nominees.

Despite common perceptions that African Americans and Latinos confront the greatest barriers to educational success, the data suggest that American Indians encounter more obstacles. While a higher proportion of Latinos has parents with low educational attainment, American Indians are the least likely group to have taken many math and science classes or AP exams. Almost one third of American Indians attend high schools that offer no AP courses, and only 46 percent of American Indian GMS nominees attended high schools offering four or more. They also have the lowest SAT and ACT scores.

A high percentage of American Indian focus group participants complained of inadequate high school academic counseling, consistent with their pattern of less specific, systematic planning and progress through the college admissions process. They also commented on delays that led to late preparation for college and postponement of the college choice process until late in the junior or senior year of high school.

Yet, judging by the performance of American Indian GMS recipients, these factors do not necessarily translate into lower academic accomplishments. Given the opportunity, American Indian students who, relative to those from other racial and ethnic groups, have been denied educational resources and preparation still are able to compete on an equal footing. On average, they have less difficulty with academic adjustment than any group except African Americans.

The weaker academic backgrounds of American Indians exact a sizable toll on their educational choices and their attitudes. American Indians are least likely to consider reputation as a "very important" factor in choosing a college and on average attend less selective institutions than do other GMS nominees. They are less confident that they will graduate from college, and have more modest academic expectations. Fewer than 80 percent of American Indian Scholars expect to earn an advanced degree, compared with 87 percent of Hispanics, 94 percent of Asian Pacific Islander Americans, and 95 percent of African Americans. Given the extreme poverty in which many American Indians grow up, some of these differences may be explained by economic factors. American Indian GMS recipients and nonrecipients both report far greater difficulty paying their college expenses than any other group.

Finally, only about one third of American Indian nominees, and 24 percent of Scholars, reported holding leadership positions, a finding that requires further exploration. One possibility is that American Indian students are engaged in tribal or community activities that they do not perceive as relevant to the context of the survey, or they may not be inclined to report such activities. Cultural factors may enter into play. Many American Indian applicants may not see calling attention to their leadership activities as appropriate.

Like Asian Americans, American Indians come from diverse and distinctive cultures. Some are far more assimilated than others into mainstream American society. However, in their focus group sessions, rather than feeling isolated, as did the Asian Pacific Islander Americans, they expressed a sense that they could learn from each other.

On average, Hispanic nominees attend large high schools. As a result, they have greater opportunities to enroll in AP courses. More than 71 percent of Hispanic nominees—a greater share than any other group—graduated from high schools offering four or more AP courses, and fully one third had taken that many. Hispanic GMS recipients tended to enroll in more selective colleges than any group other than Asian Pacific Islander Americans.

Hispanic nominees reported the second-most difficulty with academic adjustment, after Asian Pacific Islander Americans. In fact, Hispanics were the only group in which recipients were having more problems with academic adjustment than nonrecipients. Hispanics also reported a high degree of difficulty paying college expenses, behind only American Indians. This may be related to the fact that Hispanics were somewhat more likely to choose a college close to home.

Hispanic students often feel they receive mixed messages about their accomplishments and are not sure how "Latino" they should be to negotiate the system of higher education successfully. One focus group participant reflected these tensions when she recalled how adults and peers expressed pride in her academic accomplishments and, at the same time, fears that she would be separated from her family, friends, and community.

A Final Word

The Gates Millennium Scholars program is still in its early stages. By the time it has run its course, in another 17 years, it will have helped more than 20,000 talented but low-income students of color attend college, pursue their academic dreams, and embark on their careers. By that time, a goodly number of GMS alumni should have ascended to positions of leadership in their professions and their communities, and perhaps in the nation at large.

The research findings presented here on the first groups of students to compete for GMS awards and to win scholarships provides only a hint of what is to come. Already it is clear, however, that with the right kind of encouragement, nurturance, and support, students who otherwise might have been denied the opportunity to attend college; who might have trimmed their ambitions due to financial and other constraints; and who might have struggled to overcome their economic and social limitations are more than holding their own at selective academic institutions.

These findings already teach us much about the barriers these students have overcome to get where they are, and ways in which policymakers might apply these lessons more broadly. Future research, we hope, will tell us more about how these students are succeeding, the mark they are making on campus and in society, and their impact in fields where people of color have been sorely underrepresented. We eagerly await the news.

Notes

1. This section draws primarily upon Trent et al. (chapter 3) and Allen et al. (chapter 4).
2. This section draws upon St. John and Chung (chapter 5), Hurtado et al. (chapter 6), Allen et al. (chapter 4), and Trent et al. (chapter 3).
3. The eight noncognitive factors are (1) positive self-concept, (2) realistic self-appraisal, (3) understanding/navigation of social system, (4) preference for long-term goals, (5) leadership experiences, (6) community service, (7) nontraditional acquisition of knowledge, and (8) strong support person.
4. This section draws upon Sedlacek and Sheu (chapter 7).

5. This section draws upon Sedlacek and Sheu (chapter 10).

6. This section draws upon Hurtado et al. (chapter 6), Sedlacek and Sheu (chapter 7 and chapter 10), Allen et al. (chapter 4), and Trent et al. (chapter 3).

CHAPTER 2

THE SURVEY OF DIVERSE STUDENTS

Bronwyn Nichols Lodato, Michele Zimowski, Raymond M. Lodato, and Rashna Ghadialy

From the spring of 2002 to the early fall, the National Opinion Research Center at the University of Chicago (NORC) administered a baseline survey to Scholars and nonrecipients who applied to receive a Bill and Melinda Gates Millennium Scholarship (GMS) award in the inaugural (2000-01) or second year (2001-02) of the scholarship program. The survey was part of a larger effort, called the "Gates Millennium Scholar Tracking and Longitudinal Study" (GMS Longitudinal Study), designed to assess the short- and long-term effects of the scholarship program on the lives of selected cohorts of Scholars over a 20-year period. Its purpose was to gather baseline information on the educational, civic, and personal lives of all Scholars and selected nonrecipients who applied for awards during the first two years of the program.

This chapter describes the main features of the baseline survey of Cohort I (2000-01) and II (2001-02) Scholars and nonrecipients, including how the comparison samples of nonrecipients were drawn, the design and administration of the survey questionnaires, response rates to the survey, and procedures employed to weight the data from the survey. It begins by describing the design of the study and the composition of the diverse populations of Scholars and nonrecipients.

Design of the Study

In its inaugural year, GMS granted scholarships to three distinct groups of nominees: entering freshmen, continuing undergraduates, and graduate students. In the second year, GMS granted scholarships to entering freshmen only. Thus, there were four distinct populations of Scholars and four corresponding groups of nonrecipients of interest to the baseline survey of Cohort I and II nominees:

1. Cohort I freshman Scholars
   Cohort I freshman nonrecipients

2. Cohort I continuing-undergraduate Scholars
   Cohort I continuing-undergraduate nonrecipients

3. Cohort I graduate-student Scholars
   Cohort I graduate-student nonrecipients

4. Cohort II freshman Scholars
   Cohort II freshman nonrecipients

Within each nominee group (entering freshmen, continuing undergraduates, and graduate students), the nonrecipients included two broad categories of GMS applicants: applicants who were disqualified during the screening phase of the selection process, and applicants who, like the Scholars, made it past the screening phase (including the review of noncognitive criteria by the panel members), but did not receive GMS grants. The second category of nonrecipients served as the target population for the comparison samples of nonrecipients in the quasi-experimental design (e.g., Campbell & Stanley, 1963) of the study.

Often referred to as "non-equivalent control groups" in the literature (Cook & Campbell, 1979), the comparison populations of nonrecipients were selected to be as similar to the Scholars on as many key selection variables as possible, but without the benefit of random assignment of nominees to groups, differences between the groups remain. Like the Scholars, the nonrecipients met all the basic requirements of the screening phase,[1] but the final outcome of the selection process was not the same. The nonrecipients either declined to accept a GMS scholarship,[2] were disqualified or eliminated during the verification/confirmation phase,[3] or were not asked to go on to that phase.[4] Nonetheless, the nonrecipients, for the most part, represent a segment of the population of high-achieving, low-income, minority students for whom the GMS program was intended to serve.[5] The comparison populations of nonrecipients are described in detail in the next section, along with the populations of Scholars.

Composition of the Cohort I and Cohort II Populations

Cohort I Populations

Of all the nominees who applied to the program during the first year, a total of 8,547—3,473 entering freshmen, 4,762 continuing undergraduates, and 312 graduate students—made it past the screening phase of the selection process. All 8,547 nominees were asked to go on to the final verification/confirmation phase, where 1,430 entering freshmen, 2,406 continuing undergraduates, and 217 graduate students were granted scholarships. The remaining nominees, 2,043 entering freshmen, 2,356 continuing undergraduates, and 95 graduate students, defined the three corresponding populations of nonrecipients for Cohort I.

The distribution of Scholars and nonrecipients across the four racial/ethnic groups is shown in Table 1 for each nominee group. Except at the graduate-student level, scholarships were awarded to each racial/ethnic group in rough proportion to the total number of nominees who made it past the screening phase of the selection process. In the freshman group, for example, the number of scholarships awarded to African Americans, Asian/Pacific Islanders, and Hispanic Americans were roughly equal in number, as were the number of nominees in those groups.

Table 1. Population Counts for Cohort I (2000) GMS Nominees Who Made It Past the Screening Phase, by Nominee Group, Scholarship Status, and Race/Ethnicity.

Nominee Group	Race/Ethnicity	Scholarship Status		Total Nominees
		Scholars	Nonrecipients	
2000 Freshmen	African American	465	731	1196
	American Indian	87	116	203
	Asian/Pacific Islander	436	738	1174
	Hispanic American	442	458	900
	Total	1,430	2,043	3,473
2000 Continuing Undergraduates	African American	919	1,016	1,935
	American Indian	239	137	376
	Asian/Pacific Islander	578	637	1215
	Hispanic American	670	566	1236
	Total	2,406	2,356	4,762
2000 Graduate Students	African American	85	11	96
	American Indian	29	17	46
	Asian/Pacific Islander	38	2	40
	Hispanic American	65	65	130
	Total	217	95	312

Overall and within each nominee and racial/ethnic group, female Scholars outnumbered their male counterparts as shown in Table 2.[6]

Cohort II Populations

Of all the nominees applying for awards in the second year of the program, a total of 4,069 entering freshmen made it past the screening stage of the selection process. Of those nominees, 2,012 with the highest priority ranks, referred to as "Selects," were asked to go on to the verification/confirmation process, while the 2,057 remaining nominees with lower ranks, referred to as "Non-Selects," were not.

Of those selected to go to the verification/confirmation process, the first 1,000 nominees to verify their eligibility and accept the award were confirmed as Scholars. Of the 1,012 remaining Selects, three were offered a scholarship but declined to accept it, four had ineligible GPAs, four were attending ineligible institutions, 424 did not have a Pell Grant in place, and 564 had incomplete submissions at the time 1,000 Scholars were confirmed. All 3,069 nonrecipients—1,012 Selects and 2,057 Non-Selects—served as the target population for the comparison sample of nonrecipients.

Table 2. Population Counts for Cohort I (2000) Scholars, by Race/Ethnicity and Gender.

Scholar Population	Race/Ethnicity	Gender		Total Scholars
		Females	Males	
2000 Freshmen	African American	347	118	465
	American Indian	60	27	87
	Asian/Pacific Islander	299	137	436
	Hispanic American	288	154	442
	Total	994	436	1,430
2000 Continuing Undergraduates	African American	708	211	919
	American Indian	179	60	239
	Asian/Pacific Islander	363	215	578
	Hispanic American	440	230	670
	Total	1690	716	2,406
2000 Graduate Students	African American	57	28	85
	American Indian	19	10	29
	Asian/Pacific Islander	28	10	38
	Hispanic American	40	25	65
	Total	144	73	217

In contrast to the inaugural year, scholarships were awarded in equal numbers to African Americans and Hispanic Americans (350 per group), and in equal numbers to American Indians and Asian/Pacific Islanders (150 per group). The number of awards to each racial/ethnic group were roughly proportional to the number of Selects within each group, but not to the number of nominees who made it past the screening phase of the selection process (see Table 3).

Table 3. Population Counts for Cohort II (2001) Nominees Who Made It Through the Screening Phase of the Selection Process, by Race/Ethnicity, Scholarship Status, and Selection Status.

| Nominee Group | Race/ Ethnicity | Scholars (a) | Nonrecipients | | Total Non-recipients (b+c) | Total Nominees (a+b +c) |
			Selects (b)	Non-Selects (c)		
2001 Freshmen	African American	350	395	893	1,288	1,638
	American Indian	150	179	0	179	329
	Asian/Pacific Islander	150	166	758	924	1,074
	Hispanic American	350	272	406	678	1,028
	Total	1,000	1,012	2,057	3,069	4,069

Again, female Scholars outnumbered their male counterparts within each racial/ethnic group, and on the whole (see Table 4). A similar pattern was found in the target population of nonrecipients.

Sample Designs and Selection Procedures

While all 5,053 Scholars in Cohorts I and II were asked to take part in the survey, as a matter of economy, representative samples of nonrecipients, rather than the whole populations, served as the comparison groups in the baseline surveys of entering freshmen and continuing undergraduates. In the case of the graduate students, the population was too small to warrant sampling, so the entire population of nonrecipients was asked to participate in the survey. The designs for drawing the samples were developed by NORC in collaboration with the GMS Research Advisory Committee (RAC) on the basis of information currently available in electronic data files supplied by the administrator of the GMS program, the United Negro College Fund (UNCF).[7]

Table 4. Population Counts for Cohort II (2001) Scholars and Nonrecipients Who Made It Through the Screening Phase of the Selection Process, by Race/Ethnicity and Gender.

Population of Entering Freshmen	Race/Ethnicity	Gender		Total
		Females	Males	
2001 Scholars	African American	257	93	350
	American Indian	93	57	150
	Asian/Pacific Islander	101	49	150
	Hispanic American	226	124	350
	Total	677	323	1000
2001 Nonrecipients	African American	967	309	1276
	American Indian	127	51	178
	Asian/Pacific Islander	589	333	922
	Hispanic American	442	231	673
	Total	2125	924	3049*

* Gender was not available for 20 nonrecipients.

The sample designs for Cohort I entering freshmen and continuing undergraduates are shown in Tables 5 and 6, respectively, along with the sample counts in each cell of the 4-by-2 (Race/Ethnicity by Pell-Grant Status) stratified designs. In accord with the research interests of the RAC, all nonrecipients with a Pell Grant in place at the time of the verification/confirmation phase were included in the samples of both populations.[8] With the goal of obtaining about 300 complete questionnaires in each racial/ethnic group, the remaining cases for the sample of entering freshmen, and the sample of continuing undergraduates, were drawn from the pool of nonrecipients who did not have a Pell

Grant in place at the time of the verification/confirmation phase. In the case of the American Indians, the samples included the entire populations of nonrecipients.

Within each sampling stratum or cell, NORC relied on a systematic sampling procedure (e.g., Kish, 1965) in which the records were sorted by state and zip code of permanent address before the samples were drawn. The cases within each sampling stratum were divided into smaller groups or replicates of approximately equal size to allow for release of additional sample as desired.[9]

Table 5. Sample Counts for Cohort I (2000) Freshman Nonrecipients, by Race/Ethnicity and Pell-Grant Status.*

Population	Race/Ethnicity	Pell Grant Status		Total
		In Place (a)	Not in Place (b)	Sample Size (a + b)
2000 Freshman Nonrecipients	African American	24	379	403
	American Indian	1	115	116
	Asian/Pacific Islander	72	328	400
	Hispanic American	1	398	399
	Total	98	1,220	1,318

* The numbers in the shaded cells represent the entire population of non-recipients in those cells.

Table 6. Sample Counts for Cohort I (2000) Continuing-Undergraduate Nonrecipients, by Race/Ethnicity and Pell-Grant Status.*

Population	Race/Ethnicity	Pell Grant Status		Total
		In Place (a)	Not in Place (b)	Sample Size (a + b)
2000 Continuing Undergrad. Nonrecipients	African American	10	389	399
	American Indian	1	136	137
	Asian/Pacific Islander	10	389	399
	Hispanic American	3	393	396
	Total	24	1,307	1,331

* The numbers in the shaded cells represent the entire population of non-recipients in those cells.

The sample design for Cohort II nonrecipients is shown in Table 7 along with the sample counts in each cell of the 4-by-2 (Race/Ethnicity by Selection Status) design.

In accord with the research interests of the RAC, all nonrecipient Selects were included in the sample. With the goal of obtaining about 1,000 completed questionnaires, the remaining 328 nonrecipients were evenly distributed across the Non-Select cells of African Americans, Asian/Pacific Islanders, and Hispanic Americans. Again, as in Cohort I, the sample includes the entire population of American Indian nonrecipients.

Table 7. Sample Counts for Cohort II (2001) Freshman Nonrecipients, by Race/Ethnicity and Selection Status.*

Population	Race/ethnicity	Selection Status		Total Sample Size
		Selects	Non-Selects	
2001 Freshman Nonrecipients	African Americans	395	108	503
	American Indians	179	0	179
	Asian/Pacific Islanders	166	110	276
	Hispanic Americans	272	110	382
	Total	1012	328	1340

* The numbers in the shaded cells represent the entire population of non-recipients in those cells.

Within each sampling stratum, the records were sorted by gender as well as state and zip code of permanent address before the samples were drawn with a systematic sampling procedure. Again, the cases in each racial/ethnic group were divided into smaller groups, or replicates, of approximately equal size to allow for release of additional sample as desired.

In all, 4,084 nonrecipients from Cohorts I and II were asked to complete the baseline questionnaire. The next section describes the design and development of the survey instrument.

Development and Design of the Survey Instrument

NORC worked closely with The Gates Foundation and the RAC to develop a Web-based instrument that covered key areas of analytic interest primarily for The Gates Foundation and RAC, and secondarily for the education research community and broader public.

The substantive constructs identified by The Gates Foundation and the RAC to be measured in the questionnaire were

Demographic Information
High School Experience
Transition to College
College Experience
Self-Assessments
Outcomes
Attitude and Beliefs
Follow-Up Demographics

NORC prioritized the constructs based on expected analyses of the survey data by the RAC. The total item count for any given population (e.g., 2000 Freshman Scholars, 2000 Freshman Nonrecipients) was limited to 120 questions to ensure the questionnaire could be completed in no more than 30 minutes, using a 4-item-per-minute rule of thumb applied in developing questionnaires at NORC.

NORC's approach to developing the baseline instrument entailed creating an item repository composed of items tested and used in other national education surveys for the constructs provided in the framework. These studies included The National Education Longitudinal Survey: 88 Second Follow-Up; Baccalaureate and Beyond Second Follow-Up; High School and Beyond; College and Beyond; General Social Survey; Survey of Earned Doctorates 2002; and Survey of Doctorate Recipients 2001. Utilizing these source instruments also enhanced analytic comparisons between the GMS Longitudinal Study and other nationally known datasets.

New questions were developed for construct items that were not available in the referenced surveys. The new questions for the various populations were tested in cognitive interviews. Cognitive interviews are essentially "think aloud" interviews in which respondents share their thoughts on how they understand survey questions. (See Sudman, Bradburn, & Schwarz, 1996). A sample of Scholars and nonrecipients was selected from each cohort to participate in cognitive interviews to ensure the results were applicable across cohorts and populations. Data obtained from the cognitive interviews were then used to refine question texts and response categories.

The final version of the instrument was divided into eight sections in the following order:

College Enrollment
Gates (Experience with GMS Program)
Work and College Finances
Academic and Community Engagement
College Experience
Your Attitudes (Self-Assessment)
Future Plans
Background Information

Once the questionnaire item list was finalized, the Web-based, self-administered questionnaire (SAQ) was programmed. The World Wide Web enhanced the collection of high quality data by leading respondents through the questionnaire with programmed skips and prompts, thereby minimizing the instances of invalid missing data. Furthermore, instant data availability provided by high-speed data transmissions allowed immediate data-quality checks to identify and resolve any anomalies in the data.

After the instrument was programmed, iterative tests were conducted to confirm that the skip patterns were performing as intended. These skip patterns were driven by cohort affiliation (i.e., Cohort I, Cohort II), population type (e.g., Freshman, Continuing Undergraduate) and college enrollment status (i.e., enrolled, not enrolled). As a result, there were 20 different paths within the instrument. Table 8 summarizes the branches that were programmed.

Given this level of complexity, the central goal of the instrument testing was to ensure that persons assigned to specific branch categories (e.g., Never-enrolled Cohort I Freshman Scholars) were administered appropriate questions. Exhaustive tests of all skip patterns were carried out and the programmed skips were shown to function properly. Timing tests were also conducted to ensure that the instrument fell within targeted completion time range. The time test results were satisfactory, and each test respondent completed the instrument within the 30-minute time limit.

To protect the confidentiality of data during the GMS data collection effort, each respondent was issued a unique personal identification number (PIN) and password to use when accessing the instrument via the Internet. Also, each questionnaire was assigned a unique ID number, with no identifying name or address information. The instrument was launched from a secured Web server, with all appropriate firewall protections enforced. Completed questionnaires were encrypted and transmitted via a secured data line where they were stored on secured servers.

Table 8. Baseline Instrument Paths, by Cohort, Population, and College Enrollment Status.

	2000 Freshmen	2000 Continuing Undergrads	2000 Graduates	2001 Freshmen
Scholar Enrolled	X	X	X	X
Scholar Not Currently Enrolled	X	X	X	X
Scholar Never Enrolled	X			X
Nonrecipient Enrolled	X	X	X	X
Nonrecipient Not Currently Enrolled	X	X	X	X
Nonrecipient Never Enrolled	X			X

After all instrument and security programming was fully tested, the questionnaire was launched on April 15, 2002. In the next section, a summary of the design and implementation of the baseline data collection effort is presented.

Data Collection

Data collection for the baseline survey began on April 15, 2002 and concluded on October 26, 2002. This section describes the data collection design, along with a discussion of prompting and locating procedures.

Data collection began with the mailing of an advance letter to the current addresses (as defined in the UNCF database) of Scholars and nonrecipients, notifying them that they had been chosen to participate in the study. In addition, the letter to nonrecipients offered a $25 incentive for completing the survey. The Cohort I mailing was sent out in mid-April 2002, and the Cohort II letters were mailed approximately three weeks later.

Different texts were used for each mailing to the Scholar and nonrecipient populations. The mailings to Scholars described the study and its purpose, and provided a unique PIN and password to use in accessing the survey online. The nonrecipient letters also emphasized the value of the survey to policy and academic audiences who seek to improve opportunities for minority students.

Within two weeks of mailing the advance letters, NORC noted a high rate of mail returned by the USPS for undeliverable addresses, and a stagnating response rate.[10] NORC inferred that because the "current" category consisted mainly of college and university addresses, most students were in the process of moving from these addresses as the letters arrived. As a result, future mailings for the baseline survey were sent only to the permanent addresses of nonrespondents.

NORC followed the advance letter mailings with a series of prompts reminding sample members to complete the survey. A multimodal approach to prompting, roughly following the tailored design method developed by Don A. Dillman (2000), was undertaken in order to boost response rates. The modes employed included mail, telephone, and e-mail prompting. The prompting efforts, which began in mid-June 2002, but were mostly concentrated in July and August 2002, had an extremely salutary effect on response rates for both cohorts, as shown in Figure 1.

Figure 1. Data Collection Results by Month.

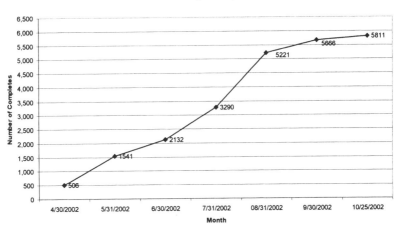

Six weeks into the data collection period, NORC conducted a nonresponse study by calling a sample of 98 nonrespondents (compiled from both cohorts) to determine their reasons for not answering the survey. The questions focused on whether the nonrespondents had received the previous mailings, where they had received the mailing (at their current or permanent address, or both), and whether they had access to the Internet over the summer. The results determined that most of those contacted had received the mailings at their permanent addresses, and nearly all had access to the Internet over the summer. In the final month of the study, the phone prompting effort was converted entirely into an effort aimed at reaching those who had only partially completed the survey ("break-offs").

At the close of data collection, sample members who did not answer the survey fell into one of four categories—those who explicitly refused to respond; those who were unlocatable;[11] those who broke off from the survey, as noted above; and those who presumably received contact from NORC, but did not respond to the survey. Table 9 below breaks out the final nonresponse categories by cohort.

Table 9. Final Nonrespondent Categories.

	Cohort I	Cohort II
Refusals	15	0
Unlocatable	390	60
Break-Offs	62	163
Reasons Unknown[12]	2013	602

Response Rates

The final response rates broken out by cohort, population, race, and gender are presented in this section. The overall response rates for the baseline survey were exceptional for a Web-based survey of postsecondary students, where research has shown that response rates generally peak between 40 and 50 percent (See Couper, Traugott & Lamais, 2001; Schaefer & Dillman, 1998; Nichols & Ghadialy, 2003). Table 10 presents a summary of the baseline response rates broken out by cohort population and race. Table 11 reviews response rates by cohort population and gender.

The next section describes how the survey weights were computed to take into account nonresponse to the survey.

Weighting for Differences in
Selection Probabilities and Unit Nonresponse

At the end of the field period, NORC generated eight separate sets of survey weights, one for each of the four Scholar populations, and one for each of the corresponding samples of nonrecipients.[14] Weights were needed for two main reasons: to compensate for differences in the selection probabilities of the nonrecipient sample members, and to compensate for subgroup differences in the participation rates of the Scholar populations and the nonrecipient samples. In the case of the Cohort II freshman nonrecipients, weights were also needed to compensate for random fluctuations from the population totals.

Table 10. GMS Tracking and Longitudinal Baseline Survey Response Rates Cohort Population Type, by Race.[13]

Population Type	Race/Ethnicity	Scholarship Status	
		Scholars	Nonrecipients
2000 Freshmen	African American	0.755	0.564
	American Indian	0.586	0.405
	Asian/Pacific Islander	0.812	0.599
	Hispanic American	0.749	0.591
	Total (percentage)	76.0	56.4
2000 Continuing Undergraduates	African American	0.627	0.468
	American Indian	0.590	0.482
	Asian/Pacific Islander	0.719	0.517
	Hispanic American	0.615	0.415
	Total (percentage)	64.2	46.9
2000 Graduate Students	African American	0.706	0.455
	American Indian	0.690	0.588
	Asian/Pacific Islander	0.790	0.000
	Hispanic American	0.754	0.508
	Total (percentage)	73.3	50.5
2001 Freshmen	African American	0.846	0.522
	American Indian	0.727	0.508
	Asian/Pacific Islander	0.913	0.681
	Hispanic American	0.826	0.598
	Total (percentage)	83.1	58.6

Table 11. GMS Tracking and Longitudinal Baseline Survey Response Rates Cohort Population Type, by Gender.

Nominee Group	Race/Ethnicity	Scholarship Status	
		Scholars	Nonrecipients*
2000 Freshmen	Male	0.720	N/A
	Female	0.778	N/A
2000 Continuing Undergraduates	Male	0.680	N/A
	Female	0.626	N/A
2000 Graduate Students	Male	0.808	N/A
	Female	0.694	N/A
2001 Freshmen	Male	0.811	0.542
	Female	0.841	0.605

*   Gender information was not available for Cohort 1 Nonrecipients.

The weighting procedure for seven of the eight populations consisted of two steps: 1) computing a base weight and 2) adjusting for nonresponse. The weighting procedure for the other population, Cohort II freshman nonrecipients, included one additional step: compensating for random fluctuations from the population totals.

Applied to all eight populations, the first step of the procedure computed a base weight for each member in the sample reflecting his or her probability (chances) of selection into the survey. In the Scholar populations, each member had the same selection probability; all Scholars in each population were asked to participate in the survey. In the nonrecipient populations, sample members within each cell of the sample design had the same selection probability, but the probabilities differed across cells.[15]

The second step of the weighting procedure, applied to all eight populations, adjusted the base weights for nonresponse to the questionnaire within each cell of an adjustment design. The adjustment cells for each population, shown in Table 12, were selected on the basis of information available in the UNCF databases. The nonresponse-adjusted weight for a case was simply the base weight inflated by the inverse of the response rate for the adjustment cell for that case.

Table 12. Adjustment Designs for Nonresponse to the Baseline Questionnaire.

Cohort	Nominee Group	Scholarship	Adjustment Design
Cohort I	Freshmen	Scholars	Race/ethnicity by gender
		Nonrecipients	Race/ethnicity by Pell-grant status
	Continuing Undergraduates	Scholars	Race/ethnicity by gender
		Nonrecipients	Race/ethnicity by Pell-grant status
	Graduate Students	Scholars	Race/ethnicity by gender
		Nonrecipients	Race/ethnicity
Cohort II	Entering Freshmen	Scholars	Race/ethnicity by gender
		Nonrecipients	Race/ethnicity by selection status by gender

Since gender was not one of the sampling strata in the Cohort II nonrecipient design, an additional adjustment was necessary to compensate for random fluctuations from the population totals. In this case, race/ethnicity, selection status, and gender defined the adjustment cells. The adjustment factor was simply the size of the population in a cell, divided by the sum of the weights for all sample members in the cell.

For all populations, the procedure was designed to yield a set of weights for completed cases that sums to the number of Scholars or the number of nonrecipients in the respective populations. Similarly, the weights within each stratum were designed to sum to the population totals within those cells.[16]

Notes

1.   During the screening phase of the selection process, nominees are disqualified for a number of reasons: incomplete or late submission of the application package, insufficient essay responses, failure to meet the qualifying criteria for GPA, race/ethnicity, financial need, or failure to pass the panel review of noncognitive criteria.

2.   In Cohort II, three candidates declined to accept the scholarship.

3.   In the verification/confirmation phase, candidates are asked to submit supporting documents to verify their GPA (high school transcripts), institution of enrollment, and other sources of financial aid. To be confirmed as Scholars, candidates must have all required documents verifying their eligibility on file. Entering freshmen and continuing undergraduates must also have a Pell Grant in place as part of their financial aid package. Since Scholars are confirmed on a flow basis as they complete the verification process, qualified candidates will not become Scholars if they complete their submissions late in the process, after the target number of confirmed Scholars is reached.

4.   In Cohort II, there were more nominees than needed to meet the goal of awarding 1,000 scholarships. Therefore, only a subset of nominees who made it past the screening phase of the selection process was asked to go on to the verification/confirmation phase.

5.   The nonrecipient populations in Cohorts I and II include sizable numbers of candidates who did not have a Pell Grant in place at the time of the verification/confirmation phase. To be

approved for a Pell Grant, candidates must submit a Free Application for Federal Student Aid (FAFSA) to the U.S. Department of Education, Federal Student Aid Programs, and meet the qualifying criteria of financial need. If a candidate does not have a Pell Grant in place, it may mean that he or she did not meet the eligibility criteria, did not submit an FAFSA, or did not submit one in time.

6. Information on the gender of nonrecipients was not available.

7. The files for Cohorts I and II included all information currently available in machine-readable form. Along with contact information, they contained race/ethnicity, nominee group (freshman, continuing undergraduate, or graduate student) and indicated whether the nonrecipient had a Pell Grant in place at the time of the verification/confirmation phase. The file for Cohort II also contained information on gender (with some missing values) and selection status (Select/Non-Select). The files served as the sampling frames (i.e., list of all members in the population) for drawing the representative samples of nonrecipients.

8. In sampling terms, all nonrecipients in those cells had selection probabilities of 1.0.

9. To divide the cases into groups, a random permutation of integers ranging from one to the number of replicates was generated for each racial/ethnic group. Then the series of integers was assigned in rotation to the cases in the file. (For example, suppose that there are five replicates and the random permutation is 5, 1, 4, 2, 3. The first 14 cases within the given racial/ethnic group will have replicate numbers of 5, 1, 4, 2, 3, 5, 1, 4, 2, 3, 5, 1, 4, 2.) The procedure produces replicates, each of which is a valid, representative sample of cases in the stratum that can be released to the field as needed to meet the sample size requirements of the survey while preserving the representativeness of the sample.

10. The database supplied by UNCF included three address categories for each individual: permanent, current, and preferred. The "permanent" listing, in general, referred to the address that the individual shared with his or her parent(s), whether during the school year or only during the summer months. The "current" listing, in general, referred to the address of the students at their particular college or university. "Preferred" addresses usually were identical to one of the other two addresses.

11. Throughout the study, unlocatable addresses were sent to NORC's locating shop, where trained personnel conducted more intensive searches using Web-based tools and, in some instances, credit bureau checks. At the conclusion of data collection, any cases without locating information or lacking contact with the respondent were coded as "final unlocatable."

12. The mode of implementation (self-administered Web-based) contributes to a high number in this category. There are limited opportunities for direct contact with potential respondents to obtain an explicit reason for nonparticipation, unlike a field-based survey or phone surveys that offer greater opportunity for direct respondent contact.

13. The response rates for the freshman and undergraduate samples of nonrecipients were weighted to take into account that the sample members were selected with unequal probabilities.

14. Generating weights to produce unbiased estimates of the population values is standard practice in survey research. When applied to the data, weights help compensate for differences in the selection probabilities of individual sample members, differences in the participation rates of subgroups in the samples, and random departures from population totals (e.g., Kish, 1965).

15. The exception to this rule is the Cohort I graduate nonrecipients, where all population members were asked to participate in the survey.

16. In the case of the Cohort I undergraduate nonrecipients, the only American Indian with a Pell Grant did not respond to the survey, leaving an empty cell in the nonresponse adjustment design for that population. In such cases, one typically collapses similar cells and makes the adjustment within the collapsed cell. In this case, that would mean giving more weight to American Indians without Pell Grants to compensate for nonresponse in the Pell-Grant-in-place cell. Instead, the subpopulation was redefined as American Indians without Pell Grants. Thus, the sum of the nonresponse-adjusted weights for the American Indians is equal to 136, rather than 137. Similarly, the only two Asian/Pacific Islanders in the population of nonrecipient graduate students did not complete the survey. Instead of giving extra weight to cases in the other racial/ethnic groups, the population was redefined, yielding a population total of 93 nonrecipients, rather than 95.

Finally, one male Asian/Pacific Islander undergraduate Scholar was deceased at the time of the survey. In this case, the weights were adjusted to account for the out-of-scope case. Thus, the sum of the sample weights was set to a population value of 2,405, rather than 2,406.

References

Campbell, D. T., & Stanley, J. C. (1963). *Experimental and quasi-experimental designs for research.* Chicago: Rand McNally.

Cook, T. D., & Campbell, D. T. (1979). *Quasi-experimentation: design & analysis issues for field settings.* Chicago: Rand McNally.

Couper, M. P., Traugott, M. W., & Lamais, M. J. (2001). Web survey design and administration. *Public Opinion Quarterly, 65*(2), 230-253.

Dillman, D. A. (2000). *Mail and Internet surveys,* 2nd ed. New York: John Wiley and Sons, Inc.

Kish, L. (1965). *Survey sampling.* New York: Wiley.

Nichols, B., & Ghadialy, R. *Achieving high response rates on Web surveys of postsecondary students.* (2003). Paper presented at 58th Annual Conference of the American Association for Public Opinion Research, Nashville, TN.

Schaefer, D. R., & Dillman, D. A. (1998). Development of a standard e-mail methodology: Results of an experiment. *Public Opinion Quarterly, 62*(3), 378-397.

Sudman, S., Bradburn, N. M., & Schwarz, N. (1996). *Thinking about answers.* San Francisco: Jossey-Bass.

CHAPTER 3

THE RELATIVE CONTRIBUTION OF HIGH SCHOOL ORIGINS TO COLLEGE ACCESS

William T. Trent, Yuqin Gong, and Dawn Owens-Nicholson

The research reported here examines factors associated with college enrollment and success for entering freshman students. This research builds on two traditions in educational attainment research: the role of high-poverty, high-minority concentrations in schools in shaping postsecondary opportunities for high-need, college eligible students and the perpetuation hypothesis (Braddock, 1980), which argues that the racial composition of the high school has important implications for postsecondary choices, especially for students who choose traditionally White colleges and universities. These analyses follow the work in status attainment research that examines school factors—size, control, and other contextual factors—that shape student outcomes (Coleman et al., 1966; Sewell, Hauser, & Featherman, 1976; Trent, Henderson, & Braddock, 1985).

The objectives of this research are twofold. First, for each racial and ethnic group we describe the social and demographic attributes of the high schools of origin of the 2001 freshman cohort of applicants to the Gates Millennium Scholars program. Second, we examine the relative contribution of individual versus school factors in shaping key educational outcomes—educational expectations, educational performance, and college selectivity.

The first objective will be especially useful in identifying the extent to which GMS recipients and nonrecipients, both of whom are high-need and academically high-performing students, have the same or different high school origins. There is a very important and persistent policy issue here regarding economic segregation in our high schools: *To what extent do high-need students and more affluent students attend the same high schools* (Chaplin, 2002; Rusk, 2002). In addition to identifying high school origins, we provide the distribution of GMS applicants across the colleges in which they initially enrolled. The three postsecondary indicators we report are the level—two-year versus four-year—of the institution, its minority serving status, and its selectivity.

Meeting the second objective will add to our understanding of the relative contribution of high school attributes to college enrollment, compared with the individual attributes of students that research clearly indicates are important for college enrollment. With these data, we are able to examine the role of selected background factors, academic self-esteem, educational expectations, and locus of control. These analyses are designed to clarify the relative role of the high school and individual factors in shaping college access.

Method

The data for this study are from the GMS 2001 freshman applicants who responded to the survey conducted by the National Opinion Research Center (NORC) in 2002. These include both recipients and nonrecipients of GMS awards. Nonrecipients were proportionately sampled and the sample weights are used in these analyses. Selected variables from the GMS-NORC dataset are used for the analyses, including demographic data; socioeconomic background variables; attitude and opinion variables; school performance measures; and self-reported postsecondary enrollment. For high school attributes, the GMS-NORC data were merged with high school attribute variables from the U.S. Office for Civil Rights Year 2000 Elementary and Secondary dataset, and with additional high school enrollment data from the Common Core dataset. The GMS-NORC data also included variables selected from the applicant files for the 2001 cohort. The merged data file resulted in data for 1609 applicants in the 2001 freshman cohort, of whom 831 are GMS recipients and 778 are nonrecipients. The cohort is more than two-thirds female—1105 (68.7%) versus 504 (31.3%) male. African Americans (576, or 35.8%) and Hispanic Americans (509, or 31.6%) make up just over two-thirds (67.4%) of the respondents, while Native Americans/Alaska Natives (200, or 12.4 %) comprise the smallest number and Asian Pacific Islander Americans (324, or 20.1%) the second smallest.

Descriptive Results

We begin with an examination of the attributes of the high schools of origin for the GMS recipients and nonrecipients. Our attention is focused on those indicators of school quality and school climate that are widely recognized as factors that influence the opportunity to learn and student performance. From the OCR E&S Survey we use *number of AP courses* offered by the school; *participation in gifted programs*; *participation in special education programs*; number of *suspensions*; and number of *expulsions* (these are reported by race and ethnicity; we use them to calculate indices of representation); *school racial composition*. *Total enrollment* and *control* (public versus private) of the high schools of origin are taken from the Common Core data. Our discussion begins with the control and size of the high schools attended by GMS applicants, followed by a discussion of one quality indicator—AP courses offered for each high school attended by GMS applicants. Following the discussion of these high school attributes, we present our findings on the participation rates for different race and ethnic groups in gifted education, special education, and suspension in the high schools of origin for GMS applicants.

High School Attributes
Applicants in the 2001 cohort represent 1308 unique high schools, 1163 of which were public. (See Table 1.) Just 109 high schools had more than one applicant. Only one high school had as many as seven applicants who became GMS recipients, and only one high school had as many as six applicants who were nonrecipients.

School Size. Table 2 shows the size of high schools attended by GMS applicants, separately for recipients and nonrecipients. Both recipients and nonrecipients come mainly from high schools in the largest quartile of high school size, with total enrollments in excess of 1123 students. Because the composition of the 2001 incoming cohort is two-thirds African American and Hispanic, this representation of large high schools seems appropriate. It is also consistent with the documented concentration of low-income, PELL-eligible students in large, primarily urban high schools.

Table 1. Unique High Schools Represented in the GMS 2001 Freshman Cohort Data.

High Schools that had...	All High Schools	U.S. Public or DOD Schools	Private, Foreign, or Home Schools
Only Recipients	613	538	75
Only Nonrecipients	586	521	65
Both Recipients & Nonrecipients	109	104	5
Total	1,308	1,163	145

Two recipients and three nonrecipients (out of 1,609) were missing high school information.
The most recipients from a single high school are seven; the most nonrecipients are six.

Our examination revealed no significant differences between recipients and nonrecipients in the size of high schools they attended. There is, however, a significant difference in school size among racial groups. On average, Native Americans attended smaller high schools than the other three groups. Asian Pacific Islander American students attended the largest high schools among the four groups. The mean school size for the four groups are African American: 1409; Native American/Alaska Native: 891; Asian Pacific Islander American: 1906; Hispanic American: 1802.

Number of AP Courses. Shaping the underlying structure of the 1965 Equality of Educational Opportunity Survey was the strong belief that the primary cause of the gap in Black-White student performance was the difference in quality between schools attended by Black students and those attended by White students. Research today frequently documents the challenges to quality faced by schools enrolling a majority of economically disadvantaged Black and Hispanic students.

One indicator of quality is the number of AP courses offered by the school the student attends. Tables 3 and 4 address this question in two ways. First, Table 3 provides a measure of quality of schools as indicated by the number of AP courses available in the schools attended by GMS applicants, both recipients and nonrecipients. The 2001 GMS applicants come mainly and disproportionately from high schools offering greater numbers of

Table 2. Size of Public High Schools in the GMS 2001 Freshman Cohort Data and All U.S. Public High Schools.

High School Size	All U.S. Public High Schools SY 2000-2001		Public High Schools in 2001 Freshman Data		Public High Schools That had a GMS Recipient		Public High Schools That Had Only Nonrecipients	
	N	%	N	%	N	%	N	%
Quartile 1 Less than 187	4,386	25.0	35	3.0	23	3.6	12	2.3
Quartile 2 187 to 515	4,392	25.0	109	9.4	67	10.5	42	8.1
Quartile 3 516 to 1,123	4,378	25.0	247	21.3	133	20.7	114	22.0
Quartile 4 Over 1,123	4,382	25.0	769	66.3	418	65.2	351	67.6
Total	17,538	100.0	1,160	100.0	641	100.0	519	100.0

Data on all U.S. public high schools comes from the U.S. Department of Education's Common Core Dataset.
Three public high schools in the GMS data had missing size information in the Common Core data.

AP courses. Fully 65 percent or more of all GMS applicants are from schools that offer four or more AP courses. Nationally, only about 19 percent of all high schools offered seven or more AP courses in the 2000-01 school year. By contrast, about 37 percent of all the schools attended by GMS recipients and nonrecipients offered seven or more AP courses. Similarly, while high schools nationally that offer four to six AP courses comprise just about 18 percent of all US public high schools, at least 27 percent of the public high schools attended by GMS applicants offered four to six AP courses.

Table 3. Number of AP Courses Offered at Public High Schools in the GMS 2001 Freshman Cohort Data and All U.S. Public High Schools.

Number of AP Courses Offered	All U.S. public h. s.'s SY 2000-01		Public h. s.'s 2001 freshman data		Public h. s.'s w/a GMS recipient		Public h.s.'s w/only non-recipients	
	N	%	N	%	N	%	N	%
None	5,758	39.2	125	11.9	71	12.4	54	11.3
1–3	3,522	24.0	241	23.0	130	22.8	111	23.3
4–6	2,626	17.9	286	27.3	156	27.3	130	27.3
7 or More	2,778	18.9	395	37.7	214	37.5	181	38.0
Total	14,684	100.0	1,047	100.0	571	100.0	476	100.0

Data on all U.S. public high schools comes from U.S. Department of Education Office for Civil Rights Data.
116 public high schools in the GMS data had no AP course information in the OCR data.

The distribution of schools offering different numbers of AP courses addresses a question about the attributes of the schools attended by the GMS applicants. A different question is examined in Table 4, which shows the distribution of GMS applicants across schools offering different numbers of AP courses. The distributions here show the racial/ethnic differences in matriculation from public high schools offering few or several AP courses. The distributions here also offer the national distributions alongside the GMS distributions. For these data, Table 4 shows that Native Americans and African Americans, both nationally and among GMS applicants, are least likely to be enrolled in schools offering seven or more AP courses. Compared with all other GMS applicants, more than twice as many Native American/Alaska Native (24.6%) applicants were enrolled in schools offering no AP courses. Asian Pacific Islander American applicants (68.2%), Hispanic American applicants (71.4%), and African American applicants (59.1%) were enrolled mainly in schools offering four or more AP courses. By contrast, the proportion of Native American/Alaska Native applicants from this sector of high schools was 45.6 percent. These percentages for GMS applicants exceed their respective national percentages for each group except Asian Pacific Islander American applicants. This appears to be mainly because of the substantial percentages from schools offering four to six AP courses.

Table 4. Number of AP Courses Offered at U.S. Public High Schools Attended by Five Racial/Ethnic Groups, SY 2000-01.

N. of AP Courses Offered at the H.S.	% White Seniors	% Native American/Alaska Native Seniors		% Asian Pacific Islander American Seniors		% Hispanic American Seniors		% African American Seniors	
	Entire U.S.	Entire U.S.	GMS 2001 Applicants	Entire U.S.	GMS 2001 Applicants	Entire U.S.	GMS 2001 Applicants	Entire U.S.	GMS 2001 Applicants
None	18.2	34.1	24.6	8.2	11.6	14.6	9.0	21.7	12.0
1-3	23.9	25.0	29.7	19.5	20.2	16.3	19.6	24.6	29.0
4-6	23.3	21.3	26.9	22.1	25.3	24.6	28.0	22.9	30.5
7 or More	34.5	19.6	18.7	50.2	42.9	44.6	43.4	30.8	28.6
Total	100.0	100.0	100.0	100.0	100.0	100.0	100.0	100.0	100.0
N	1,754,156	26,260	111	120,258	391	301,359	334	335,967	566
Missing	78,785	4,106	19	12,393	34	58,421	72	34,417	81

Data on AP course offerings comes from U.S. Department of Education Office for Civil Rights Data.
The GMS N's and proportions have been weighted by the adjusted weight.

In addition to the above measure of school quality, the OCR E&S survey also contains data on participation in Gifted Education, Special Education, Suspensions, and Expulsions by race and ethnicity. A substantial body of research (Coleman et al., 1966; Lee, 1996, 1997, 2000) argues for the explicit examination of school effects. Such effects are believed to be critical in shaping student outcomes. Early on, the findings of such explorations yielded counterintuitive results, suggesting that school-to-school differences were of less significance than other social background measures. We continue this tradition of examining school effects, focusing here on four measures that are constructed in a way that arguably depicts the "fairness" or "equity" climate in the schools attended by GMS applicants (see Appendix for the construction of the measures). These measures, identifying over- and underrepresentation in gifted education, special education, suspension from school, and expulsion from school, are constructed separately for each race and ethnic group represented by GMS applicants. This next section presents the results for each of these indicators of school quality for schools attended by GMS applicants. We begin with our results for Gifted Education.

Gifted Education. Compared with White representation in Gifted Education enrollment, two-thirds of African American GMS applicants came from schools where African American students were underrepresented (see Figure 1). Over 50 percent of the Native American/Alaska Native applicants were from schools where Native American/Alaska Native students were underrepresented. About one-third of Asian Pacific Islander American applicants were from schools where Asian Pacific Islander American students were underrepresented, and over 70 percent of Hispanic American applicants from school where students in the same category were underrepresented.

On average, three racial groups (African American, Hispanic American, and American Indian/Alaska Native) were underrepresented in gifted education compared with White students in the same school. Asian Pacific Islander American students are the only group that on average was not underrepresented compared with White students (mean indices are: 0.68, 0.46, 0.32, and -0.25, respectively).

The racial composition of schools attended by GMS applicants is found to be related to the representation of racial groups in gifted education. Schools with the highest percentage of African American enrollment (75%-100%) were more likely to have a higher representation of African Americans in the gifted program (underrepresented index 41.7 versus 67-72). The same pattern holds for American Indians/Alaska Natives (18.2 versus 48.7-65.3). Schools with Asian Pacific Islander American enrollment above 50 percent were more likely to have Asian Pacific Islanders underrepresented in gifted programs, which is counterintuitive and contrasts sharply with the results for other racial and ethnic groups.

Figure 1. Percentage Distribution of Gates High Schools by Representation in Gifted Education for Each Race/Ethnicity.

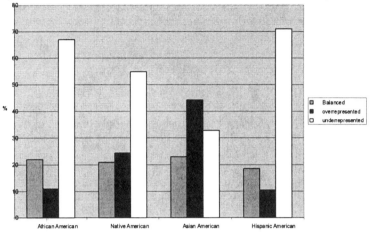

Special Education. For Special Education (see Figure 2), the results also show differences across the four racial/ethnic groups in these data. Compared with White representation in special education, a little over two-thirds of African American GMS applicants attended schools where students of their racial group are overrepresented. Forty-seven percent of Native American/Alaska Native applicants were from schools where Native American/Alaska Native students were overrepresented. About 6 percent of Asian Pacific Islander American applicants were from schools where their group was overrepresented, and one-half of Hispanic American applicants were from schools where Hispanic American students were overrepresented.

On average, for all the high schools attended by the respondents, and compared with Whites, African Americans were overrepresented in special education while Asian Pacific Islander Americans were quite underrepresented in special education programs. American Indian/Alaska Native and Hispanic students were also underrepresented in special education programs, but not as much as Asian Pacific Islander Americans. (The means are 0.24, -0.81, -0.14, and -0.25).

Applicants from schools with the highest percentage of African American enrollment (75%-100%) were more likely to have lower rates of African American disproportionality in special education programs (the underrepresention index percentage is 53.3 versus 21.0-33.7). The opposite pattern holds for American Indian/Alaska Native students (27.3 versus 43.6-55.7). Asian Pacific Islander Americans and Hispanic Americans show no clear patterns.

Suspension. Suspension from school or within-school suspension costs students valuable instructional time. Moreover, the fairness communicated by the use of suspensions is an important component of school climate. Compared with White representation in suspensions, 85 percent of African American GMS applicants are from schools where African American students were overrepresented. About half of Native American/Alaska Native applicants were from schools where their group was overrepresented. About one-fourth of Asian Pacific Islander American applicants were from schools where Asian Pacific Islander students were overrepresented, and one-third of Hispanic American applicants were from schools where Hispanic Americans were overrepresented (see Figure 3).

Figure 2. Percentage Distribution of Gates High Schools by Representation in Special Education for Each Race/Ethnicity.

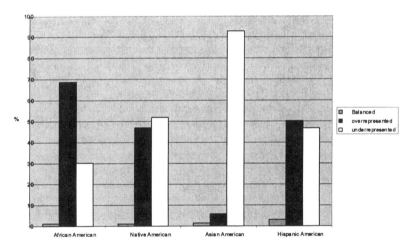

On average, three racial groups (American Indians/Alaska Natives, African Americans, and Hispanic Americans) were overrepresented when compared with Whites in the same school. Asian Pacific Islander American students are the only ones who were, on average, underrepresented compared with White students (mean indices are: 0.54, 0.96, 0.39, and -0.20, respectively). Schools with higher percentages of Asian Pacific Islanders were more likely to have Asian Pacific Islanders overrepresented in suspension.

Figure 3. Percentage Distribution of Gates High Schools by Representation in Suspension for Each Race/Ethnicity.

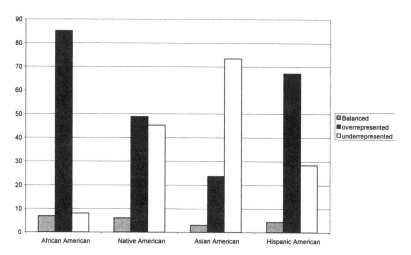

Expulsions. Expulsions, even more so than suspensions, severely restrict and prevent educational growth. Compared with White representation in expulsions, over one-third of African American GMS applicants attended schools where African Americans were overrepresented; 21 percent of Native American/Alaska Native applicants were from schools where Native American/Alaska Native students were overrepresented; 16 percent of Asian Pacific Islander American applicants were from schools where Asian Pacific Islander students were overrepresented, and 35 percent of Hispanic American applicants attended schools where students from their group were overrepresented (see Figure 4).

On average, the same three racial/ethnic groups (Native Americans/Alaska Natives, African Americans, and Hispanic Americans) were overrepresented in expulsion when compared with White students in the same school. Asian Pacific Islander Americans, again, are the only group that on average was not overrepresented compared with White students (the mean indices are 0.43, 0.40, 0.18, and -0.03 respectively).

Schools attended by GMS applicants that have more than 25 percent African American enrollment are likely to have more African Americans expelled. A similar pattern holds for Native Americans/Alaska Natives, Asian Pacific Islander Americans, and Hispanic Americans.

Figure 4. Percentage Distribution of Gates High Schools by Representation in Expulsion for Each Race/Ethnicity.

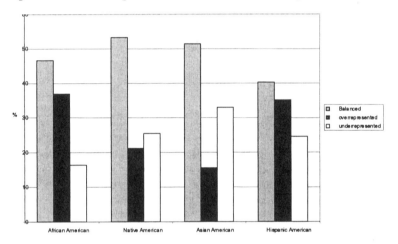

There are no significant differences between GMS recipients and nonrecipients for the four indexes for representation in gifted programs, special education programs, suspensions, or expulsions.

Summarizing this section on school climate factors, some observations are warranted. There are important ways in which respondents' race has implications for participation in gifted programs, special education, rates of suspension, and expulsions. For example, Asian Pacific Islander American applicants are more likely to come from schools where Asian Pacific Islander Americans are either equally or overrepresented in gifted programs. By contrast, applicants from the other three racial groups are less likely to come from schools where students like themselves are equally or overrepresented in gifted programs.

For representation in special education programs, 92.8 percent of Asian Pacific Islander American applicants were from schools where they were underrepresented in special education programs. By contrast, the percentages for African Americans, Native Americans/Alaska Natives, and Hispanic Americans are 30.1, 52.1, and 46.7 respectively.

The results for suspensions and expulsions are not surprising: African American applicants have the greatest likelihood of coming from high schools where their race group was overrepresented in suspension, and Asian Pacific Islander American applicants have the least likelihood of coming from schools where their race group was overrepresented in suspensions (85.1% versus 23.7%). The other two groups are in the middle (Native Americans/Alaska Natives: 48.7 percent, Hispanic Americans: 67.1%). The same pattern holds for expulsions, although the likelihood for each racial group is smaller than for suspension.

College Enrollment

In addition to the general characteristics of the high schools, we explored the college enrollment outcomes for the 2001 GMS applicant cohort. Figures 5 through 7 present the descriptive results for three "types of colleges" measures.

Figure 5. First College/University Type (4-year versus 2-year) by Gates Status (N=3934).

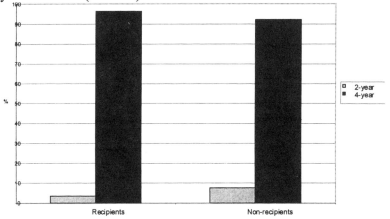

Figure 5 shows that about 93 percent of respondents went to four-year colleges. A significantly higher proportion of nonrecipients than recipients went to two-year colleges (7.7% versus 3.6%). On a second measure, minority serving status (see Figure 6), about 19.5 percent of all applicants enrolled in Minority Serving Institutions (MSIs). There was no statistically significant difference between recipients and nonrecipients in the rates of enrollment in MSIs.

Figure 6. First College Type (MSI versus Non-MSI) By Gates Status (N=3934).

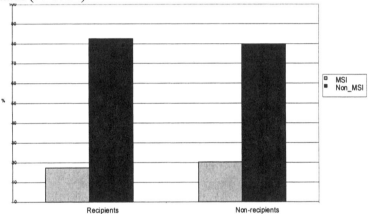

The College Selectivity for colleges attended by GMS applicants, as measured by the acceptance rate reported to U.S. News & World Report by each college or university, is shown in Figure 7. A significant difference was found between recipients and nonrecipients in the selectivity of the first college/university in which they enrolled. Recipients attended more selective institutions than did nonrecipients (the mean acceptance rate is 58.4% versus 63.1%). There is a significant difference in the degree of college selectivity of first college enrolled in among the four racial groups of applicants without controlling for other relevant variables. Native American/Alaska Native students, on average, enrolled in the least selective colleges, while Asian Pacific Islander American students went to the most selective colleges among the four groups. The mean acceptance rates—college selectivity—for African American, Native American/Alaska Native, Asian Pacific Islander American, and Hispanic American students are: 63.1 percent, 72.8 percent, 58.3 percent, and 60.6 percent respectively.

Figure 7. First College Acceptance Rate for Gates Applicants (N=3622).

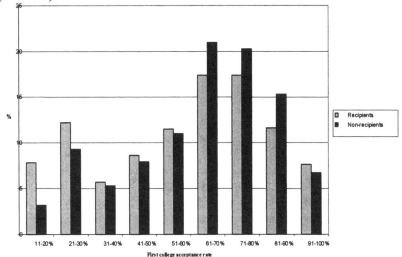

These descriptive results show that there were differences in college-going outcomes for GMS recipients and nonrecipients. These data also show differences across race on two of the above measures: attendance at high schools offering different numbers of AP courses and attending selective colleges. Notably, in both instances, Native American/Alaska Native and African American students are more disadvantaged on these measures.

Regression Analyses Results

The following discussion presents results from regression analyses focusing on the relative contributions of individual versus school factors in shaping selected outcomes. The results, based on the examination of the descriptive analyses, are informative and set the stage for examining the relative contribution of the high school origin measures and individual level measures. While such analyses are conducted more frequently using statistical approaches that explicitly estimate "nested" coefficients, the data here do not accommodate such an approach because the GMS student is mainly one case per school. Rather, we employ standard ordinary least squares (OLS) estimates for continuous dependent variables and maximum likelihood estimates for binary dependent variable. Table 5a and 5b presents a summary of the findings from our regression analyses.

Academic Self-esteem

Academic self-esteem has been shown to be an important factor in explaining educational attainment. We explore its role for GMS applicants. There is a significant association between GMS status and students' academic self-esteem scores. Of the four items comprising the index (see Appendix II for the construction of the index), there is a significant difference between recipients and nonrecipients on three items (the exception is the item regarding "students like me do not do well in this college/university"). GMS recipients tend to have a higher level of academic self-esteem than do nonrecipients. The T-test reveals a statistically significant difference in the overall score on academic self-esteem items between recipients and nonrecipients.

School attributes explained a statistically significant and substantively meaningful proportion of the variance in students' levels of academic self-esteem, along with parents' education and respondents' race and gender. More specifically, respondents from schools with higher Hispanic American enrollments have lower academic self-esteem, while respondents from schools with higher African American enrollment tend to have higher levels of academic self-esteem. Other school attributes such as size, number of AP courses offered, the student-teacher ratio, and gifted/SPED enrollment also are statistically significant. Students from bigger schools, schools offering more AP courses, and schools that have a smaller student-teacher ratio have higher academic self-esteem. Students from schools that have greater parity in gifted program enrollment also have higher academic self-esteem. Students from schools where minorities are less represented in special education programs have higher levels of academic self-esteem. Overrepresentation in neither suspensions nor expulsions is statistically significant.

GMS respondents' mother's educational levels, race, and gender are all significant predictors of levels of academic self-esteem. Compared with Asian Pacific Islander Americans, African American, Hispanic American and Native American/Alaska Native respondents all have higher levels of academic self-esteem. Males have lower levels of academic self-esteem than females. Mother's educational level has a positive effect on academic self esteem-esteem. These results are informative and mainly consistent with expected patterns of effects for school and background variables. At the same time, the set of predictors explains just 8 percent of the total variance in academic self-esteem. Because of the importance of academic self-esteem for subsequent academic pursuits, the impact of school measures on this outcome is an important finding.

Locus of control

Attribution theory seeks to explain how individuals assign causes for the outcomes and experiences they have. Locus of control is the construct that summarizes such attributions. The theory holds that, in general, an "internal" (individual/personal acceptance of responsibility) locus of control is more supportive of higher attainment. Some research (Gurin & Epps, 1975; Gurin et al., 1978) suggests that externality might be more appropriate for some populations. We explore the role of attribution for these respondents.

There is a significant difference between GMS recipients and nonrecipients in the ratings on all five items comprising our measure of locus of control (see Appendix II for the construction of the index). GMS recipients are more likely to feel that they have control over their plans and their lives compared with nonrecipients.

School attribute measures contribute significantly to the explained variance for locus of control for GMS applicants, along with parents' education and respondents' race and gender. Specifically, higher Hispanic American enrollment levels are found to be negatively associated with students' locus of control. Respondents from schools with closer parity between White and minority students in gifted program enrollment exhibit higher locus of control scores.

Table 5a. Summary of Coefficients from the Regressions on Selected Independent Variables.

Independent Variables	Academic Esteem Model 1	Academic Esteem Model 2	Locus of Control Model 1	Locus of Control Model 2	Educational Expectation Model 1	Educational Expectation Model 2	Educational Expectation Model 3	SAT Score Model 1	SAT Score Model 2	SAT Score Model 3	SAT Score Model 4
Male	—	—			+	+	+	+	+	+	+
Rs father's education attainment	+	+	+	+		+	+	+	+	+	+
Rs mother's education attainment		—			+	+	+	+	+	+	+
African American	X	+	X		+	+	+	X	—	—	—
Native American	X	+	X	+	—	—	—	X	—	—	—
Hispanic American	X	+	X	+	+	+	+	X	+	+	+
% Black students in school	X		X		X	—	—	X	—	—	—
% Hispanic students in school	X	—	X		X	—	—	X	—	—	—
School total enrollment	X	+	X	+	X			X		+	+
No. AP courses offered	X	+	X	+	X			X			—
Student-teacher ratio	X	+	X	+	X	+	+	X			
Gifted program index¹	X	+	X	+	X	—	—	X	+	—	—
Special education index¹	X	—	X		X	+	+	X	+		+
Suspension index¹	X	+	X	+	X	—	—	X	+		+
Expulsion index¹	X	+	X	+	X	—	—	X	+	+	+
Locus of control	X	X	X	X	X			X	+	—	
Academic esteem	X	X	X	X	X	+	+	X	+	+	+
Educational expectation	X	X	X	X	X	X	X	X	+	+	+
SAT score	X	X	X	X	X	X	X	X	X	X	X
Constant	+	+	+	+	+	+	+	+	+	+	+
R²	.05	.08*	.03	.06*	.03	.05*	.06*	.23*	.30*	.31*	.33*

* R-square change from previous model is significant at α < .05 or better.
† —significant positive coefficient at α = 0.05 or better ; — —significant negative coefficient at α = 0.05 or better ;
X—variable was not included in the equation.
Student-teacher ratio = total enrollment/# of full- time teachers. ¹Refer to appendix I for the constructions of these indices.

Table 5b. Summary of Coefficients from the Regressions on Selected Independent Variables.

Independent Variables	Dependent Variables									
	College Acceptance Rate					GMS Status				
	Model 1	Model 2	Model 3	Model 4	Model 5	Model 1	Model 2	Model 3	Model 4	Model 5
Male	–	–	–	–						+
Rs father's education attainment					+					
Rs mother's education attainment										
African American						–	–	–	–	–
Native American						–				
Hispanic American	–					+	+	+	+	+
% Hispanic students in school						+	+	+	+	+
% Black students in school		–	–	–	–	+		+	+	+
School total enrollment		–	–	–	–		+			–
No. AP courses offered				–	–	–	–	–	–	–
Student-teacher ratio		–	–	–						
Gifted program index[1]		+	+	+	+				+	+
Special education index[1]		–	–	–	+	+	+	+	+	+
Suspension index[1]							–	–	–	–
Expulsion index[1]									+	
Locus of control	X	X	+	+	–			+	+	+
Academic esteem	X	X	X	+			+	+	+	+
Educational expectation	X	X	X	X	+	X	X	X	X	+
SAT score	X	X	X	X	+	X	X	X	X	+
Constant	+	+	+	+	+	+	–	–	–	–
R^2	0.02	.07*	.08*	.09*	.27*					
χ2						137.67*	51.96*	20.87*	16.89*	28.70*
Degree of Freedom						6	9	2	1	1

* R-square or Chi-square change from previous model is significant at α = 0.05 or better.
† —significant positive coefficient at α = 0.05 or better. | —significant negative coefficient at α = 0.05 or better ; X—variable was not included in the equation.
[1] Refer to appendix 1 for the constructions of these indices.
Student-teacher ratio = total enrollment/# of full time teachers.

Mother's educational level has positive implications for applicants' locus of control. Father's educational level does not have a significant effect. Other things being equal, African American, Native American/Alaska Native, and Hispanic American students have higher levels of locus of control than do Asian Pacific Islander American students. Again, however, all variables in the equation explained only 6 percent of total variance in locus of control. Still, the noted role of school factors for locus of control suggests the importance of school factors for subsequent outcomes.

Educational Expectations

Students' educational expectations have been shown repeatedly to be consequential for subsequent educational attainment. In our analyses, we find that school attributes, along with background information, added significantly to the prediction of educational expectations. Respondents from schools with higher percentages of African American or Hispanic American students tend to have higher educational expectations. Schools where minority students are less often suspended or expelled have favorable implications for students' educational expectations.

In addition, higher academic self-esteem is found to be beneficial for educational expectations. In contrast to the preceding variables, father's educational level has a positive effect on educational expectations, while mother's educational level does not. However, being male is negatively related to educational expectations, and Native American/Alaska Native and Hispanic American students are found to have lower levels of educational expectations than Asian Pacific Islander Americans.

SAT Scores

GMS applicants were not selected on the basis of their SAT or ACT scores. Nonetheless, we would expect that SAT scores would be especially susceptible to school effects. For these data, attributes of schools attended by GMS applicants contribute significantly to the predication of SAT scores after controlling for other variables in the equation. All school attribute variables except school size are statistically significant for SAT scores. Applicants from schools with higher proportions of African American or Hispanic American students have lower SAT scores. Those from schools with a smaller student-teacher ratio or more AP courses have higher SAT scores. Schools with greater parity in gifted program participation or those favoring minorities in the gifted program have a positive effect on SAT scores. Schools with fewer minorities suspended or expelled have a positive effect on SAT test scores also. Finally, both higher levels of students' educational expectations and academic self-esteem correspond positively with their SAT scores.

In contrast to earlier occurring outcomes, being male is positively related to students' SAT scores. Finally, Native Americans/Alaska Natives, African Americans, and Hispanic Americans have lower SAT scores than Asian Pacific Islander Americans.

College Selectivity

One critical outcome variable we examine is college selectivity. We are especially interested in identifying high school effects for the degree of selectivity of the first college enrolled in by the applicants. Column 5 of Table 5 presents the results.

Students' background information, school variables, SAT/ACT score, educational expectation, and self-concepts (academic self-esteem and locus of control) all explained significant amounts of the variance in college selectivity. When school variables were added to the model (number of AP courses, the student-teacher ratio, parity of gifted program participation, and special education program enrollment), all were found to be significant predictors of college selectivity. Respondents from schools offering more AP courses, and those from schools where gifted program participation is more equally distributed compared with White students, are more likely to enroll in more-selective colleges. The effect of school attribute measures remains the same even after controlling for locus of control, academic self-esteem, and educational expectations. However, after entering SAT scores, the parity in special educational program enrollment is not significant. Respondents who have higher levels of academic self-esteem are in less selective colleges. This is true even after controlling for all other variables considered. SAT score is also significant; students with higher SAT scores are in more-selective colleges. After controlling for school, individual attributes, and SAT score, African American and Hispanic American students enrolled in more selective colleges than Asian Pacific Islander students, and male students enrolled in less-selective colleges than females.

GMS Status

The final outcome measure we assess here is GMS status, that is, whether or not the applicant received a GMS award. Here, again, understanding the role of school factors in the selection of an applicant as a Scholar has important implications for the program as well as for the identification and selection process itself. For example, admissions offices at colleges and universities traditionally often use such findings to build a list of high schools that will offer the "yield" of applicants they desire.

When adding all nine school variables into the model with background information, the change in the explained variance is significant. Therefore, school attributes make a substantial contribution to the prediction of the probability of being selected as a Gates Millennium Scholar. Students from schools with more AP courses or schools with a higher percentage of African American enrollment have a greater likelihood of being selected as Scholars. Students from schools where minorities are more represented in gifted programs than Whites or where minorities are less represented in expulsions have a better chance of being Scholars. Even after controlling for other variables, the effect of the percentage of African American enrollment, gifted program participation, special education enrollment parity, and expulsion parity all remain statistically significant. The effect of number of AP courses, however. is not statistically significant.

Students' race, gender, SAT scores, and educational expectations are important in a favorable way for becoming a GMS recipient. After controlling for school and individual background, students with higher SAT scores have a greater likelihood of being selected as Scholars. After controlling for all other variables considered in the model, females have a slightly better chance of being recipients than males. African American, Hispanic American, and Native Americans/Alaska Natives each have a greater likelihood of selection as recipients compared with Asian Pacific Islander Americans. Those whose parents have less education have a better chance to receive a GMS award, which may reflect the GMS policy requiring applicants to be Pell-eligible. And finally, the higher one's educational expectations are, the greater the chance of becoming a Scholar is. This is true after controlling for all other variables.

Conclusion

The findings reported here are both illuminating and important. It is especially important to note the role of the school factors as determinants of selection as a Scholar. In short, schools do make a difference. In addition to schools offering the opportunity to learn at high levels, as indicated by the number of Advanced Placement courses they offer, it also is important, based on these data, that schools maintain a climate of fairness as referenced by equitable rates of participation in gifted programs and parity in rates of representation in special education, expulsion, and suspension across racial and ethnic groups.

These school factors that are shown to be consequential for antecedent outcomes also are determinants of these later academic outcomes. Finally, this set of findings provides evidence that there are high schools that produce solid performers who are minority students with high economic need. It will be important to learn more about why and how the school factors are important in order to determine the extent to which the attributes of these high schools are replicable.

References

Braddock, J. H, II. (1980, Jul). The perpetuation of segregation across levels of education: A behavioral assessment of the contact-hypothesis. *Sociology of Education, 53*, 178-186.

Chaplin, D. D., & Century Foundation Task Force on the Common School. (2002). *Divided we fail: Coming together through public school choice.* New York: Century Foundation Press.

Coleman, J. S. (1966). *Equality of educational opportunity.* Washington, DC: Office of Education, U.S. Department of Health, Education, and Welfare.

Gurin, P., et al. (1978, December). Personal and ideological aspects of internal and external control. *Social Psychology, 41*, 275-296.

Gurin, P., & Epps, E. (1975). *Black consciousness, identity, and achievement: A study of students in historically black colleges.* New York: John Wiley.

Lee, V. E., Smith, J. B., & Croninger, R. G. (1997, April). How high school organization influences the equitable distribution of learning in mathematics and science. *Sociology of Education, 70,* 128-150.

Lee, V. E., & Smith, J. B. (1996, February). Collective responsibility for learning and its effects on gains in achievement for early secondary school students. *American Journal of Education, 104,* 103-147.

Lee, V. E. (2000). School size and the organization of secondary schools. In M. T. Hallinan (Ed.), *The handbook of the sociology of education.* New York: Kluwer Academic/Plenum Publishers.

Rusk, D., & Century Foundation Task Force on the Common School. (2002). *One nation, one school.* New York: Century Foundation Press.

Sewell, W. H., Hauser, R. M., & Featherman, D. L. (Eds.) (1976). *Schooling and achievement in American society.* New York: Academic Press.

Trent, W., Braddock, J., & Henderson, R. (1985). Sociology of education: A focus on education as an institution. *Review of Research in Education, 12,* 295-333. Washington, DC: American Research Association.

Appendix I. Construction of indices of representation of minority groups in gifted education, special education, suspension, and expulsion.

Gifted program index = % of White in Gifted program/% of White in school – % of Black (Native, Asian, Hispanic) in gifted program/% of Black (Native, Asian, Hispanic) in school

Special education index = % of Black (Native, Asian, Hispanic) in SPED/% of Black (Native, Asian, Hispanic) in school – % of White in SPED/% of White in school

Suspension index = % of Black (Native, Asian, Hispanic) in suspension/% of Black (Native, Asian, Hispanic) in school – % of White in suspension/% of White in school

Expulsion index = % of Black (Native, Asian, Hispanic) in expulsion/% of Black (Native, Asian, Hispanic) in school – % of White in expulsion/% of White in school

Appendix II. Construction of indices of academic self-esteem and locus of control.

Item	Response Range	Scale Scores	
		Minimum	Maximum
Academic Self-esteem			
Students like me do not usually do well	Strongly agree to strongly disagree	0	3
I expect to be an honor student at this college/university	Strongly disagree to strongly agree	0	3
I could get higher grades in a major that suited me better	Strongly agree to strongly disagree	0	3
I am afraid that I may not make it in college or in a university	Strongly agree to strongly disagree	0	3
Total		0	12
Cronbach's Alpha			0.579
Locus of Control			
I don't have enough control over the direction my life is taking	Strongly agree to strongly disagree	0	3
In my life, good luck is more important than hard work for success	Strongly agree to strongly disagree	0	3
Every time I try to get ahead, something or somebody stops me	Strongly agree to strongly disagree	0	3
My plans hardly ever work out, so planning only makes me unhappy	Strongly agree to strongly disagree	0	3
When I make plans, I am almost certain I can make them work	Strongly disagree to strongly agree	0	3
Total		0	15
Cronbach's Alpha			0.700

CHAPTER 4

WHO GOES TO COLLEGE? HIGH SCHOOL CONTEXT, ACADEMIC PREPARATION, THE COLLEGE CHOICE PROCESS, AND COLLEGE ATTENDANCE

Walter R. Allen, Marguerite Bonous-Hammarth, and Susan A. Suh

> *Success results when preparation meets opportunity.*
> Joseph B. Wirthlin

> *Shoot for the moon . . . a miss will put you among the stars.*
> African American Proverb

Together these epigrams convey the importance of preparation as a prior condition for success. In this paper, we examine the relationship between high school preparation and college attendance. The assumption underlying this study was that adequate preparation is necessary for success. The group studied represents some of this nation's most talented and accomplished high school graduates. The fact that not all of these applicants for the 2001 Gates Millennium Scholars (GMS) awards were successful in their quest for financial support does not detract from the overall academic excellence of the pool. Thus, it is reasonable to search for explanations for links between high school context, high school preparation, college choice, and college attendance in the experiences of these exemplary students. Perhaps the answer to the puzzle confronting teachers, parents, researchers, and policy makers of how best to improve educational achievement for all youth is contained in the life stories of the select group of students who are sufficiently bold and qualified to apply for (and, in some instances, win) the extraordinarily competitive Gates Millennium Scholarships.

Background

The path to college begins early and is influenced by a variety of factors. Sometimes the presence of strong parental influence is the major determinant for students preparing for college attendance (Hearn, 1984; Stage & Hossler, 1989). At other times, personal aspirations or fears, peer influence, or sheer enjoyment of learning are the major determinants of students' academic preparation (Galotti & Mark, 1994; Hossler, Braxton & Coopersmith, 1989). These determinants, however, reflect only the level of student commitment to learning. They do not account for such factors as the learning environments students encounter, the rigor of the curriculum presented, or the degree to which the schools they attend expect and encourage high academic achievement and advanced learning (Hearn, 1991; McDonough, 1997).

The literature on college choice suggests that opportunities to learn differ for students of different races, ethnicities, social classes, and regional urbanicities, as specific resources provided in academic settings vary between and within schools (Garet & DeLany, 1988; Oakes, 1985; Oakes, Quartz, Ryan & Lipton, 2000; Pachon, Federman & Castillo, 2000). This research demonstrates that urban, low-income students of color encounter unique challenges gaining access to rigorous academic courses, adequate educational resources, quality instruction, early college counseling, and other college prerequisites. School-managed strategies, such as academic tracking, selective distribution of information about college prerequisites, and access to other college planning resources, determine the knowledge and social capital students have to guide subsequent college choices and selections.

Purpose of the Study

The purpose of this study is to examine patterns of high school preparation related to college choice and enrollment for students from different high school learning environments. First, the study examines differences across racial/ethnic, gender, social class, and regional groups with regard to college destinations for Scholars. Second, it explores the influence of background characteristics, such as college aspirations and decisions/behaviors of students prior to college enrollment, on college destination. In particular, we propose to analyze the pathways to college for students and how factors related to college preparation accumulate to influence college enrollment and successful transition to college. Although student admission to a first-choice college and student selection of a first-choice college may refer to different factors (e.g., student admissibility vs. student preferences and ability to pay), we investigate student enrollment in first-choice colleges as one outcome. As discussed further below, we are interested in the factors that influenced the enrollment decisions of these high-achieving grant applicants.

Several elements of a larger picture must be considered in order to comprehend fully the multilayered, dynamic aspects of college access and success for different groups of students. Therefore, we propose to address various research questions related to secondary preparation and postsecondary opportunities. A developmental life course perspective provides the foundation for this study; thus, we examine academic plans, preparation, achievement, and performance for different groups of students during the critical years of high school and transition to college.

The research questions guiding this study are as follows:

1. What factors facilitate or hinder students' preparation in high school for application to college or university?

2. What effect, if any, does high school context have on the academic preparation and post-secondary plans, decisions, and outcomes of students from different racial/ethnic and gender subpopulations?

3. If there are observed racial/ethnic, gender, and social class differences in high school preparation, college choice, and college outcomes among different subgroups of students, what are the research, practice, and policy implications?

Data and Methods

The study employed quantitative and qualitative methods, drawing on two major sources of data: 1) national survey data from the applicant pool for the 2001 GMS program, and 2) interview data from a subsample of Fall 2001 Scholars in their freshman year of college.

Fall 2001 GMS Freshman Applicants
Data were collected by the National Opinion Research Center (NORC) at the University of Chicago, which included survey responses from 1,500 applicants to the Fall 2001 GMS freshman class. Of the applicants who reported racial background, 510 are African American, 135 are Native American/Alaska Native, 312 are Asian Pacific Islander American, 114 are White[1], and 219 are Hispanic American.[2] The survey included questions on first-, second-, and third-choice colleges, degree aspirations, beliefs and values, family support for college, high school academic preparation, undergraduate activities, and background information.

These data were subjected to quantitative analyses in order to identify differences between student cohorts by background characteristics and to determine how background preparation and high school context are correlated with college choice, transition, and success. Using the Fall 2001 GMS Applicant Data Set, we analyzed descriptive data including means, standard deviations, correlations, and cross-tabulations to determine the relationships across racial/ethnic, gender, and socioeconomic student cohorts. Four regression models were developed:[3] The first regression model (logistic) examined associations among independent variables and the outcome measure enrollment in student's first-choice college. The second regression model (ordinary least squares regression) examined the associations among independent variables and an outcome measure indicating extent of adjustment to college life. A third regression model (ordinary least squares regression) examined the influence of independent variables on the outcome measure educational aspirations, while a fourth regression model examined the influence of independent variables on the outcome measure college persistence (i.e., likelihood of dropping out of college prior to graduation).

GMS Interview Sample
The researcher solicited interviews with Scholars attending a November 11, 2002, GMS Leadership Conference in Los Angeles, California. Invitations to participate in the interviews were sent via electronic correspondence along with background information on the study. A total of 56 students were in the interview study. The gender and racial/ethnic breakdown of the interview sample was as follows: gender—43 females and 13 males; race/ethnicity—14 African Americans, 11 Native Americans/Alaska Natives, 19 Asian Pacific Islander Americans, and 12 Hispanic Americans.

Interviewees were grouped by ethnicity and divided into six focus groups: African American (2 groups), Native American/Alaska Native, Asian Pacific Islander American (2 groups), and Hispanic American. Participants completed a research survey that included questions on high school achievement, standardized tests completed, assessments of levels of preparation for college, and background information. (See Appendix A.) Focus group interviews lasted approximately one and one-half hours and included questions about sources of information concerning college and major challenges in addition to barriers and facilitators for college preparation. (See Appendix B.) At the conclusion of the focus groups, participants were given $5 gift cards from Starbucks coffee shops as a gratuity.

Qualitative data enhanced the researcher's understanding of patterns revealed in the broader quantitative study. We analyzed patterns from the GMS Interview Sample and identified several themes related to high school preparation and transition to college. ATLAS.ti software was used to examine the focus group interview transcripts for major themes and key patterns. The goal was to elucidate themes revealed by quantitative analyses and to uncover overlooked patterns/factors.

Results

Generally speaking, descriptive statistics reveal stark racial contrasts. (See Appendix C.) The results sometimes are surprising in that our findings often refute common stereotypes of racial groups. For example, stereotypes and monolithic conceptions, such as the presumed high achievement and "success" of Asian Pacific Islander Americans as a whole and assumptions that African American and Hispanic American students consistently have more academic and social difficulties, fail to represent adequately the rich dynamics and diversity within the different groups.

Indicators of socioeconomic status, such as parents' education, point to Asian Pacific Islander Americans and Hispanic Americans as the groups with the greatest proportion at the lower end of the economic spectrum. Despite this, Asian Pacific Islander Americans tend to hold the highest professional degree aspirations of all racial/ethnic groups. They also are most likely to have taken many high school math and science classes as well as Advanced Placement (AP) exams. Asian Pacific Islander Americans also are most likely to have experienced being the racial minority in their high school classes and are the most likely to report lower self-esteem or sense of control over their lives. Although Asian Pacific Islander Americans have the highest mean admissions test scores and the highest mean of time spent studying of any racial group, they are the most likely to report difficulties keeping up with college homework. The tendency of Asian Pacific Islander Americans to attend their first-choice college is not significantly different from other racial/ethnic groups.

Disputing common perceptions that African American and Hispanic American students confront the most barriers to educational success, these data suggest that Native American/Alaska Native students often encounter more obstacles than their African American and Latino counterparts. While it is true that, overall, Hispanic Americans have higher proportions of parents with low educational attainment than Native Americans/Alaska Natives, the latter students are the least likely of all racial groups to have taken math and science classes or AP exams. Further, Native American/Alaska Native students also have the lowest mean SAT and ACT scores. Challenging widespread stereotypes, African American students are the least likely to believe that planning does not work out and the least likely to report difficulty in keeping up with college homework. African Americans also are more likely to express higher doctoral degree aspirations compared with other racial/ethnic groups. Below are specific racial and gender differences (all statistically significant cross-tabulations are significant at the .001 level unless otherwise noted):

Father's Education. While African Americans and Native Americans/Alaska Natives have similar patterns of father's education (64% and 70% high school or some college, respectively), Asian Pacific Islander American and Hispanic American students show extremely bifurcated patterns. A sizeable percentage of fathers from these two groups are at the lowest levels of education (20% of Asian Pacific Islander Americans and 18% of Hispanic Americans have less than high school). Comparable percentages of fathers for these groups are at the highest levels of education (18% of Asian Pacific Islander Americans and 17% of Hispanic Americans have graduate degrees). Females are more likely than males to have fathers with less than a high school degree (20% vs. 16%) and are less likely to have fathers with an advanced degree (10% vs. 16%) ($p < .01$).

Mother's Education. Similarly, Asian Pacific Islander Americans are much more likely to have mothers with less than a high school education (27%), followed by Hispanic Americans

(19%), African Americans (5.6%), Native Americans/Alaska Natives (5.3%), and Whites (6.2%). Asian Pacific Islander American students are least likely to have mothers with graduate degrees (40-50% lower than all other students). No significant gender differences were found in mother's education; about half of all male and half of all female respondents had mothers with no more than a high school education.

Racial Composition of High School Classes. Almost half of all African American and Asian Pacific Islander American students strongly disagree when asked if their racial group was the majority in their high school classes (46% and 47%, respectively). Surprisingly, 42 percent of Native American/ Alaska Native students agreed or strongly agreed that their racial group was the majority, higher than Whites responding similarly (32%). There were no significant gender differences in high school racial composition; less than one-third of both male and female students said most of their high school classes were with students of the same racial group.

Mathematics and Science Curriculum. While most African Americans and Asian Pacific Islander Americans reported four or more years of high school math (91% and 90%, respectively), fewer Native Americans/Alaska Natives said the same (72%), with Whites (82%) and Hispanic Americans (85%) in the middle. Native American/Alaska Native students were also the least likely to have taken four or more science classes: 58 percent on the low end versus 79 percent of Asian Pacific Islander Americans on the high end (p<.01).[4] Slight gender differences were shown; females were slightly less likely to have taken four or more years of math than their male counterparts and slightly more likely to have taken three years instead (p<.05). However, it was impressive that in this sample, about two-thirds of both males and females took at least four years of high school science.

SAT or ACT Scores. Not surprisingly, there are statistically significant racial and gender differences in mean scores for both the SAT (Asian Pacific Islander American = 1247, White = 1192, Hispanic American = 1161, African American = 1110, Native American/Alaska Native = 1094; male = 1185, female = 1136) and the ACT (Asian Pacific Islander American = 26.2, White = 25.6,

Hispanic American = 24.5, Native American/Alaska Native = 23.1, African American = 22.9; male = 25, female = 24).

Advanced Placement Exams. Nearly half of White and Native American/Alaska Native students had not taken any AP exams (45.0% and 45.7%, respectively), while Asian Pacific Islander American students were most likely to have taken at least four (50.0%) and least likely to have not taken any. Surprisingly, a high proportion of Hispanic American students took at least four AP exams (33.6%), and Hispanic Americans were less likely not to have taken any (24.4%) compared with the other groups. There were no statistically significant gender differences; about one-third of each gender did not take any AP exams, while another one-third took four or more.

High School Affiliation. Hispanic Americans were most likely to have attended a private school (19%) or religious school (17%). Asian Pacific Islander Americans were least likely to have attended either type (4% and 3%, respectively). No gender differences were seen; about one-tenth or fewer of all students (regardless of gender) attended a private or religious school.

Self-esteem and Locus of Control. Although many reported highest self-esteem (36%), Asian Pacific Islander Americans were most likely to report low self-esteem (disagree or strongly disagree, 9.1%), almost two times more likely than Native Americans/Alaska Natives (4.7%), Hispanic Americans (4.6%), and African Americans (5.5%). Whites were second most likely to report low self-esteem, at 7.3%. However, Asian Pacific Islander Americans were the least likely to report highest level of self-esteem compared with all other groups (42% of Whites, 59% of African Americans, 50% of Native Americans/Alaska Natives, and 56% of Hispanic Americans). Regarding locus of control, again, Asian Pacific Islander Americans were most likely to say that planning does not work out (13% agree or strongly agree). On the other hand, African Americans were the least likely to believe that planning does not matter (6.2%). There were no significant racial differences in academic self-esteem (all mostly high). Similarly, significant gender differences were absent; more than 90 percent of male and female students report high self-esteem and locus of control. Slightly fewer of both genders disagreed with the statement that people like them do not do well academically, evidencing high academic self-concepts across the group.

Reasons for Choosing College. Native American/Alaska Native students were least likely to consider reputation as "very important," while Asian Pacific Islander Americans were the most likely to place a high value on this factor (67% vs. 86%, respectively). There were no gender differences on the importance attributed to college academic reputation. There were no significant racial/ethnic or gender differences over low cost as reason for college choice; low expenses proved very important to all students.

Academic difficulties. Although all groups had sizeable proportions reporting difficulties keeping up with homework as first-year college students, Asian Pacific Islander American students were most likely to say they found it "difficult" or "very difficult," while African Americans were the least likely (47% vs. 29%). Asian Pacific Islander Americans and African Americans also were the least and most likely to report no difficulty with freshman homework (15% vs. 28%, respectively). No gender differences were found; a little over one-third of males and females reported difficulty with homework. There were no significant racial/ethnic or gender differences in difficulty managing time or paying for college; all groups were split about half-and-half.

Educational Aspirations. Compared with all other racial/ethnic groups, African American and Asian Pacific Islander American students were more likely to have the highest education aspirations. They were the least likely to want a bachelor's degree or less (the proportion was nearly half that for other racial groups). However, the type of advanced degree sought was different for each group. African American students tended to want to pursue doctoral degrees (38%) more than professional degrees (22%). In contrast, about the same number of Asian Pacific Islander Americans planned to pursue doctoral degrees (27%) as to pursue professional degrees (26%).

Other. Racial/ethnic and gender differences for the average proportion of time spent studying were statistically significant (Asian Pacific Islander American = 53.9% of time, Hispanic American = 49.8%, African American = 47.1%, Native American/Alaska Native = 46.1%, White = 42.3%; male = 48.2%, female = 50.3%, p<.05). There were no statistically significant differences by race, neither as to whether students were attending their first-choice school (most are) nor in their overall college adjustment (most adjusted well). However, there were notable gender differences; overall, females were less likely than males to be attending their first-choice college (68% vs. 79%). Whites and Native Americans/Alaska Natives reported slightly less often than other groups that they were "very unlikely" to drop out of college before graduating (p<.05) (there were no gender differences on this question).

Turning our attention to multivariate relationships in the data, we used regression in an attempt to discover which factors were the most powerful determinants or correlates of the college choice outcomes. All regression results were relatively straightforward and make sense intuitively. First, we used logistic regression in order to examine the multiple predictors of attending the first-choice college. Each subsequent block of variables added to the model increased the model's explanatory power. (See Table 1.) However, the attitudes, time use, college persistence, and educational aspirations variable blocks did not significantly alter the model statistically. In the final model, it is clear, holding all other variables constant, that needing to attend a low-expense school (Exp(B)=.58) and having less difficulty with college homework (Exp(B)=.71) are both associated with decreases in the odds that a student will attend his/her first-choice college. Being African American (Exp(B)=.58) gave a significant coefficient at the .05 level until the college adjustment variables were introduced into the model. Variables that *increase* the odds of attending the first-choice school, holding all other variables constant are:

- Being male more than doubles the odds of attending the first-choice school (Exp(B)=2.01).
- As reputation of school becomes increasingly important to the student, the odds of going to first-choice college more than doubles with each incremental increase in importance (Exp(B)=2.03).

When we used linear regression to explore multivariate predictors of college adjustment (does not feel like part of campus community; strongly agree to strongly disagree), the results were enlightening. (See Table 2). Each subsequent block of variables added to the model and increased the model's explanatory power. This was especially true for variables in the attitudinal block. The indicators in the high school characteristics, college persistence, and educational aspirations variable blocks did not significantly alter the model statistically. Holding all other variables constant in the full model, the largest effects were found with increases in the level of importance of school reputation in selecting the school (β=.164, p<.001), academic self-concept (β=.136, p<.01), and self-esteem (β=.132, p<.01). Increasing levels of proportion of time devoted to study in college have a negative effect on college adjustment (β=-.120, p<.01). Being Hispanic American increases college adjustment slightly (β=.106, p<.05) in addition to not having difficulties with college expenses (β=.105, p<.01) and having higher education aspirations (β=.093, p<.05).

Linear regression of educational aspirations showed that each subsequent block of variables added to the model increased the model's explanatory power to the final model. (See Table 3.) The effect of more time devoted to study was especially strong. The attitudes, college choice, specific college adjustment indicators, and college persistence (i.e., likelihood of dropping out of school) variable blocks did not significantly alter the model, statistically speaking. Holding all other variables constant, the strongest predictors of educational aspirations according to our full regression model are proportion of time devoted to study (β=.167, p<.001), number of science courses taken in high school (β=.127, p<.01), and *not* being Asian Pacific Islander American (β=-.142, p<.01) or Hispanic American (β=-.098, p<.05).

Table 1. Logistic Regression Model Predicting Attendance at First-Choice College: African American, Asian Pacific Islander American, and Hispanic American Students, Gates Millennium Scholars Freshman Applicants, Fall 2001 (N=668).

	B	S.E.	Wald	Sig.	Exp(B)
Constant	.176	1.837	.009	.924	1.193
Independent Variables					
Background/Demographics					
Father's Education	-.058	.088	.427	.514	.944
Mother's Education	.037	.095	.155	.694	1.038
African American	-.442	.266	2.767	.096	.643
Asian Pacific Islander American	-.181	.286	.403	.525	.834
Hispanic American			2.575	.109	
Male	.699**	.213	10.772	.001	2.012
High School Characteristics					
Of Majority Race in H.S. classes	.050	.091	.303	.582	1.051
Years of H.S. Math	-.116	.290	.159	.690	.891
Years of H.S. Science	.167	.184	.823	.364	1.182
SAT score	.001	.001	.752	.386	1.001
Number of H.S. AP Exams	.057	.067	.728	.394	1.059
Private H.S.	.425	.503	.713	.398	1.529
Religious H.S.	-.937	.550	2.901	.089	.392
Attitudes					
General Self-Esteem	.183	.120	2.330	.127	1.201
Locus of Control	.217	.153	2.010	.156	1.243
Academic Self-Concept	-.257	.141	3.304	.069	.773
College Choice					
Selecting for low expenses	-.553***	.157	12.401	.000	.575
Selecting for strong reputation	.708**	.221	10.238	.001	2.030
College Adjustment					
Difficulty with schoolwork	-.345*	.147	5.494	.019	.708
Difficulty with time management	.136	.130	1.089	.297	1.145
Difficulty paying for expenses	.107	.097	1.222	.269	1.113
Time Use	.610	.516	1.400	.237	1.841
College Persistence	-.017	.380	.002	.965	.983
Educational Aspirations	-.070	.097	.524	.469	.932

NOTE: Statistically significant at the following levels: *$p<.05$; **$p<.01$; ***$p<.001$.

Model Summary	
Omnibus Tests of Coefficients	Chi-square = 82.520, df(23) $p<.001$
-2 Log Likelihood	717.030
Cox & Snell R^2	.116
Nagelkerke R^2	.167

Table 2. Linear Regression Predicting College Adjustment Overall, All Variables, African American, Asian Pacific Islander American, and Hispanic American Students, Gates Millennium Scholars Freshman Applicants, Fall 2001 (N=683).

	B	S.E.	β	Sig.
Constant	.943	.543		.083
Independent Variables				
Background/Demographics				
Father's Education	-.007	.026	-.012	.787
Mother's education	.027	.028	.043	.325
Asian Pacific Islander American	.081	.072	.050	.263
Hispanic American	.192*	.075	.106	.011
Male	-.016	.059	-.010	.785
High School Characteristics				
Of Majority Race in H.S. classes	.012	.027	.017	.642
Years of H.S. Math	.010	.083	.004	.907
Years of H.S. Science	-.030	.055	-.020	.590
SAT score	-.000	.000	-.023	.621
Number of H.S. AP Exams	-.013	.020	-.027	.516
Private H.S.	.064	.136	.027	.639
Religious H.S.	-.080	.155	-.030	.607
Attitudes				
General Self-Esteem	.118**	.036	.132	.001
Locus Control Planning	.087	.045	.078	.056
Academic Self-Concept	.139**	.040	.136	.001
College Choice				
Selecting for low expenses	-.032	.043	-.028	.463
Selecting for strong reputation	.305***	.069	.164	.000
College Adjustment				
Difficulty with schoolwork	.009	.042	.011	.830
Difficulty with time management	-.051	.038	-.066	.178
Difficulty paying for expenses	.080**	.029	.105	.005
Time Use	-.486**	.152	-.120	.001
College Persistence	.211	.111	.072	.057
Educational Aspirations	.070*	.028	.093	.013

NOTE: Statistically significant at the following levels: *$p<.05$; **$p<.01$; ***$p<.001$.

Model Summary			
R	.405	Adjusted R^2	.135
R^2	.164	S.E.	.700

Finally, linear regression of college persistence (drop out before graduation; strongly agree to strongly disagree) also helped to clarify complex multivariate relationships. Each subsequent block of variables added to the model and increased the model's explanatory power up to the final model. (See Table 4.) The high school characteristics, college choice, time use, and educational aspirations variable blocks did not significantly alter the model statistically. Holding all other variables constant, those with a stronger locus of control were more confident in their ability to persist in college (β=.108, p<.01). Students whose mothers have higher education levels also tended to have stronger college persistence, net of all other effects (β=.092, p<.05). Finally, the degree to which students have problems adjusting to homework loads in their first years at college also predicts college persistence, net of other effects (β=.113, p<.05).

Gates Millennium Scholars Interviews

Of the 56 Scholars who participated in focus group interviews, the majority were female (77%). By race/ethnicity, the scholars included 14 African Americans (25%), 11 Native Americans/Alaska Natives (19%), 19 Pacific Islander Americans (34%), and 12 Hispanic Americans (21%). These students reported a spectacular 3.9 grade point average in high school and continued to do very well in their first year of college (3.5 GPA). The majority had aspirations to pursue advanced degrees and to enter high-status professions, with 9 African Americans (64%), 7 Native Americans/Alaska Natives (64%), 12 Asian Pacific Islander Americans (63%), and 6 Hispanic Americans (50%) aiming for doctorates or degrees in medicine or law.

Among the focus group participants, females reported lower scores on standardized tests than males, particularly for SAT I math (correlation coefficient, r=-.37, p<.05). Similarly, African Americans in this sample reported lower standardized test scores for SAT I verbal (r=-.61) and math (r=-.42). By contrast, Asian Pacific Islander American Scholars in this sample reported higher SAT I math scores (r=.53, p<.01). As one would expect, students' scores on different standardized tests were highly and positively inter-correlated. Students from higher income backgrounds tended to be more satisfied with their high school academic preparation for college (r=.40, p<.01) and with the quality of teaching at their high school (r=.40, p<.01). Finally, students who were satisfied with the quality of their high school teachers and academic counseling tended to report satisfaction with the availability of college information at their high schools.

Table 3. Linear Regression Predicting Educational Aspirations, All Variables, African American, Asian Pacific Islander American, and Hispanic American Students, Gates Millennium Scholars Freshman Applicants, Fall 2001 (N=691).

	B	S.E.	β	Sig.
Constant	.710	.746		.341
Independent Variables				
Background/Demographics				
Father's Education	.055	.035	.070	.123
Mother's education	-.044	.038	-.053	.241
Asian Pacific Islander American	-.299**	.098	-.142	.002
Hispanic American	-.236*	.102	-.098	.022
Male	-.047	.081	-.022	.559
High School Characteristics				
Of Majority Race in H.S. classes	.004	.037	.004	.908
Years of H.S. Math	.162	.114	.055	.155
Years of H.S. Science	.244**	.075	.127	.001
SAT score	.000	.000	.079	.099
Number of H.S. AP Exams	.020	.027	.033	.455
Private H.S.	-.111	.187	-.036	.553
Religious H.S.	.160	.214	.045	.455
Attitudes				
General Self-Esteem	.004	.049	.004	.931
Locus Control Planning	.022	.062	.015	.726
Academic Self-Concept	.038	.055	.028	.490
College Choice				
Selecting school for low expenses	-.014	.059	-.009	.818
Selecting school for strong reputation	-.043	.095	-.017	.653
College Adjustment				
Difficulty keeping up with schoolwork	.062	.058	.056	.283
Difficulty with effective time management	.010	.052	.009	.851
Difficulty paying for expenses	.007	.039	.006	.868
Time Use	.888***	.206	.167	.000
College Persistence	.007	.010	.029	.452

NOTE: Statistically significant at the following levels: *p<.05; **p<.01; ***p<.001.

Model Summary			
R	.295	Adjusted R^2	.057
R^2	.087	S.E.	.964

Table 4. Linear Regression Predicting College Persistence, All Variables, African American, Asian Pacific Islander American, and Hispanic American Students, Gates Millennium Scholars Freshman Applicants, Fall 2001 (N=691).

	B	S.E.	β	Sig.
Constant	2.222***	.169		.000
Independent Variables				
Background/Demographics				
Father's Education	.008	.009	.039	.384
Mother's education	.019*	.010	.092	.042
Asian Pacific Islander American	-.021	.025	-.039	.393
Hispanic American	.011	.026	.017	.686
Male	-.022	.020	-.042	.271
High School Characteristics				
Of Majority Race in H.S. classes	-.000	.009	-.001	.969
Years of H.S. Math	.041	.029	.054	.157
Years of H.S. Science	.029	.019	.059	.133
SAT score	.000	.000	.035	.461
Number of H.S. AP Exams	.001	.007	.006	.882
Private H.S.	.004	.047	.005	.927
Religious H.S.	-.000	.054	-.068	.250
Attitudes				
General Self-Esteem	.015	.012	.050	.222
Locus Control Planning	.040**	.016	.108	.010
Academic Self-Concept	.043	.013	.125	.001
College Choice				
Selecting school with low expenses	.010	.015	.027	.486
Selecting school with strong reputation	-.015	.024	-.025	.522
College Adjustment				
Difficulty keeping up with schoolwork	.033*	.015	.113	.027
Difficulty with time management	-.004	.013	-.016	.748
Difficulty paying for expenses	-.006	.010	-.022	.563
Time Use	.047	.053	.034	.377
Educational Aspirations	.115	.153	.029	.452

NOTE: Statistically significant at the following levels: $*p<.05$; $**p<.01$; $***p<.001$.

Model Summary			
R	.322	Adjusted R^2	.074
R^2	.104	S.E.	.244

In a further look at how Scholars compare in terms of their academic backgrounds and perceptions about academic preparation in high school, Appendix F shows the distribution of mean test scores, high school GPA, and college GPA by race/ethnicity. In general, the students have comparable mean

GPAs, despite the fact that African Americans and Native Americans/Alaska Natives in this data set reported lower SAT I math scores compared with their Asian Pacific Islander American and Hispanic American peers.

Cross-tabulation of student satisfaction with high school academic counseling showed the value of disaggregating among focus group participants. We found that a majority of African Americans (42.9%) and nearly half of Native Americans/Alaska Natives (45.5%) in this sample were not satisfied with the quality of their high school academic counseling. By contrast, the majority of Hispanic Americans were very satisfied (66.7%) with high school counseling and the majority of Asian Pacific Islander Americans (52.6%) were somewhat satisfied with this important component of their academic preparation.

With this backdrop, we now turn our attention to the qualitative data from the Scholar interviews. Presumably, Scholar responses, comments, and discussions will provide a richer consideration of issues raised in the surveys conducted with Freshman 2001 applicants and with GMS recipients.

Understanding the High School Contexts and College Preparation
To understand better how various factors come into play in student preparation for college and throughout the transition to college, we examined verbatim responses from focus group participants to identify themes related to college preparation. Systematic analyses of scholar focus group interview transcripts were conducted using ATLAS.ti software.

The focus group discussions on college preparation identified three common themes related to implicit family support for college goals, student desire for a "better life," strong motivation for college, and student recognition of a "hidden curriculum" in terms of differential treatment from school personnel regarding college preparation. Specifically, students in all groups confirmed parental support that considered college as a requirement, and not an option. In many instances, parental support of college goals was as much "implicit" as explicit. Most students indicated that this support for college was emphasized beginning in elementary school and carried throughout their academic careers. As an example, one student shared how parents and family, through remarks and behaviors, communicated the expectation of college attendance.

> And, for me, college was always something like my parents always told me, "Oh, yeah, you gonna go to college." So, I always grew up thinking, Oh, I'm going to college, I'm going to college. Junior high, I'm going to college and going to college. Like high school, I was like, okay, I'll take hard classes so I can go to college. And then, like when I started thinking about SAT, and that's when I really got serious about, you know, I'm gonna go to college. There are things that I have to do if I really wanna go.

Students from low socioeconomic backgrounds understandably emphasized motives for college attendance that reflected desires to overcome or rise above current economic circumstances. These aspirations often exceeded their current living conditions and were expressed as "wanting more." These students routinely referred to lessons learned from parents who did not complete college.

> I feel my parents just wanted me to have something more than they had . . . so they were pushing me, get in college. 'Cause like my mom graduated college, but my dad never did so I feel that they kind of . . . like they're kind of living through me what they couldn't have.

Students across all racial/ethnic cohorts recognized not only between-school inequities, but also "within-school" inequities in educational resources and experiences during their high school years. In this respect, they saw how formal academic tracking and informal mechanisms prevented certain groups of students from accessing college preparatory tracks with rigorous coursework. Moreover, informal interactions with counselors and teachers often were colored by negative racial/ethnic stereotypes. The result was the creation-perpetuation of racial/ethnic inequalities within the school, hindering access to information and courses essential for college preparation. One high-achieving student commented,

> As far as prepping for college, I think they [the teachers and counselors] are kind of biased, like the school and everything because the school like even in elementary, they're kinda divided. You have kinda the smart kids and the like not so smart kids. And, when I was in high school, like all the kids who were in the good classes, they got the benefits of everything. We got the college tours, we got mentors, we got tutoring, like helping with our financial aid package and everything. And you know, telling us what classes to take. But as far as the other kids, they didn't get any help toward preparing for college and that's why the majority of them don't even attend college after graduating.

In addition, there were comments from certain racial/ethnic student groups that revealed how their special circumstances (i.e., racial, cultural, social, historical, and economic) were linked with educational inequities. African American and Hispanic American students voiced concern over how negative racial/ethnic stereotypes caused school personnel and students from other cultural backgrounds to unfairly question their academic abilities. One young woman related her experiences with and triumph over racial discrimination:

> My dad worked there [at school] as a janitor, and so, like, I always felt like I had a little bit of an advantage. It seems kinda funny but I always felt that I had this little bit of an advantage because he was there, talking to the faculty. Everybody there underestimated me, nobody believed in me but it was...it was like there was no support that I . . . but he was there to tell them, you know, "This is my daughter . . . you have to believe in her." And, he was there to

pressure them into letting me into the classes that could take, and that I wanted to take and that I needed to take.

These students also reported how economic and life hardships motivated them to be more committed and to prepare more rigorously for college. Having experienced limited opportunities in their communities, these students were determined to gain a better life through educational advancement.

I guess I realized I wanted to go to college after working in the fields for 11 years. In my final year of my junior year in high school then I realized that I didn't want to work 16 hours a day, you know, all during the week, during the summer. Coming home from the fields with, you know, cut fingers, bleeding and stuff like that, you know. I didn't like it. And, I figured, you know, I needed to do something else besides work the fields, you know, earning $5.50 an hour. So that's when I decided, you know, to get more serious [about school].

However, rather than dwell exclusively on negative factors that shaped their educational aspirations, African American and Hispanic American Scholars acknowledged important mentors who made the difference in their lives. They pointed to mentors and supporters who were "the wind beneath their wings" as they sought to rise above educational disadvantage, poverty, despair, and hardship.

She [a counselor] was a big influence. Any time you needed information, she was there. If you wanted to know about a specific college, she'll have a huge folder with your name on it—the school you wanted and she'll just like, "Here's the stuff you needed and a little extra on the side." . . . I'd say maybe 20 percent of the high school seniors graduating never thought in their lifetimes that they would ever attend a college. And they were, they're on, you know, class night, they were announcing like whose college you're going to and which university, you know.

At the same time, an Hispanic American female highlighted the ambivalence that sometimes exists for "first-generation" students of color as they pursue their goals of college attendance. The tensions were manifest in mixed messages from adults and peers who expressed pride in her academic accomplishments and, at the same time, expressed fears that she would be separated from her family, friends, and community.

> I also was encouraged and both discouraged at the same time. I was always encouraged by like older adults saying, "You know, you can make it" and stuff. But a lot of peers would always tell me, "Oh, you can't make it," you know. Most Mexicans don't make it, and a lot of my Hispanic peers would always tell me, "You're acting White now." And I felt some kind of racism in my classes 'cause I was usually the only Mexican in my honors classes.

Responses from Native American/Alaska Native Scholars reflected different patterns of planning and progress through the college admissions process that seemed at points less specific and systematic. For example, while all Scholars identified college and occupational success as important goals, Native Americans/Alaska Natives provided less definitive plans for attaining these goals. Beyond less specific articulation of the specific steps leading to college, Native Americans/Alaska Natives also more often reported late preparation for college and postponement of the college choice process until late in the junior or senior year of high school.

> I always knew I wanted to go to college. And when I finally got to high school, it came down to like where you wanna apply in my senior year

the college I'm going to now. Yeah, they were offering a program where like a visitation program so I flew out there to visit the campus. And I just fell in love with it and so I came back to my high school and I learned that they had given us an extension for like early decisions, so I went ahead and applied and then I got in. So, yeah, so I kinda made the final choice of my college my senior year afterward.

Finally, Asian Pacific Islander Scholars also offered unique responses. These students consistently voiced very traditional ideals about college choice, overwhelmingly preferring four-year, selective universities. Asian Pacific Islander students who did not prefer four-year institutions often were reluctant to discuss alternative plans to attend junior colleges or, worse yet, the decision not to attend college at all, they said. An Asian Pacific Islander American scholar commented on the importance of the prestige factor in college choice.

It's like even if you did go to college, like, some went to junior colleges and that was like disaster. "Where are you going to college?" And people would be like, "Um, nowhere really," because it was almost like a badge of shame that you were going to a community college. Like if you weren't going to college at all, that was like unheard of.

In addition, there was much discussion about the negative consequences associated with the definition and treatment of Asian Pacific Islander American students as a whole as a "model minority." In general, students felt the obligation to live up to the myth, to strive and to achieve because of others' raised expectations. However, students also recognized a negative side to the myth in that often they were steered away from student support systems, tutoring, and other vital academic resources because stereotypic beliefs (i.e., "model minority") suggested that they either did not need or would not benefit from such services.

Perversely, in some instances, the seemingly positive images of Asian Pacific Islander American students produced negative consequences. Students sometimes found it more difficult to take advantage of campus academic and social support services.

> They [teachers] think every Asian gets things, like that they understand everything really well. And so, like when I go talk to my professor, [he] expects me to understand what he's talking about. And, I just say to him, like, "I don't understand." He's like, "What don't you understand?" ... He's like, "You're supposed to understand, you're smart." I'm like, "No." It's like, I don't know, there's this . . . false expectation that I'm supposed to be good at so-and-so, so they kinda like cheat me on teaching me the simple way.

Summary, Discussion, and Implications

The assumption underlying this study is that adequate preparation is a necessary foundation for academic success. More specifically, we hypothesized that successful college choices and schooling experiences are influenced by many factors. To be successful, students must have a network of individuals and resources (educational, social, and cultural) for information on college preparation and access available to them. These students also must have available precollegiate school contexts conducive to and supportive of high academic achievement (Post, 1990; Allen, 1992). Students who have more human, social, cultural, and economic capital of this sort also are more likely to succeed in school (Stanton-Salazar, 2001).

Arguably, applicants for the prestigious and lucrative Gates Millennium Scholarships are among the nation's most accomplished graduating high school seniors. So, it is fitting that this study uses data from the Fall 2001 GMS applicant pool to explore critical influences on high school preparation and college choice. These survey data provide information about educational background, family demographics, attitudes, and the college choice process for 1,500 multiple race/ethnicity applicants. Supplemental data (questionnaires and focus group interviews) came from an interview study of 56 African American, Asian Pacific Islander American, and Hispanic American Scholars in the 2001 cohort. Together, these data sets provide broad and specific views (based on quantitative and qualitative data) of the college choice process spanning from high school preparation to college selection to academic adjustment in the first year of college.

The key findings from this study convey important lessons. First and foremost, we see ample reason to challenge conventional wisdom about race/ethnicity and achievement in this society. In point of fact, the applicant pool data reveal across all racial/ethnic groups that students who are high achievers and who worked hard to prepare themselves take advantage of opportunities when and wherever presented. Equally important, however, is the clear, ample evidence that for reasons of economics, race, ethnicity, and gender, opportunities continue to be distributed differentially among these equally highly talented and highly motivated young people.

The American creed places great weight on individualism. Our ideals presume the American Dream to be equally available to all who possess the necessary desire, moxy, talent, and energy. However, success ultimately is based not only on individual ability or initiative, but also on factors outside individual control (e.g., social institutions and their actors, social setting). What we see revealed in these data—for a group where effectively all/any questions about their personal qualifications are removed—is the power of societal factors to shape individual outcomes. Educational barriers, rooted in this country's historic (and present) customs and structures of racial/ethnic discrimination, continue to frustrate the educational ambitions of far too many qualified students of color.

In general, the successful transitions of these scholars into college hinged on their academic preparation, internal motivation, and access to key sources of support (parents, friends, school personnel, scholarship programs). As noted in GMS focus group responses, these students acknowledged the many barriers to postsecondary opportunities, but they were resilient, knowing that the alternative to enrollment was continued economic and social hardship. In some cases, these students went beyond their limited knowledge about college and access to college-educated people to petition teachers and counselors for information and access to a rigorous curriculum. They capitalized on their limited information to build connections among friends and greater networks of support in school.

Most notably, we see how financial constraints can set the trajectory of a talented young student's educational opportunities and goals, with clear consequences for his or her future professional accomplishments. To the degree that sufficient economic resources are made available, as with the GMS awards, students are better able to pursue their educational and occupational dreams to the maximum extent of their ability. Over the course of their lives, many of these students experienced economic disadvantage and hardships that most certainly restricted their educational opportunities. Rather than succumbing, these students, their families, and key mentors adopted resistance strategies that made lemonade from lemons. The consistent response to economic hardship was to realize the promise that educational achievement held as a means to overcome and rise above economic deprivation. Subsequently, these students held on to the brass ring that was education for all they were worth.

Another lesson we learn is that human potential is not easily reduced to simplistic measures like standardized test scores or the number of Advanced Placement courses taken. African Americans and females had lower test scores compared with Whites and males; however, their academic achievements were comparable. Similarly, the fact that Native American/Alaska Native and female students had taken fewer high school science classes than Asian Pacific Islander American and male students did not automatically translate into lower academic accomplishments. Finally, given the opportunity, Native American/Alaska Native students who, relative to other racial/ethnic students, had been denied educational resources and preparation were able (when circumstances permitted) to compete on an equal footing.

These findings remind us that educational achievement is a social process, shaped by human exchanges within definitive sociocultural contexts. If the answers to individual outcomes are indeed to be found neither "in the stars" nor "in ourselves," then they can be found in institutional contexts and social relationships. John Ogbu's study (1978) of educational achievement differences between majority and minority groups across several societies reinforces this point. He found that while educational achievement levels for Vietnamese in Australia were quite low, the opposite was true in the United States. Similar contradictions were revealed for Black West Indians in England versus the United States. Dramatic cross-national differences in the academic success rates of the same cultural group are best explained in terms of contextual differences. Where the aspirations and preparation of individuals of certain groups are supported, successful outcomes will be the result. On the other hand, where these opportunities are blocked, underachievement will be the result. It is just that simple (Allen, 1992; Allen, Spencer & O'Connor, 2002).

Ultimately, the implications of this study pose a challenge to our society. Will the society embrace its ideals and eliminate the vast educational inequities that continue to deny opportunities for a better life to certain excluded racial/ethnic and economic groups, or will it allow these inequities to persist? The future of our nation is tied up in the answer to this question. Over this century and the next, the United States must rely on a population that is increasingly female, of color, immigrant, and poor. Investments in creating opportunities for educational development and advancement among these disproportionately excluded groups will pay handsome dividends in the development of a skilled, financially viable labor force. The Bill & Melinda Gates Foundation is investing one billion dollars in the education of the next generation; however, we need billions more. Too many bright, talented, and motivated poor students and students of color are still denied educational opportunities. In this sense, we must confront an age-old question, a question confronted by many great societies before the United States. Which will it be—"Swords or plowshares?" "Bombs or butter?" "Smart weapons or smart children?" History has taught us that how a society answers this simple question determines that society's future and its fate.

Notes

1. The sample for the survey was drawn from the GMS applicant pool, all the members of which had been identified as belonging to the target racial/ethnic groups. However, on the survey, respondents were allowed to self-identify their race or ethnicity. Some multiracial respondents may have selected White as their racial category.

2. The numbers of respondents who answered each survey question differ. As a result, total counts for the descriptive statistics found in Appendix C may not be the same as the above.

3. For all regression models, only the African American, Asian Pacific Islander American, and Hispanic American respondents were included due to the low counts of the remaining two racial groups in the final models.

4. Hispanic Americans (68%) and African Americans (72%) were between the two extremes in four-year science enrollment.

References

Allen, W. R. (1992). The color of success: African-American college student outcomes at predominantly white and historically African American public colleges and universities. *Harvard Educational Review, 62,* 26-44.

Allen, W. R., Spencer, M. B., & O'Connor, C. (Eds.). (2002). *African American education: Race, community, inequality, and achievement—a tribute to Edgar G. Epps.* London: JAI Press, Inc.

Galotti, K. M., & Mark, M. C. (1994). How do high school students structure an important life decision? A short-term longitudinal study of the college decision-making process. *Research in Higher Education, 35,* 589-607.

Garet, M. S., & DeLany, B. (1988). Students, courses, and stratification. *Sociology of Education, 61,* 61-77.

Hearn, J. C. (1984). *Impacts of undergraduate experiences on educational aspirations and plans.* (ERIC Document Reproduction Service, No. ED245651.)

Hearn, J. C. (1991). Academic and non-academic influences on the college destinations of 1980 high school graduates. *Sociology of Education, 64,* 158-171.

Hossler, D., Braxton, J., & Coopersmith, G. (1989). Understanding student college choice. In J. C. Smart (Ed.), *Higher education: Handbook of theory and research,* Vol. 5 (pp. 231-238). New York: Agathon Press.

McDonough, P. M. (1997). *Choosing colleges: How social class and schools structure opportunity.* Albany, NY: SUNY.

Oakes, J. (1985). *Keeping track: How schools structure inequity.* New Haven, CT: Yale University Press.

Oakes, J., Quartz, K. H., Ryan, S., & Lipton, M. (2000). *Becoming good American schools: The struggle for civic virtue in education reform.* San Francisco: Jossey-Bass.

Ogbu, J. (1978). *Minority education and caste: The American system in cross-cultural perspective.* New York: Academic Press.

Pachon, H. P., Federman, M., & Castillo, L. (2000). *An analysis of Advanced Placement courses in California high schools.* Claremont, CA: Tomás Rivera Policy Institute.

Post, D. (1990). College-going decisions by Chicanos: The politics of misinformation. *Educational Evaluation and Policy Analysis, 12,* 174-187.

Stage, F., & Hossler, D. (1989). Differences in family influences on college attendance plans for male and female ninth graders. *Research in Higher Education, 30,* 301-315.

Stanton-Salazar, R. D. (2001*). Manufacturing hope and despair: The school and kin support networks of U.S.-Mexican youth.* New York: Teachers College Press.

APPENDIX A

Survey for Gates Millennium Scholars Focus Groups

1. What is your gender?
    a) Male
    b) Female

2. Are you: (Please check all that apply)
    a) African American
    b) Native American
    c) Arab American
    d) Caucasian
    e) Chinese
    f) Filipino
    g) Japanese
    h) Korean
    i) Other Asian (please specify) _____
    j) Mexican/Chicano
    k) Puerto Rican
    l) Central American
    m) Cuban
    n) South American
    o) Other Hispanic/Latino (please specify) _____
    p) Other _____

3. What is your best estimate of your parents' or total household income last year? Please consider income from all sources before taxes. (Mark <u>one</u> only)

    a) Less than $6,000   _____
    b) $6,000 to $9,999   _____
    c) $10,000 to $15,999   _____
    d) $16,000 to $19,999   _____
    e) $20,000 to $24,999   _____
    f) $25,000 to $29,999   _____
    g) $30,000 to $39,999   _____
    h) $40,000 to $49,999   _____
    i) $50,000 to $59,999   _____
    j) $60,000 to $69,999   _____
    k) $70,000 to $74,999   _____
    l) $75,000 to $99,999   _____
    m) $100,000 to $149,999_____
    n) $150,000 to $199,999_____
    o) $200,000 or more   _____

4. Citizenship status: (Mark <u>one</u>)
    a) U.S. citizen
    b) Permanent resident (green card)
    c) Neither

5. Are your parents: (Mark <u>one</u>)
    a)   Both alive and living with each other?
    b)   Both alive, divorced or living apart?
    c)   One or both deceased?

6. What is your parent's highest level of education? Father   Mother
    a)   Grammar school or less........................( )   ( )
    b)   Some high school..............................( )   ( )
    c)   High school graduate..........................( )   ( )
    d)   Postsecondary school other than college.....( )   ( )
    e)   Some college..................................( )   ( )
    e)   College graduate..............................( )   ( )
    f)   Some graduate school..........................( )   ( )
    g)   Graduate degree...............................( )   ( )

7. What is your mother's job title? _____

8. Where does your mother work (for example - automotive shop, elementary school, hospital, or other industry)? _____

9. What is your father's job title? _____

10. Where does your father work (for example - automotive shop, elementary school, hospital, or other industry)? _____ _____

11. What is your probable career choice?
    Please specify: _____

12. Highest level of education you plan to complete:
    a)   Bachelor's degree (B.A., B.S., etc.)
    b)   Master's degree (M.A., M.S., etc.)
    c)   Ph.D. or Ed.D.
    d)   M.D., D.O., D.D.S., or D.V.M. degree
    e)   LL.B. or J.D. (law)
    f)   B.D. or M.DIV (Divinity)
    g)   Other (specify) _____

13. Circle the answer that best describes your overall high school grade point average:
    a) A+ or A   d) B   g) C
    b) A-   e) B-   h) C-
    c) B+   f) C+   i) D+ or below

14. Circle the answer that best describes your overall college grade point average:
    a) A+ or A   d) B   g) C
    b) A-   e) B-   h) C-
    c) B+   f) C+   i) D+ or below

15. Have you taken the following standardized exams? (If the answer is "yes" to any of these items, please list your highest score)
    a) SATI   Circle: Yes   No   Math: ___   Verbal: ___
    b) SATII   Circle: Yes   No   Math: ___   Verbal: ___

    Elective on SATII (give name and score):_____
    c) ACT   Circle: Yes   No   Score: _____

16. Please circle how many College Advanced Placement (A.P.) courses you completed in high school?
a) None	d) 4-6	g) 11 or more
b) 1-2	e) 5-7	
c) 3-5	f) 8-10	

17. How well do you feel your high school has prepared you academically for college?
    a) Extremely well
    b) Fairly well
    c) Somewhat
    d) Not too well
    e) Not at all

18. How satisfied were you with the following at your high school: (Mark <u>one</u> for each item)

    a) The quality of teach at your high school?_____   Not satisfied   Somewhat Satisfied   Very satisfied

    b) The quality of academic counseling at your high school?   Not satisfied   Somewhat Satisfied   Very satisfied

    c) Availability of college-related information at your high school?   Not satisfied   Somewhat Satisfied   Very satisfied

    d) Quality of personal counseling?   Not satisfied   Somewhat Satisfied   Very satisfied

19. Where did you get most of your college information from?
    a) Parents
    b) Siblings
    c) Other family members
    d) Peers
    e) Teachers
    f) Counselors
    g) Internet
    h) Other (please specify): _____

20. Of your closest friends, how many of them went to college?
    a) None
    b) Less than half
    c) About half
    d) More than half
    e) All

21. What types of colleges did you apply to?
    a) Community college
    b) State college
    c) Public 4 year university
    d) Private 4 year university
    e) Other (specify): _____

22. What was the primary reason for applying to the college type in Question #21?

    _____

    _____

23. On a scale of 1 (low) and 10 (high), please rate the following activities:

    a. AMOUNT OF TENSION: Current ability to learn new material quickly_____ _____

    b. LEVEL OF RELEVANCE: Relevance of campus social clubs and activities at your college to meet your needs _____

    c. AMOUNT OF PRESSURE: Pressure felt in high school to complete academic college preparation _____

    d. AMOUNT OF PRESSURE: Pressure felt in high school to participate in honors/AP or accelerated curriculum _____

    e. AMOUNT OF PRESSURE: Pressure felt in high school to maintain effective communication with teachers _____

    f. AMOUNT OF TENSION: Establishing effective communication and mentorship with college professors _____

    g. AMOUNT OF TENSION: Ability in high school to learn new material quickly _____

APPENDIX B

Protocol for Focus Group Interviews with Gates Millennium Scholars.

1. What high school did you attend (location, type of school)?

2. When did you first realize your desire to attend college?

3. What actions did you take (and when did you take these actions) to realize your college plans?

4. Describe some of the individuals who were most informative in helping you to realize your college attendance.

5. Describe some of the individuals who were least informative in helping you realize your college attendance.

6. What structures were in place at your high school to assist with your search for information about college and about specific colleges?

7. What structures were in place in your high school to help you complete college prerequisite courses?

8. Describe the interactions between you and representatives from your first-choice, second-choice and third-choice colleges when they visited your high school. (PROMPT: What information did they share with you about the prospective college, college costs, and your competitiveness in their applicant pool?)

9. If you had the opportunity to replay your college planning process, what would you handle differently and why?

10. At what point in your college search process did you find out you were a GMS recipient and how did this award impact your college choice?

APPENDIX C

Descriptive Statistics of Fall 2001 Gates Millennium Scholars Freshman Applicants by Race.

	White	African American	Native American/ Alaska Native	Asian Pacific Islander American	Hispanic American
Father's education					
Less than high school	8.9%	8.5%	9.2%	20.1%	17.7%
High school graduate/GED	26.8	36.1	32.3	23.8	30.4
Some college	27.7	27.8	36.9	17.7	22.0
College graduate/B.A.	20.5	16.0	13.8	20.7	15.3
Graduate degree/M.A. or Ph.D.	16.1	11.6	7.7	17.7	16.7
Total N	*112*	*449*	*130*	*294*	*209*
Mother's education					
Less than high school	6.2%	5.6%	5.3%	27.0%	19.4%
High school graduate/GED	28.3	26.2	26.3	24.3	25.8
Some college	30.1	36.3	36.8	19.0	25.8
College graduate/B.A.	23.0	21.6	19.5	23.7	19.8
Graduate degree/M.A. or Ph.D.	12.4	10.3	12.0	6.0	9.2
Total N	*113*	*504*	*113*	*300*	*217*
Sex					
Female	69.3%	73.7%	70.4%	67.9%	58.0%
Male	30.7	26.3	29.6	32.1	42.0
Total N	*114*	*510*	*135*	*312*	*219*
Race majority of h.s.					
Strongly disagree	36.0%	46.4%	25.6%	46.8%	34.4%
Disagree	32.4	22.7	32.3	35.5	30.7
Agree	22.5	12.0	27.1	12.9	22.0
Strongly agree	9.0	18.9	15.0	4.8	12.8
Total N	*111*	*507*	*133*	*310*	*218*
N.yrs math comp. in h.s.					
Two	.9%	1.0%	1.5%	.6%	1.8%
Three	17.5	8.1	26.7	9.0	13.2
Four or more	81.6	91.0	71.9	90.4	84.9
Total N	*114*	*509*	*135*	*311*	*219*
N. yrs science comp. in h.s.					
One	-	-	-	.3%	.5%
Two	3.5	2.9	6.7	.6	4.1
Three	23.7	25.1	35.6	20.6	27.9
Four or more	72.8	71.9	57.8	78.5	67.6
Total N	*114*	*509*	*135*	*311*	*219*

APPENDIX C

Descriptive Statistics of Fall 2001 Gates Millennium Scholars Freshman Applicants by Race (continued).

	White	African American	Native American/ Alaska Native	Asian Pacific Islander American	Hispanic American
Took SAT					
Yes	61.1%	79.1%	39.1%	90.9%	82.9%
No	38.9	20.9	60.9	9.1	17.1
Total N	*113*	*506*	*133*	*309*	*217*
SAT score					
Mean	1192	1110	1094	1247	1161
SD	(155)	(162)	(153)	(176)	(158)
Total N	66	382	42	272	174
Took ACT					
Yes	69.6%	64.7%	86.5%	46.4%	57.0%
No	30.4	35.3	13.5	53.6	43.0
Total N	*112*	*504*	*133*	*302*	*214*
ACT score					
Mean	25.6	22.9	23.1	26.2	24.5
SD	(3.8)	(3.8)	(4.2)	(4.4)	(4.3)
Total N	*77*	*316*	*112*	*134*	*117*
No. of AP exams taken					
None	45.0%	36.7%	45.7%	12.1%	24.4%
One	13.5	18.1	19.7	12.1	13.4
Two	16.2	15.5	18.9	11.1	15.2
Three	6.3	10.8	6.3	14.7	13.4
Four or more	18.9	18.9	9.4	50.0	33.6
Total N	*111*	*502*	*127*	*306*	*217*
Attended private h.s.					
No	86.8%	90.2%	92.6%	95.8%	81.2%
Yes	13.2	9.8	7.4	4.2	18.8
Total N	*114*	*510*	*135*	*312*	*218*
Attended religious h.s.					
No	91.2%	93.3%	96.3%	97.1%	83.5%
Yes	8.8	6.7	3.7	2.9	16.5
Total N	*114*	*509*	*135*	*312*	*218*
Self-esteem					
Strongly disagree	-	1.2%	-	1.6%	2.3%
Disagree	7.3	4.3	4.7	7.5	2.3
Agree	50.5	35.4	45.3	55.4	39.5
Strongly agree	42.2	59.1	50.0	35.5	55.8
Total N	*109*	*506*	*128*	*307*	*215*

APPENDIX C

Descriptive Statistics of Fall 2001 Gates Millennium Scholars Freshman Applicants by Race (continued).

	White	African American	Native American/ Alaska Native	Asian Pacific Islander American	Hispanic American
Locus of control planning					
Strongly agree	.9%	1.6%	2.4%	1.6%	3.7%
Agree	10.9	4.6	6.4	11.4	5.1
Disagree	56.4	52.1	56.0	53.6	44.9
Strongly disagree	31.8	41.8	35.2	33.4	46.3
Total N	*110*	*505*	*125*	*308*	*214*
Select school for strong reputation					
Not important	-	1.4%	3.1%	.6%	1.4%
Somewhat important	25.0	17.7	29.8	13.8	23.3
Very important	75.0	80.9	67.2	85.5	75.3
Total N	*112*	*509*	*131*	*311*	*215*
Use of time in school					
Mean	42.3%	47.1%	46.1%	53.9%	49.8%
SD	(16.4)	(18.0)	(17.8)	(18.6)	(18.1)
Total N	*109*	*505*	*125*	*308*	*212*
Difficulty with schoolwork					
Very difficult	8.1%	6.1%	3.1%	8.8%	8.8%
Difficult	26.1	23.0	33.6	38.6	28.8
Not very difficult	44.1	42.9	43.0	37.3	40.5
Not difficult	21.6	28.0	20.3	15.3	21.9
Total N	*111*	*508*	*128*	*308*	*215*
Likelihood of dropping out					
Very or somewhat likely	.9%	.4%	.8%	1.0%	1.4%
Somewhat unlikely	8.1	2.8	9.2	3.6	2.8
Very unlikely	91.0	96.8	90.1	95.4	95.8
Total N	*111*	*506*	*131*	*303*	*213*
Educational aspirations					
Less than B.A.degree	2.0%	.8%	3.2%	.3%	-
B.A. or post-B.A. certificate	15.7	6.7	16.8	8.2	15.6
M.A. degree	36.3	32.9	39.2	38.4	35.5
Professional degree	19.6	21.8	16.0	26.2	16.6
Doctoral degree	26.5	37.7	24.8	26.9	32.2
Total N	*102*	*477*	*125*	*294*	*211*

APPENDIX C

Selected Descriptive Statistics of Fall 2001 Gates Millennium Scholars Freshman Applicants by Gender.*

	Female	Male
Father's education		
Less than high school	20.3%	15.7%
High school graduate/GED	29.5	28.7
Some college	23.6	23.2
College graduate/B.A.	16.3	16.0
Graduate degree/M.A. or Ph.D.	10.3	16.4
Total N	*1020*	*470*
No. of years of math completed in high school		
Two	.9%	1.2%
Three	13.7	9.2
Four or more	85.4	89.6
Total N	*1105*	*501*
Attending first-choice school?		
Mean	31.8%	21.4%
SD	68.2	78.6
Total N	*1058*	*485*

* Only those cross-tabulations by gender that were statistically significant, at least the $p<.05$ level, are included in this table.

Means, Standard Deviations and Correlations for Variables, Gates Millennium Scholars Freshman Applicants, African American, Asian Pacific Islander American, and Hispanic American Students Fall 2001 (N=660).

		M	S.D.	1	2	3	4	5	6	7	8	9	10	11	12	13
1.	FATHEDUC	2.95	1.27													
2.	MOTHEDUC	2.95	1.19	.516***												
3.	AFRICAN AMERI	.46	.50	.177***	-.019											
4.	ASIAN	.32	.47	.041	-.122**	-.634***										
5.	LATINO	.22	.41	-.024	-.075	-.489***	-.365***									
6.	MALE	.34	.47	.083*	-.008	-.108**	.000	.130**								
7.	HSMRITY	1.94	1.05	-.093*	-.017	.033	-.101**	.074	-.045							
8.	HSMATHYR	3.90	.33	.067	.054	.030	.018	-.056	.098*	-.015						
9.	HSSCIEYR	3.71	.51	.020	.001	-.023	.086*	-.070	.013	-.048	-.200***					
10.	SATSCORE	1171.68	177.30	.278***	.124**	-.326***	.333***	.016	-.181***	.133**	.104**	.156***				
11.	APEXAM	2.30	1.58	.110**	.013	-.302***	.285***	.041	.015	.035	.100**	.146***	.466***			
12.	HSPRIV	1.12	.32	.096*	.129**	-.008	-.131**	.157***	-.148***	.023	.043	-.049	.095*	-.045		
13.	HSREL	1.08	.28	.068	.090*	-.040	-.116**	.180***	-.070	.034	.029	-.082*	-.008	-.130**	.764***	
14.	ESTGOOD	1.37	.83													
15.	LCPLANNI	3.32	.68													
16.	AENOTWEL	3.37	.74													
17.	RSNLOWEX	2.39	.66													
18.	RSNSTREP	2.83	.40													
19.	UDIFFSCW	2.77	.88													
20.	UDIFFTIM	2.44	.96													
21.	UDIFFEXP	2.50	.98													
22.	TIMEUSE	.50	.19													
23.	DROPCOLL	2.95	.25													
24.	HIGHDEGR	3.79	.99													
25.	FCHOICE	.71	.45													
26.	NPARTCAR	3.32	.75													

NOTE: Correlations significant at the following levels: * p<.05; ** p<.01; *** p<.001 (2-tailed).

Means, Standard Deviations and Correlations for Variables, Gates Millennium Scholars Applicants, African American, Asian Pacific Islander American, and Hispanic American Students Fall 2001 (N=660) (continued).

		M	S.D.	14	15	16	17	18	19	20	21	22	23	24	25	26
1.	FATHEDUC	2.95	1.27	.020	.028	.066	-.042	.026	-.014	.028	.064	-.011	.105**	.079*	.008	.038
2.	MOTHEDUC	2.95	1.19	.047	.075	.087*	-.113**	.047	.033	.071	.038	-.071	.139***	.016	.007	.088*
3.	AFRICAN AMERI	.46	.50	.048	.016	-.087*	.012	.006	.158***	.064	.016	-.097*	.033	-.116**	.070	-.038
4.	ASIAN	.32	.47	-.129**	-.052	.056	.022	.072	-.032	.016	.000	.033	.094*	.094*	.070	-.041
5.	LATINO	.22	.41	.088*	.039	.042	-.040	-.088*	-.045	-.050	-.019	-.043	-.048	-.048	.061	.092
6.	MALE	.34	.47	.029	-.017	-.034	-.074	.032	.055	.000	.000	.009	.009	-.059	.092	-.001
7.	HSMJRTY	1.94	1.05	.015	-.038	-.042	.036	-.037	.028	.013	.033	-.048	-.011	-.020	.008	.008
8.	HSMATHYR	3.90	.33	-.048	.030	-.018	-.001	.025	-.011	.004	.001	.003	-.048	-.006	.010	.008
9.	HSSCIEYR	3.71	.51	.094*	.076	-.012	.016	.019	.021	-.027	.006	.032	.089*	.091*	.004	.010
10.	SATSCORE	1171.68	177.30	-.047	.076	.059	-.198***	-.157***	-.058	-.048	.113**	.073	.054	.161***	.151***	.033
11.	APEXAM	2.30	1.58	.003	.047	.055	-.086*	.091*	.054	.032	.032	.057	.057	.054	.122**	.000
12.	HSPRIV	1.12	.32	-.012	-.011	.020	-.069	.054	.049	-.021	-.008	-.008	.003	.003	.020	.020
13.	HSREL	1.08	.28	.014	-.037	.032	-.042	.037	.099*	.076	-.035	-.026	.000	.000	.016	.016
14.	ESTGOOD	1.37	.83		.357***	.236***	.036	.054	.142***	.076	.009	-.090*	.131**	.042	.058	.217***
15.	LCPLANNI	3.32	.68			.323***	-.054	.113**	.092*	.144***	.009	-.012	.189***	.073	.077*	.201***
16.	AENOTWEL	3.37	.74				-.113**	.064	.057	.099*	.115**	-.035	.171***	.050	-.014	.242***
17.	RSNLOWEX	2.39	.66					-.158***	-.053	-.018	.022	-.113**	-.027	.007	-.036	-.085*
18.	RSNSTREP	2.83	.40						.057	.082*	.032	.090*	-.003	.024	.065	.049
19.	UDIFFSCW	2.77	.88							.669***	.181***	-.155***	.129**	.065	.015	.049
20.	UDIFFTIM	2.44	.96								.160***	-.079*	.087*	.050	-.036	.049
21.	UDIFFEXP	2.50	.98									-.134**	.013	.017	.029	.015
22.	TIMEUSE	.50	.19										.017	.163***	.075	-.117**
23.	DROPCOLL	2.95	.25											.094*	-.008	.139***
24.	HIGHDEGR	3.79	.99												-.022	.131**
25.	FCHOICE	.71	.45													.130**
26.	NPARTCAR	3.32	.75													

NOTE: Correlations significant at the following levels: *p<.05; **p<.01; ***p<.001 (2-tailed).

APPENDIX E

Description of Fall 2001 Gates Millennium Scholars Freshman Applicants Variables Used in Regression Models.

Dependent Variables	Description	Coding
Fchoice	Currently attending first-choice college	0=No; 1=Yes
Npartcar	Student <u>does not</u> feel part of campus community	1=Strongly agree; 2=Agree; 3=Disagree; 4=Strongly disagree
Dropcoll	Likelihood to drop out	1=Very likely; 2=Somewhat likely; 3=Somewhat unlikely; 4=Very unlikely
Highdegr	Highest degree expected	1=Less than two years of college; 2=Two or more years of college; 3=Bachelor's degree; 4=Post-baccalaureate certificate; 5=Master's degree; 6=First professional degree; 7=Doctoral degree
Fatheduc	Highest grade or level of father's education	1=Less than high school; 2=High school graduate/GED; 3=Some college; 4=College graduate/B.A; 5=Graduate degree/M.A. or Ph.D.
Motheduc	Highest grade or level of mother's education	1=Less than high school; 2=High school graduate/GED; 3=Some college; 4=College graduate/B.A; 5=Graduate degree/M.A. or Ph.D.
African Amer., Asian, Latino	Race of respondent	0=Not of racial group; 1=Member of racial group
Male	Student gender	0=female; 1=male
Hsmjrity	Took majority of h.s. classes with same race	1=Strongly disagree; 2=Disagree; 3=Agree; 4=Strongly agree
Hsmathyr	N. of years of h.s. math courses taken	0=None; 1=One; 2=Two; 3=Three; 4=Four or more
Hsscieyr	N. of years of h.s. science courses taken	0=None; 1=One; 2=Two; 3=Three; 4=Four or more
Satscore	SAT scores	
Apexam	N. of AP exams taken	0=None; 1=One; 2=Two; 3=Three; 4=Four or more
Hspriv	Attended private h.s.	0=No; 1=Yes
Hsrel	Attended religious h.s.	0=No; 1=Yes
Estgood	Student feels good about herself/himself	1=Strongly disagree; 2=Disagree; 3=Agree; 4=Strongly agree
Lcplanni	Plans do not work out/planning leads to unhappiness	1=Agree strongly; 2=Agree; 3=Disagree; 4=Disagree strongly
Aenotwel	Do not do well in college	1= Agree strongly; 2=Agree; 3=Disagree; 4=Disagree strongly

APPENDIX E

Description of Fall 2001 Gates Millennium Scholars Freshman Applicants Variables Used in Regression Models (continued).

Dependent Variables	Description	Coding
Rsnlowex	Select school with low expenses	1=Not important; 2=Somewhat important; 3=Very important
Rsnstrep	Select school with strong reputation	1=Not important; 2=Somewhat important; 3=Very important
Udiffscw	Difficulty keeping up with schoolwork	1=Very difficult; 2=Difficult; 3=Not very difficult; 4=Not difficult
Udifftim	Difficulty with time management	1=Very difficult; 2=Difficult; 3=Not very difficult; 4=Not difficult
Udiffexp	Difficulty paying for college	1=Very difficult; 2=Difficult; 3=Not very difficult; 4=Not difficult
Timeuse	Time spent studying	Calculated by time spent studying divided by sum of time spent studying, time spent participating in college-sponsored extracurricular activities, and time spent relaxing or socializing
Dropcoll	Likelihood to drop out	1=Very likely; 2=Somewhat likely; 3=Somewhat unlikely; 4=Very unlikely
Highdegr	Highest degree expected	1=Less than two years of college; 2=Two or more years of college; 3=Bachelor's degree; 4=Post-baccalaureate certificate; 5=Master's degree; 6=First professional degree; 7=Doctoral degree

APPENDIX F

Comparison of Academic Indicators by
Focus Group Race/Ethnicity.

	African American	Native American/ Alaska Native	Asian Pacific Islander American	Hispanic American
	(N=14)	(N=11)	(N=19)	(N=12)
INDICATORS				
Mean HS GPA	3.93	3.93	3.92	3.79
(S.D. HS GPA)	(.15)	(.16)	(.12)	(.21)
Mean College GPA	3.46	3.50	3.47	3.45
(S.D. College GPA)	(.58)	(.42)	(.31)	(.38)
Mean SAT I Math	506	545	667	630
(S.D. SAT I Math)	(69)	(7)	(84)	(67)
Mean SAT I Verbal	513	600	590	591
(S.D. SAT I Verbal)	(54)	(85)	(90)	(52)

CHAPTER 5

THE IMPACT OF GMS ON FINANCIAL ACCESS: ANALYSES OF THE 2000 FRESHMAN COHORT

Edward P. St. John and Choong-Geun Chung

The Gates Millennium Scholars (GMS) program, implemented in the fall of 2000, was created to improve educational opportunity for low-income minorities who are qualified for college. Begun following two decades of erosion in the purchasing power of federal need-based grants (Advisory Committee on Student Financial Assistance, 2001, 2002; St. John, 2002, 2003), GMS represents a distinctive national experiment in providing adequate need-based grant aid. Research on the effect of GMS awards on financial access can inform policymakers on the potential impact of reinvesting in need-based grants.

Because policy analysts disagree about the role of financial aid in promoting college access, it is important to situate the GMS program within a national policy context. The competing explanations for the disparity in college enrollment rates for low-income high school students compared with middle- and high-income high school students were considered in the design of this study. This report situates GMS in the policy debate about alternative explanations for disparities in college access. Next, the research approach and findings are presented. The report concludes by discussing the implications of the findings for changes in federal and state finance policies that could better promote college access.

Situating the GMS Program

Historically, need-based federal student financial aid programs were created to ensure equal opportunity for low-income students (Gladieux & Wolanin, 1976). By 1975, there was a consensus that financial aid was central to providing equal opportunity for college enrollment. The Pell Grant program[1] had been fully implemented and enrollment rates for Hispanic Americans and African Americans who had graduated from high school were essentially equal to the enrollment rates for Whites (St. John, 2003). At the time, the policy debates were about how best to provide funding for middle-income families: through grants or tax subsidies. The *Middle Income Student Assistance Act of 1978* (MISAA) expanded eligibility for Pell Grants and other federal grants to include middle-income students, but these more liberal provisions were never fully funded.

However, the administrations of Ronald Reagan and George H. W. Bush shifted the emphasis in federal aid from grants to loans. Loans provided student aid to middle-income students at a lower cost to taxpayers than would have been possible if grants had been used consistent with MISAA. The Clinton administration created savings programs and tax credits that further increased financing opportunities for middle-income students. By 2000, when the GMS program was implemented, the net cost of attending a public four-year college had increased dramatically for low-income students due to the decline in the value of federal need-based grants and increases in tuition changes.

By 2000, even market-oriented economists recognized that a new imbalance in public financing of higher education had become problematic (e.g., Fogel, 2000). Economists and higher education scholars also had argued that the decline in the value of federal grants had reduced opportunity for low-income students (Heller, 1997; McPherson & Schapiro, 1991, 1997; St. John, 1994; St. John, Paulsen & Starkey, 1996). Yet, the preponderance of official[2] policy literature after 1980 simply overlooked the role of need-based aid in promoting access (Adelman, 1995, 1999; Gladieux & Swail, 1999; King, 1999; NCES, 1996, 1997a, 1997b, 1998).

When the Bill & Melinda Gates Foundation announced in 1999 that it would dedicate one billion dollars to grants to low-income minority students, it did so in a contested policy context. Federal officials consistently argued that the failure of the public schools explained the lagging college enrollment rates for minority students. At the same time, they advocated for loans, tax credits, and savings programs—strategies that favored middle-income students. Yet, some advocates of minority access continued to point to financial barriers (St. John, 1991, 1997).

The GMS Program

Initiated in the fall of 2000, the GMS program has given scholarships to college students and aspiring college students. Low-income African Americans, Hispanic Americans, Asian Pacific Islander Americans, and American Indians and Alaska Natives are eligible for the awards. Pell Grant award eligibility is used as an indicator of financial need, while noncognitive measures are used in selection.[3] During the first year, awards were given to entering college students, continuing students, and graduate students in selected high-demand fields. Undergraduate students chosen as Gates Minority Scholars would continue to receive awards throughout their undergraduate education and could receive fellowships for graduate education if they went on in the fields of mathematics, science (including computer science), engineering, education, and library science.

Ambiguities in the award process during the 2000 academic year had the effect of creating a "quasi-random" distribution of first-year awards. Students were required to have a 3.3 grade point average (GPA) in high school. A set of noncognitive criteria (Sedlacek, 2004) was used to determine student eligibility: selection considered information related to self-concept and long-range plans, among other things. All of the students included in the 2000 surveys—both the GMS recipients and the nonrecipients who compose the comparison group—met both the cognitive and noncognitive selection criteria.

The final stage of selection considered financial need. The financial criterion (i.e., Pell eligibility) was applied in the third stage of the selection process. Due to delays in the award process, some students were notified of their awards after the start of the fall term. However, the majority were notified before they made their final college choice. Students with high scores on the noncognitive criteria were notified first of their eligibility. These students had to have substantial financial need (i.e., be Pell eligible) to receive GMS awards. In making its final selections, the GMS program also sought to maintain racial balance in award distribution. Thus, some students with high scores on the noncognitive criteria did not receive awards.

Since the selection process sorted first on the noncognitive criteria, the two groups are relatively similar with respect to the selection criteria. Thus, respondents include students who met the noncognitive criteria in both the GMS recipient group and the comparison group. Further, Pell-eligible students were included in both the GMS recipient and nonrecipient groups, although Pell eligibility is more strongly represented in the recipient group. This means that there was substantial variation in both groups. Different levels of financial need and different scores on the noncognitive criteria were represented in both the GMS recipient and nonrecipient groups in the 2000 cohort. However, all of the students surveyed in the 2000 cohort met the noncognitive eligibility criteria. GMS recipients were eligible to receive financial awards throughout their undergraduate education and, if they went to graduate school in one of the selected fields, through their graduate education as well.

The financial criteria for awards were more clearly communicated during the second year of the program, which means that awardees had consistently higher scores on the award criteria than the nonrecipients. Therefore, for the 2000 freshman cohort there was a quasi-random distribution of awards. Research on this cohort is crucial to building an understanding of the impact of supplemental need-based grant aid on financial access for college-prepared low-income students.

The GMS awards cover the amount of financial need that remains after other grant aids—federal, state, and institutional—is awarded. These "last-dollar" grants are intended to eliminate the need for loans. The actual amounts of GMS awards vary substantially, depending on the tuition charges at the colleges and universities students attend and the amount of aid they receive. Students enrolled in private colleges receive much larger awards, on average, than do students who attend public colleges. Thus, GMS functions as a need-based grant program, filling the need remaining after other grant aid.

In addition to financial support, the GMS program also provides leadership opportunities for students receiving awards. This includes attending national meetings and receiving other support services offered by the foundation. These elements of the GMS program were designed to promote persistence, success in college, and professional experience after college.

Evolving Arguments about Access

Arguments by economists about financial need had a substantial influence on federal student financial aid programs through the 1970s (Breneman, Finn, & Nelson, 1978; Finn, 1978; Gladieux & Wolanin, 1976). However, after 1980, new rationales were used to refocus the policy debates on academic preparation for college. Most recently, efforts have been made to build balanced approaches for research and policy on college access. The assumptions used in these three stages of research merit review as a means of further situating this study.

Early Analyses of Financial Access. Economists began to study the impact of tuition on college enrollment in the 1960s (Becker, 1964; Hansen & Weisbrod, 1969). Early studies used both time-series data and samples of high school students to examine the impact of prices on enrollment. Reviews of these early studies found that tuition charges reduced enrollment rates, a finding that often was used to argue that student aid was the most efficient possible means of promoting college access. Later, substantial progress was made in analyzing the impact of student financial aid on college enrollment using national longitudinal databases. Jackson (1978) and Manski and Wise (1983) found that student aid expanded access for students in the high school class of 1972. Manski and Wise concluded that implementation of Pell Grants had expanded access to two-year colleges more than to four-year colleges because of constraints on academic preparation. Subsequent analyses found that student grants were positively associated with enrollment by low-income students in the early

1980s, as they had been a decade earlier (Jackson, 1988; St. John, 1990, 1991; St. John & Noell, 1989). Recent analyses that consider trends in federal need-based and non-need grants, trends in state grants, and trends in school reform find a correspondence between changes in grant funding and college enrollment rates by high school graduates [4] in the 1970s, 1980s, and 1990s (Perna & Titus, 2002; St. John, 2003).

Recent Analyses of Academic Preparation. During the past two decades, many policy analysts have considered the role of academic preparation for college in efforts to build a better understanding of college access. The focus on the role of academic preparation grew out of efforts by the Reagan administration to respond to concerns about gaps in enrollment rates for White students and African American students after 1978. The official report prepared in response to this concern examined the relationship between courses taken in high school and college enrollment (Pelavin & Kane, 1988, 1990). While previous studies had controlled for the impact of taking a college preparatory curriculum (e.g., Jackson, 1978; St. John, 1991; St. John & Noell, 1989[5]), they did not examine the impact of specific high school courses, such as algebra. The Pelavin and Kane study focused on specific math courses, but did not consider the direct effects of student financial aid on enrollment, even though analyses of the effects of student aid were available to the authors.[6]

In the late 1990s, the National Center for Education Statistics' analyses of longitudinal databases consistently focused on the association between high school courses and college enrollment (Adelman, 1995, 1999; NCES, 1996, 1997a, 1997b, 1998). These reports sometimes acknowledged that financial aid played a role in college access, but they consistently avoided analyzing the direct effects of financial aid on college enrollment. This approach to the analysis of access overlooks large numbers of prepared students who cannot afford to enroll (Fitzgerald, 2004; Lee, 2004).

Seeking Balance in Access Research. Recently, several researchers have begun to reexamine the NCES study with the intent of using a more balanced approach. Their findings have important implications for research on the GMS program.

First, reanalysis of statistics reported by NCES (1997a) revealed that there are large numbers of low-income, college-qualified students who did not enroll in college (Advisory Committee on Student Financial Assistance, 2002; St. John, 2002). These analyses used a balanced access model that considered whether students' perceptions of financial need could influence academic preparation, as well as the direct effects of finances on college enrollment. Based on this reanalysis, the Advisory Committee on Student Financial Assistance (2002) estimated that four million college-qualified, low- and middle-income students would be left behind in the 2000s because of inadequate grant aid.

Second, at the request of the Advisory Committee, Don Heller (2004) recently reexamined the logical models and statistical methods used by NCES. He concluded that these studies did not adequately consider the relationship between income and parents' education when assessing the impact of family finances on access. His review points to fundamental problems with the basic conception of access used in the NCES and ACE studies. A follow-up study by William Becker (2004), also commissioned by the Advisory Committee, examined the consequences of these oversights from a statistical and econometric perspective. It is clear from these reviews that the NCES reports underestimated the impact of family income on college access (Becker, 2004; Heller, 2004).

This study of the impact of GMS grants on financial access adds to this newest wave of research that considers the impact of student financial aid on access for low-income, college-qualified students. Most GMS applicants were high-achieving students in high school. Because selection was based on noncognitive variables, the level of achievement (i.e., test scores, grades) did not influence the selection process.

The New Inequality. There has been a widening gap in college enrollment opportunity for minorities compared with Whites. The gap in college enrollment rates for African American and Hispanic American high school graduates compared with White high school graduates grew after 1975 (See Figure 1). In 2000, the year GMS was implemented, the differential between Whites and African Americans was 6.1 percentage points; in 1975, the gap had been only 0.8 percentage points. For Hispanic American high school graduates, the change was even more dramatic. In 1975, Hispanic American high school graduates attended college at a rate 3.2 percentage points higher than Whites; by 1999, they had fallen behind Whites by 13.7 percentage points. Thus, the GMS program was implemented at a critical time.

Figure 1. College Enrollment Rates of All 18- to 24-Year-Old High School Graduates, With Differential Enrollment Rates for African American and Hispanic Gaps Compared to White.

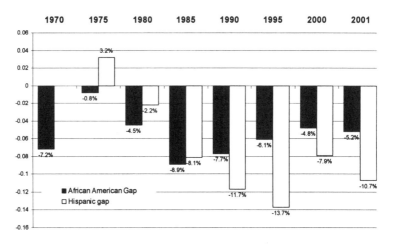

Trend analyses also point to a similar opportunity gap for low-income students compared with upper-income students during the 1980s and 1990s (Ellwood & Kane, 2000). About 29 percent of low-income high school seniors in 1980 and 1987 attended four-year colleges in the fall after high school graduation. Similarly, in 1992, 28 percent of this group attended public four-year colleges. However, the percentage of high-income students attending four-year colleges increased from 55 percent in 1980 and 1982 to 66 percent in 1992. The gap between low-income and high-income students grew from a 26 percentage point differential for the 1980 and 1982 cohorts to 37 percentage points for the 1992 cohort. The trend indicates that the new inequality in opportunity was related to income.

A decline in the purchasing power of Pell Grants and other federal need-based grants also paralleled the emergence of the new inequality (Figure 2). In 1975-76, the cost of attending a public four-year college (tuition, room and board, and other expenses) was only $2,348 higher than the maximum Pell award (in constant 1997-98 dollars). In contrast, in 1999-2000, the gap after maximum Pell was $4,738. These changes suggest that the new inequality in college opportunity could be related to trends in college costs and federal grants. In addition, the cost of attending college increased faster than Pell Grants in the first two years of the twenty-first century (College Board, 2002a, 2002b).

Figure 2. Financial Trends: Decline in Purchasing Power of Pell Grants.

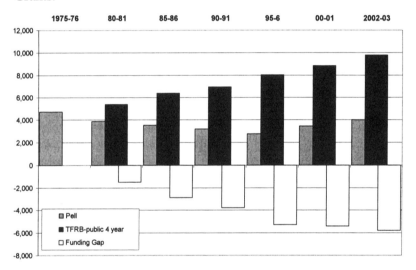

Framing the Study

This study examines the impact of GMS awards on financial access by students in the 2000 cohort. It uses a national sample of students who received GMS awards along with applicants who did not receive awards. We start with an understanding that both forms of access—financial and academic—are important policy issues. Consistent with recent analyses (St. John, 2003), we define the two forms of access as follows:

- *Academic access* refers to *whether students are academically prepared for initial and continued enrollment.*
- *Financial access* is defined as *the ability to afford continuous enrollment in the lowest cost two-year and four-year programs available to applicants, given their ability and prior performance.*

Using these definitions, the applicants for GMS awards uniformly met the requirement for academic access. Most of the students in the sample took the steps to become college qualified: they aspired to attend college, took appropriate preparatory courses,[7] applied for college, and applied for government aid. In addition, they applied to GMS for supplemental student financial assistance. Therefore, the current study examines whether low-income minority students who met or exceeded the threshold for academic access made gains in financial access as a result of receiving a GMS award. This paper focuses on the following questions:

- Did receipt of a GMS award improve the chances that low-income, college-qualified minority students would enroll in four-year colleges?
- Were recipients of GMS awards more likely to maintain continuous enrollment than were applicants who did not receive GMS awards?

It is necessary to address both questions to build an understanding of the impact of GMS awards on financial access. Since the definition of financial access includes access to four-year colleges for which students qualify, it is important to consider the impact of the program on college destination. Further, the analysis of the impact of GMS awards on continuous enrollment represents the essential test of the effect of these awards on college access. The analyses of the impact of GMS awards on financial access have implications for the current policy debates about college access. If college-qualified, low-income minority students lack access to four-year colleges and/or if they lack the opportunity to maintain continuous enrollment, then the threshold of financial access has not been met. Conversely, if GMS is positively associated with enrollment in four-year colleges and/or continuous college enrollment, then Pell Grants are no longer adequate to ensure financial access. If Pell Grants were adequate to support enrollment in public four-year colleges, we might expect that the additional support provided by GMS would have had an additional influence on enrollment in private four-year colleges but not on whether students enrolled in public two-year or public four-year colleges. NCES has rested its arguments about access on the notion that low-income students and minority students who prepare for college have access to four-year colleges (NCES, 1997a).

Research Approach

This study used a survey of the 2000 first-year GMS cohort to examine the impact of GMS awards on financial access. The surveys, statistical methods, and limitations are described below.

The GMS Surveys

The base year for the GMS surveys was 2002-03. The National Opinion Research Center (NORC) at the University of Chicago developed the survey instruments and conducted the survey. Students included in these surveys would have been enrolled for four semesters if they had maintained continuous enrollment.

NORC also collected longitudinal studies for NCES and could draw from the questions from these surveys to design the GMS questionnaire. In addition, the GMS research advisory panel[8] collaborated with NORC on the study design and questionnaire development. The intent of the GMS survey was to follow a longitudinal design similar to NCES's longitudinal studies so that the long-term effects of GMS awards could be examined. The long-term effects of the program could be due to the leadership training, as well as to the additional financial resources Scholars received.

The NORC surveys included samples of both GMS award recipients and applicants who did not receive awards. While the response rates for the two first-year cohorts were slightly higher for recipients than for nonrecipients, both groups had a sufficient response[9] level:

- A 76% response rate for GMS recipients in the 2000 freshman year cohort.
- A 56.4% response rate for nonrecipients in the 2000 freshman year cohort.

In developing the databases for the researchers, NORC added weights to adjust the sample for the probability of selection.[10] Statistical analyses for the current study were conducted using SASS (Statistical Application for the Social Sciences). The sample for the 2000 cohort included 1,829 responses. Given that an extremely low number—only 41—in the sample did not enroll in college, it was not possible to examine the effects of GMS awards on whether students enrolled in any type of institution.[11] The analyses of the 2000 cohort used the 1,788 responses by students who enrolled in college.

Statistical Methods and Specifications

College Destination. The analysis uses multinomial logistic regression to examine the impact of GMS on enrollment in public two-year colleges or in private colleges[12] compared with public four-year colleges. The analysis examined the influence of the following independent variables:

- GMS award (compared with students who did not receive an award).[13]
- High achievement (students in the highest quartile on the ACT/SAT were compared with students in the middle two quartiles, as a control for the influence of prior academic achievement).[14]
- Low achievement (students in the lowest quartile on the ACT/SAT were compared with students in the middle two quartiles, as a control for achievement).
- Low costs (students who rated "chose college for low tuition" as a 5 on a 5-point scale were coded as "1," others were coded as "0." This variable provides a control for choosing a college for low costs).

- Reputation (students who rated "chose college for academic reputation" as a 5 on a 5-point scale were coded as "1;" others as "0." This variable provides a control for choosing a college for academic reasons).
- Parental contribution (students whose parents are contributing their "expected contribution" were coded as "1" for yes; those who were not were coded as "0" for no. This variable provides a control for the effects of parental support).
- Male (compared with female).
- African American (compared with Asian American).[15]
- Hispanic (compared with Asian American).
- American Indian and Alaska Native (compared with Asian Pacific Islander American).
- Father has a bachelor's degree (compared with students' fathers who did not have this level of attainment; this variable provides a control for parents' education).

The multiple outcomes in this analysis allow us to consider the implications for the federal government and states. Since the early 1980s, federal student financial aid has not been sufficient to ensure financial access to four-year colleges. Examining whether GMS awards influenced students who attended public two-year colleges provides an indicator of whether this minimum threshold was maintained. However, the analysis of whether GMS awards influenced students to enroll in private colleges has implications for all states, since many states provide need-based grant aid for low-income students in both public and private colleges.

Statistical Methods

To assess the effects of GMS on these outcomes, three statistical methods were used:

- Breakdown analyses were used to assess whether there were differences for GMS recipients compared to nonrecipients in the rates of enrollment in different types of colleges and in continuous enrollment.

- Logistic regression analyses were used to examine whether GMS has a statistical association with the outcome, controlling for the influence of other variables.
- Simulations using the regression results were used to estimate the percentage difference in outcomes, holding other variables in the model constant.

Breakdown Analyses are a generally accepted means of comparing the rates of student outcomes for students in certain categories, an approach frequently used in the NCES studies of student access (Heller, 2004). In these analyses we break down the GMS recipients and nonrecipients by SAT scores (high quartile, middle two quartiles, and low quartile) to illustrate differences in rates related to SAT and GMS. This steps helps illustrate differences in rates in relation to achievement for recipients and nonrecipients.

Logistic regression analyses using the model specifications described above provided a method of assessing whether GMS was significantly associated with the outcomes, controlling for other variables with a logical relationship. We used multinomial logistic regressions for destination (an appropriate approach for multiple outcomes) and logistic models for continuous enrollment (appropriate for dichotomous outcomes). This is an analytic step that NCES failed to use appropriately in its studies of student enrollment and persistence (Becker, 2004; Heller, 2004). These analyses establish whether or not there was a statistical association, controlling for other logically related variables, a step necessary to establish whether the additional aid had an influence on the outcome. We present both change-in-probability measures (delta-p statistics) and odds ratios for each independent variable, appropriate methods for presenting associations (Peng, So, Stage, & St. John, 2002).

Finally, we used *simulations* with the logistic regression models to present estimates of the differences in rates of enrollment and persistence related to the receipt of GMS, holding other variables constant. In these simulations, we set all of the variables at the average, then present different rates controlling for ability categories and receipt of GMS.

We use this three-step approach because such careful analyses are appropriate for establishing relationships between independent variables and outcomes in analyses that use sound logical models (Peng et al., 2002). Not only did NCES fail to use these steps when they reached the conclusion that parents' education and high school math explained the variance in enrollment and persistence (Becker, 2004; Heller, 2004), but they also failed to even consider the whether there was an association between aid and attainment outcomes (St. John, 2002, 2003).

<u>Continuous Enrollment</u>. The analysis of continuous enrollment compares students who maintained continuous enrollment (coded as "1") with students who did not (coded as 0) in a logistic regression model. The independent variables in the continuous enrollment model were:

- GMS award (compares students who received the GMS award with the comparison group [students who were not Pell-eligible and were GMS-eligible or who were not GMS-eligible]).
- Pell only (compares students who received Pell awards and were GMS-eligible and did not receive GMS with the comparison group).
- High achievement (students in highest ACT/SAT quartile compared with students in the middle two quartiles).
- Low achievement (students in the lowest ACT/SAT quartile compared with students in the middle two quartiles).
- Male (compared with female).
- African American (compared with Asian Pacific Islander American).
- Hispanic American (compared with Asian Pacific Islander American).
- Father had bachelor's degree (compared with not having degree).
- Private college (compared with attending a public four-year college).[16]

- Public two-year college (compared with attending a public four-year college).

This analysis allows us to examine the effects of GMS awards on financial access, defined as the ability to maintain continuous enrollment in a public two-year or four-year college to which students can gain financial access. The first step of the analysis assesses the impact of GMS awards on college destination. It provides a basis for judging whether GMS awards influence the ability to enroll in public four-year colleges,[17] as well as whether they furnish additional support for enrolling in private colleges.[18] The second step examines whether students had adequate financial resources to maintain continuous enrollment.

Limitations
This study used the most appropriate available approach for assessing the effects of GMS and Pell awards on financial access. However, a few constraints on the current study merit consideration by readers.

First, the ratings of the noncognitive measures used to make GMS awards were not available for the current study. While efforts are under way to make these measures available to the research advisors, this has not yet happened. This information void is somewhat problematic because the selection criteria can have an indirect effect on the outcomes measured here. This problem is mitigated at least partially by the quasi-random nature of the first-year award process.[19]   Therefore, subsequent analyses should include variables that control for the effects of the selection process.

Second, the information that can be collected appropriately from student self-reports is limited. Generally, students know about the type of grant aid that they receive, so it was appropriate to ask whether they had received Pell awards. However, we could not depend on the accuracy of responses to questions about the amount of state and federal grants received, so these questions were not asked on the survey.[20]   In the future, we plan to use information on state financial indicators in a multi-level analysis.

Third, a number of additional questions about the monetary effects of GMS awards were beyond the scope of this initial study.

For example, the continuing student file can be used to examine the impact of accumulated debt[21] on continuous enrollment, since GMS was designed to eliminate debt burden. In addition, it will be important to examine the impact of GMS on persistence by graduate students, a subject that is not studied frequently.

Fourth, while these analyses document whether GMS awards and these outcomes are associated, it is not possible to discern whether documented relationships are causally linked. Specifically, significant relationships could be attributed to the selection process, the finances provided, or other features of the GMS program. Further analyses are needed to discern the reasons for the statistical relationships reported here. However, the analysis is more than a simple comparison, because the logistic regression controlled for many of the other independent variables that influenced these outcomes. Proven logical models guided the selection of the independent variables.

Finally, while the GMS program was not a true experiment with random assignment, the 2000 study has some similarity to experimental studies. The population for this study includes only students who met the noncognitive selection criteria. The second stage of selection considered need, but there were students who met the need criteria in both groups. Therefore, logistic regression analyses of survey responses that control for the financial selection criterion (i.e., Pell award) are as valid as policy studies that use experimental designs. Further, since these analyses control for other factors that influence the selected outcomes, this approach includes better statistical controls than studies that compare only means for treatment and control groups, a much simpler approach to statistical analysis.

Findings

The analyses of financial access are presented in two steps. The analysis of college destination is followed by the analyses of continuous enrollment. These analyses present descriptive statistics along with the regression analysis and analysis of effect size.[22]

College Destinations

<u>The Sample</u>. Most of the students in the sample (Table 1) attended four-year colleges: 42.1 percent attended private colleges and 55.7 percent attended public four-year colleges. Only 2.2 percent of the sample attended public two-year colleges. The highest achievement group (23.5%) and the lowest achievement group (27.5%) each represented about one quarter of the population.

At a prima facie level, the basic notion put forward by NCES (1997a)—that students who take the steps to prepare for college have the opportunity to attend four-year colleges—appears to hold.

However, such descriptive statistics do not establish that those students who took the steps to prepare for college and who attended two-year colleges were not influenced by their financial circumstances, as some analysts conclude when they do not consider the direct effects of student aid (Choy, 2002; NCES, 1997a).

There was a great deal of racial/ethnic diversity in this sample. Fewer than half the respondents in the 2000 sample were GMS recipients (40.5%). Fewer than half were male (31.5%). African Americans comprised 34.9 percent of the 2000 sample, compared with 5.6 percent for American Indians and Alaska Natives, 25.3 percent for Hispanic Americans, and 34.2 percent for Asian Pacific Islander Americans. More than one third (36.3%) had fathers whom had completed their college degrees.[23]

Finances were more central to college choices for students in the sample than were academic reputations. While slightly less than half (44.3%) of the 2000 sample indicated that reputation was a very important reason for choosing their colleges, most (80.2%) indicated that costs were very important.

Federal need analysis estimates the expected parental contribution. Students in the study were asked whether their parents contributed to college finances. The majority responded affirmatively (53.8%), indicating that their parents tried to fulfill their expected contribution. However, in cases where parents did not or could not fulfill this obligation, their children could have been influenced by this shortfall.

Table 1. Descriptive Statistics for Variables in the Multinomial Logistic Regression for College Choice: 2000 Freshman Cohort.

Variable	Value	Frequency	%
Institution Choice in 2000 Fall	Private	701	42.1
	Public 2-year	37	2.2
	Public, 4-year or above	928	55.7
Gates Scholarship	Recipient	674	40.5
	Nonrecipient	992	59.5
SAT-ACT Crosswork Score Group	Lowest quartile	459	27.5
	Highest quartile	392	23.5
	Mid quartiles	816	48.9
Reason select school low expenses	Very important	738	44.3
	Other	928	55.7
Reason select school strong reputation	Very important	1,337	80.2
	Other	329	19.8
Parents contributing college finances	Parents are contributing college finances	897	53.8
	No	770	46.2
Gender	Male	525	31.5
	Female	1,142	68.5
Ethnicity	African Americans	581	34.9
	American Indians/Alaska Natives	94	5.6
	Hispanic Americans	422	25.3
	Asian Pacific Islander Americans	569	34.2
Father's Education Attainment	Bachelor's or Higher	604	36.3
	Other	1,062	63.7
Valid cases		1,666	
Cases with missing values		163	
Total number of cases with relative weight		1,829	

Breakdown Analyses. The breakdown analyses (Table 2) indicate that there are differences in the rate of enrollment in both two year colleges and private colleges compared to public four-year colleges. There was a clear relationship between SAT scores and enrollment in each type of college. However, very few of these students—a group that attended rigorous high schools (Trent, Gong & Owens-Nicholson, chapter 3) and had high grades in preparation courses—enrolled in two-year colleges. In these analyses we see the more substantial differences in rates related to enrollment in private colleges. Both SAT scores and GMS appear to be related to enrollment in four-year colleges, although these analyses would seem to indicate the GMS had a more substantial association with this outcome. We test this proposition below.

Logistic Regression. Receipt of a GMS award was one of several variables influencing college destinations (Table 3). Receiving a GMS award increased the odds of attending a private college compared with a public college and reduced the chances of being enrolled in a public two-year college. Students receiving GMS awards were 1.37 times more likely to enroll in private colleges than in public four-year colleges. In contrast, GMS awardees were only .359 times as likely to enroll in two-year colleges. Conversely, GMS recipients were more likely to enroll in public four-year colleges than in two-year colleges.

Table 2. Enrollment Rates by College Type, Broken Down by GMS Award and SAT-ACT Group: 2000 Freshman Cohort.

GMS	SAT-ACT Crosswork Score Group	Private Count	Private Row%	Public 2-Year Count	Public 2-Year Row%	Public 4-Year Count	Public 4-Year Row%
				College Choice			
Recipient	Lowest quartile	70	30.5	7	2.8	153	66.6
	Highest quartile	63	56.2			49	43.8
	Mid quartiles	160	47.9	3	0.8	171	51.2
Nonrecipient	Lowest quartile	57	24.6	9	4.0	164	71.4
	Highest quartile	175	62.4	1	0.4	105	37.3
	Mid quartiles	177	36.7	18	3.7	287	59.6
Total		701	42.1	37	2.2	928	55.7

Since some GMS recipients received awards after enrolling, it is conceivable that the significance of GMS for college choice is an artifact of selection.[24] However, because all students in the study met the selection criteria, it is highly unlikely that this artifact (the delay of some awards) explains the significance of the GMS variables, especially given the other statistical controls in this analysis. Therefore, there is a sound basis for concluding that this significance is related to the GMS program, both to its funding and to other design features. These findings have implications for state and federal policy, as is discussed in the concluding section.

Student achievement also was associated with college destination. Students with high scores were more likely to attend private colleges than public four-year colleges and less likely to attend two-year colleges. In contrast, students with low scores were less likely to enroll in private colleges. This finding is consistent with a long history of research on college choice (Hossler, Schmit, & Vesper, 1999; Paulsen, 2001a, 2001b).

Table 3. Multinomial Logistic Regression for College Destinations: 2000 GMS Freshman Cohort.

Variable		Private			Public 2-year		
		Odds Ratio	Delta P	Sig.	Odds Ratio	Delta P	Sig.
GMS	Recipient	1.3692	0.0779	***	0.3589	-0.0141	**
SAT-ACT	Lowest quartile	0.5436	-0.1377	***	1.1885	0.0041	
	Highest quartile	2.2479	0.1994	***	0.1644	-0.0185	*
Low exp.	Very important	0.4284	-0.1834	***	0.8333	-0.0036	
Reputation	Very important	1.3947	0.0825	**	0.4286	-0.0126	**
Parents	Contributed	1.4158	0.0862	***	1.5972	0.0128	
Gender	Male	0.7198	-0.0774	***	1.1471	0.0032	
Ethnicity	African Americans	1.4672	0.0952	***	0.9301	-0.0015	
	American Indians	0.4996	-0.1545	**	2.6547	0.0347	
	Hispanic Americans	1.4881	0.0987	***	3.0427	0.0424	**
Father's Ed.	Bachelor or Higher	1.0127	0.0031		0.3149	-0.0151	**
Number of cases with weight =		1,666					
Model χ^2 =		259					
-2 Log Likelihood =		1,186					
Cox & Snell Pseudo R^2 =		0.144					

Note: *** $p<0.01$, ** $p<0.05$, * $p<0.1$

Choosing a college because of low expenses was negatively associated with enrollment in private colleges but was not significantly associated with enrollment in public two-year colleges. Minority students who chose public four-year colleges differed from students who chose private colleges on this variable, but did not differ from students who attended two-year colleges. Therefore, these findings indicate that costs were central in the choice of college destination for students enrolling in public colleges, both two year and four year.

Gender and ethnicity were associated with enrollment in private colleges. Males were less likely to enroll in private colleges, but gender was not associated with enrollment in two-year colleges compared with public four-year colleges. African Americans were 1.47 times more likely to enroll in private colleges than were Asian Pacific Islander Americans. Hispanic Americans were significantly more likely to enroll in private colleges, while American Indians and Alaska Natives were significantly less likely to enroll in private colleges.

Hispanics were more likely to enroll in public two-year colleges than were Asian Pacific Islander Americans, but the other ethnicity variables were not significant for the 2000 cohort. This confirms other research indicating that college choices are more constrained for Hispanic Americans than for other ethnic groups (Paulsen, St. John, & Carter, 2002).

Parents' education was not associated with enrollment in private colleges, but did influence enrollment in two-year colleges for the 2000 cohort. Compared with their peers whose parents had not received a degree, students whose fathers had bachelor's degrees were less likely to enroll in public two-year colleges than in public four-year colleges. Thus, while parents' education does influence the college choice process for these minority students, it does not appear to be the most important determinant, as some have proposed (Choy, 2002).

Analysis of Effects. The simulations (Table 4) compare two of the predictor variables at the average for the population, then estimate the enrollment rates for GMS recipients and nonrecipients broken down by income group. These analyses again show a stronger amount of rate differential attributable to GMS than to SAT differences. These analyses further verify that adequate student financial aid makes a substantial difference in college destination, even among highly qualified students who take all of the steps necessary to enroll in the four-year college.

The comparison of Tables 2 and 5 illustrates the difference for simple differences in rates and predicted differences, controlling for other factors. Note that in Table 2, 56.4 percent of the GMS students in the high-GMS quartile enrolled in private colleges. However, when we control for other variables (set them as constant with the average for the data set), then the predicted percentage of high-achieving GMS recipients attending private colleges is 65.4 percent. However, the differential between the two tables is much smaller. Given these findings we conclude that GMS had substantial effects on improving the odds of enrolling in private colleges, but other factors inhibited the choice of private colleges for GMS recipients with high SAT-ACT scores. More specially, the simple rate differences from the breakdown analyses are not a good indicator of the effect of the receipt of GMS or achieving high scores on college entrance tests.

Table 4. Predicted Probability on Enrollment by Type of Institution by GMS and SAT-ACT Group: 2000 Freshman Cohort.

GMS	SAT-ACT Crosswork Score Group	Private		Public 2-year	
		Predicted Log Odds	Predicted Probability	Predicted Log Odds	Predicted Probability
Recipient	Lowest quartile	-0.7807	31.4%	-4.0611	1.7%
Recipient	Highest quartile	0.6389	65.4%	-6.0393	0.2%
Recipient	Mid quartiles	-0.1711	45.7%	-4.2338	1.4%
Nonrecipient	Lowest quartile	-1.0949	25.1%	-3.0363	4.6%
Nonrecipient	Highest quartile	0.3247	58.0%	-5.0146	0.7%
Nonrecipient	Mid quartiles	-0.4853	38.1%	-3.2090	3.9%

These analyses illustrate further the problems with the prior NCES analyses, as reviewed by Becker (in press) and Heller (in press). NCES rested its conclusions about the role of preparation on breakdown statistics, a method that does not provide a sufficient set of statistical controls to reach the types of conclusions that have been reached from these analyses. However, the more serious problem was that NCES failed to control for the role of finances (St. John, 2002, 2003). This three-step analysis verify that finances have a direct association with the opportunity to enroll in four-year colleges and private colleges, a topic NCES failed to consider even though their conclusions excluded this explanation for the inequalities now evident.

Continuous Enrollment
    Sample Characteristics. Most of the sample (96.6%) enrolled continuously, indicating a high degree of financial access. Table 5 summarizes the descriptive data, which, of course, is similar to that in Table 1. This table provides a further breakdown of recipient categories. Only a small percentage of the sample was Pell eligible and GMS eligible but did not receive GMS awards (2.8%). Comparing these students and GMS recipients with others in the sample refines our ability to understand the impact of GMS. The comparison group included students who were eligible for GMS but not Pell, and students who did not meet the GMS eligibility criteria. No Pell information was available on students who did not meet the GMS criteria.[25]
    Breakdown Analyses. The breakdown of persistence rates differentiates the population, sorted for SAT group and GMS (Table 6). These analyses reveal that GMS was associated with more substantial differences in persistence rates, as measured by continuous enrollment during the first two years of college. Variation in rates was small, but there were differences for the two groups. The logistic regressions were needed to determine whether this association was significant, controlling for other independent variables.
    Logistic Regression Analysis. Controlling for other variables, receiving a GMS award was positively associated with continuous enrollment (Table 7). GMS recipients were 2.7 times more likely than were nonrecipients to maintain continuous enrollment. However, non-GMS recipients who received a Pell award and were eligible for GMS did not differ statistically from the comparison group. This indicates that the added financial resource provided by the GMS award, rather than meeting the noncognitive selection criteria, was the reason GMS students persisted better.

The finding that GMS improved continuous enrollment is important, given the substantial statistical controls in this study. Both the recipient and comparison groups met the selection criteria. Controlling for other factors influencing enrollment, GMS recipients were substantially more likely to persist. These findings confirm that providing adequate financial assistance along with other support services improves the odds that low-income, high-achieving students will maintain continuous enrollment.

In contrast, achievement, as measured by the design variables for test scores, was not related statistically to continuous enrollment. Typically, a high correlation is found between college grades and scores on ACT and SAT tests (St. John, Hu, Simmons, & Musoba, 2001). However, most colleges do not have policies that preclude lower-division students from continuing if they have low grades for up to two terms. Thus, the finding that achievement was not related to continuous enrollment indicates that the students in this sample did not have substantial academic problems.

African American respondents were less likely to enroll continuously than were Asian Pacific Islander Americans who met the noncognitive selection criteria, a finding that merits further analysis. However, other ethnic groups did not differ significantly. Neither gender nor fathers' education was associated with continuous enrollment.

The type of college attended did influence persistence, however. Compared with students in public four-year colleges, those attending private colleges were more likely to persist, while students attending public two-year colleges were less likely to persist. Thus, students starting out in two-year colleges had less opportunity to maintain continuous enrollment and their financial access was further constrained.

Table 5. Descriptive Statistics for Variables in the Logistic Regression on Continuous Enrollment: 2000 Freshman Cohort.

Variable	Value	Frequency	%
Continuous Enrollment	Continuous Enrollment	1,645	96.6
	Stop or Drop-Off	58	3.4
GMS/Pell Eligibility	GMS and Pell Eligible	685	40.2
	Non-GMS and Pell/GMS Eligible	47	2.8
	Non-GMS Scholar and Pell Ineligible	972	57.0
SAT-ACT Crosswork Score Group	Lowest quartile	471	27.6
	Highest quartile	398	23.4
	Mid quartiles	835	49.0
Gender	Male	536	31.5
	Female	1,167	68.5
Ethnicity	African Americans	593	34.8
	American Indians/Alaska Natives	97	5.7
	Hispanic Americans	432	25.3
	Asian Pacific Islander Americans	582	34.1
Father's Ed	Bachelor's or Higher	612	36.0
	Other	1,091	64.0
Institution Type in 2000 Fall	Private	710	41.7
	Public 2-year	43	2.5
	Public, 4-year or above	950	55.8
Valid cases		1,703	
Cases with missing values		126	
Total number of cases with relative weight		1,829	

Analysis of Effects. The simulations (Table 8) present the estimates of persistence rates for GMS recipients and nonrecipients in different SAT groups. These analyses further illustrate the differentials in rates, but build in appropriate statistical control. When we take these steps, it is abundantly apparent that GMS improved the odds that recipients would persist. However, when we compare across the two tables, it is apparent the the percentage is very nearly equal to the actual percentage—the odds that GMS recipients would persist was around 98-99 percent in both actual (Table 6) and predicted (Table 8). Yet the predicted percentages of nonrecipients who persisted were lower than the actual, indicating that not receiving GMS was a larger comparative disadvantage in persistence than indicated by the simple breakdown. This further illustrates that (a) GMS had a modest positive influence on the opportunity to persist, and (b) the simple statistical breakdowns typically used to reporting on policy studies are poor indicators of program effects.

Table 6. Continuous Enrollment Rate, Broken Down by GMS Award and SAT-ACT Group: 2000 Freshman Cohort.

Pell Eligibility	GMS	SAT-ACT Crosswork Score Group	Count	Row %	Count	Row %
				Continuous Enrollment		Stop or Drop-off
Yes	Recipient	Lowest quartile	228	98.2	4	1.8
		Highest quartile	111	98.1	2	1.9
		Mid quartiles	334	98.5	5	1.5
	Nonrecipient	Lowest quartile	17	89.5	2	10.5
		Highest quartile	11	100.0		
		Mid quartiles	16	100.0		
No	Nonrecipient	Lowest quartile	204	93.3	15	6.7
		Highest quartile	266	97.5	7	2.5
		Mid quartiles	456	95.1	23	4.9
Total			1,645	96.6	58	3.4

Table 7: Logistic Regression Analysis of Continuous Enrollment by Students in the 2000 Freshman Cohort.

	Variable	Odds Ratio	Delta P	Sig.
Gates Scholarship GMS and Pell Eligibility	GMS Gates Scholar and Pell Eligible	2.7380	0.0213	***
	GMS Non Gates Scholar and Pell Eligible	1.0397	0.0013	
SAT-ACT Group	Lowest quartile	0.8787	-0.0045	
	Highest quartile	0.9353	-0.0023	
Gender	Male	1.4708	0.0106	
Ethnicity	African Americans	0.4956	-0.0324	*
	American Indians/Alaska Natives	0.5563	-0.0255	
	Hispanic Americans	1.2549	0.0067	
Father's Ed.	Bachelor's or Higher	1.4058	0.0096	

Table 7: Logistic Regression Analysis of Continuous Enrollment by Students in the 2000 Freshman Cohort (continued).

Variable	Odds Ratio	Delta P	Sig.
Institution Type Private	2.0932	0.0175	**
in 2000 Public 2-year	0.1607	-0.1459	***
Number of cases with relative weight =	1,703		
Model χ^2 =	49		
-2 Log Likelihood =	459		
Cox & Snell Pseudo R^2 =	0.028		

Note: *** $p<0.01$, ** $p<0.05$, * $p<0.1$

Table 8: Predicted Probability on Enrollment Rates by GMS and SAT-ACT Group: 2000 Freshman Cohort.

Pell Eligibility	GMS	SAT-ACT Crosswork Score Group	Predicted Log Odds	Predicted Probability
Yes	Recipient	Lowest quartile	4.2291	98.6%
Yes	Recipient	Highest quartile	4.2915	98.7%
Yes	Recipient	Mid quartiles	4.3584	98.7%
Yes	Nonrecipient	Lowest quartile	3.2607	96.3%
Yes	Nonrecipient	Highest quartile	3.3232	96.5%
Yes	Nonrecipient	Mid quartiles	3.3900	96.7%
No	Nonrecipient	Lowest quartile	3.2218	96.2%
No	Nonrecipient	Highest quartile	3.2842	96.4%
No	Nonrecipient	Mid quartiles	3.3511	96.6%

Findings and Implications

These analyses strongly suggest that GMS awards improved financial access. GMS recipients were better able to afford to attend a four-year college and especially private colleges. Further, starting in a two-year college was negatively associated with continuous enrollment and change of college. Thus, receiving a GMS award improved the odds that college-qualified, low-income minority students would enroll in a four-year college and maintain continuous enrollment.[26]   In addition to meeting a minimum threshold set by our definition of financial access, the GMS recipients had an increased ability to enroll and persist in private colleges. Thus, college choices were expanded for GMS recipients.[27]

These findings also add to a general understanding of the access challenge facing educational policymakers in the United States. In the 1970s, the rates of college enrollment by Hispanic Americans, African Americans, and Whites who had graduated from high school were essentially equal, but a substantial gap opened after 1980 (St. John, 2002, 2003). Growth in the enrollment gap corresponded with the decline in the purchasing power of Pell Grants. However, since NCES failed to use its massive databases to examine the impact of student aid on access, little information was publicly available on the relationship between the gap in enrollment opportunity and the decline in federal need-based grants. Thus, the extra support provided by GMS awards created additional financial access for college-qualified, low-income minority students.

This study of the GMS 2000 freshman cohort reduces substantially the information void created by NCES's failure to examine the consequences of the decline in need-based grants. By comparing students who received awards with students who did not, controlling for variables other than educational choices, we assessed the impact of GMS on financial access. For high-achieving minority students, receiving adequate (last-dollar) financial aid improved their odds of attending four-year colleges and their ability to maintain continuous enrollment, two important indicators of financial access for college-prepared students.

Low-income students who received additional need-based financial support had a greater probability of enrolling in four-year colleges and of maintaining continuous enrollment. Only a few states provide sufficient additional need-based financial aid to offer low-income students the opportunity to enroll in college (St. John, Chung, Musoba, Simmons, Wooden, & Mendez, 2004). This GMS study further confirms that providing additional need-based student aid is an effective strategy and merits serious consideration by states.

These findings will have important policy implications. The primary policy lesson is that greater investment is needed in need-based financial aid. High-achieving, low-income students lack adequate financial resources to enroll in four-year colleges and to persist during the first two years.

Further analyses are necessary to untangle the reasons why GMS improved financial access. Studies should examine the relative contribution of the selection criteria and process, the monetary awards, and the other features of the GMS program. However, these initial analyses strongly indicate that a relationship exists between providing adequate financial aid and enrollment opportunity.

Notes

1.   The Pell program was created as "Basic Educational Opportunity Grants" (BEOGs) in the Education Amendments of 1972, but was subsequently renamed "Pell Grants." This report uses the current name for the program even though it was known as "BEOGs" before 1980.

2.   By "official" literature, we refer to policy reports written by the U.S. Department of Education and its contractors, along with reports published by national higher education associations.

3.   The United Negro College Fund administered both the program and the award process for African Americans. Other national organizations with commitments to Hispanic Americans, Asian Pacific Islander Americans, and American Indians/Alaska Natives were contracted with to administer the scholarship award process for these groups.

4.   High school graduation represents an appropriate indicator of academic preparation for a two-year or four-year college. Other analysts have examined the role of college preparatory courses in preparing high school students for enrollment in four-year colleges (Adelman, 1999; NCES, 1997a; Pelavin & Kane, 1990).

5.   The publications (St. John, 1991; St. John & Noell, 1989) originally were completed as reports for Pelavin Associates, prior to the release of Pelavin and Kane (1988).

6.   Professor St. John was a Senior Associate with Pelavin Associates when the Pelavin and Kane study (1988) was

conducted. He completed analyses of the relative effects of academic preparation, aspirations, and student aid on enrollment (St. John, 1991).

7. Students in these analyses enrolled in college. So, by definition, they took sufficient or appropriate courses to gain financial access. Since we lacked variables on high school experience, we could not examine high school courses.

8. The advisory panel included Walter Allen, Sylvia Hurtado, William Sedlacek, Edward St. John, and William Trent.

9. The advisory panel was concerned that NORC reach at least a 50 percent response level for each group, a threshold that was met consistently.

10. The GMS recipients may be more "self-selected." For example, it is conceivable that students who dropped out may not have responded. Nevertheless, we must assume that the use of the weights compensates for this possible bias.

11. Earlier studies of access using longitudinal databases have examined if students enrolled in college (Becker, 1988; St. John, 1989). However, since students in this sample had achieved a threshold for financial access, it is not surprising that most actually enrolled in college. Therefore, our analyses focus on continuous enrollment, consistent with our definition of financial access (St. John, 2003).

12. A very small sample of members enrolled in proprietary schools. These students were included in the group that went to private colleges, because these colleges have private control (albeit for profit) and have higher cost than public two-year colleges. Public two-year colleges were treated as a distinct category because they have lower tuition than other types of colleges.

13. In the multinomial logistic analysis, it was not possible to maintain a distinct coding for Pell without GMS award. There was no information on Pell awards for students who did not meet GMS award criteria.

14. We did not have information on high school courses and grades in this file. We were limited to ACT/SAT scores as a measure of prior achievement.

15. Asian Pacific Islander Americans were used as the comparison group in these analyses because Asian Pacific Islander Americans generally attend college at a rate comparable with

Whites and, on average, they have higher parental educational attainment levels than other minority groups (Paulsen, St. John, & Carter, 2002).

16. These variables—private college and public two-year college—are included to provide a basis for comparing across the two models. The multinomial analysis of college destinations considers financial and academic reasons for college choice. Therefore, it is possible logically to consider the indirect effects of college choice on persistence (in the logic regression) when the choice variables had a significant association with college destinations (in the multinomial logistic regression).

17. This represents a minimum threshold of access. For students in states with high need-based state grants, the GMS awards usually are of modest size.

18. Originally, Pell was created to subsidize college choice by low-income students, including the choice to attend private colleges. When MISAA extended Pell eligibility to children of middle-income families, the intent of subsidizing choice for private colleges was liberalized. However, since the mid-1980s, Pell Grants have not reached a threshold that would ensure financial access to public four-year colleges in most states (St. John, 2002).

19. The quasi-random nature of the first-year award was discussed as part of the background on GMS, above.

20. This issue was the subject of a great deal of discussion by the research advisors with the NORC team. Ultimately, we agreed to a constrained set of questions about student financial assistance as a means of ensuring that there was adequate room to ask a broader range of questions on other topics of importance for research on minority students.

21. We are reliant on self-reported information about debt, but these questions were included in the survey of continuing students because they were central to the interest of the Bill & Melinda Gates Foundation.

22. The tables presented in this report have different numbers of cases. This variation is attributable to differences in response rates for the questions on the survey.

23. Most students who had a mother with a college degree also had a father with a college degree. This study used father's

education as the indicator, but mother's or both would have had similar results.

24. We do not know the exact number of GMS recipients who were notified after the beginning of the academic year, but verbal communications indicate that a relatively small number of recipients were affected by the delay.

25. Therefore, it was not fully possible to assess the direct effects of Pell. However, the method of coding provides a basis for assessing the effects of GMS monetary awards.

26. The GMS selection criteria and process may have played a role in the findings on college destination, so this finding should be interpreted with caution.

27. Historically, the goal of federal student financial aid programs was to equalize choice of college (Gladieux & Wolanin, 1976).

References

Adelman, C. (1995). *The new college course map and transcript files: Changes in course-taking and achievement, 1972-1993*. Washington, DC: National Center for Education Statistics.

Adelman, C. (1999). *Answers in the tool box: Academic intensity, attendance patterns, and bachelor's degree attainment*. Washington, DC: National Center for Education Statistics.

Advisory Committee on Student Financial Assistance. (2001). *Access denied: Restoring equal educational opportunity*. Washington, DC: Author.

Advisory Committee on Student Financial Assistance. (2002). *Empty promises: The myth of college access in America*. Washington, DC: Author.

Becker, G. S. (1964). *Human capital: A theoretical and empirical analysis with special reference to education*. New York: Columbia University Press.

Becker, W. E. (2004). Omitted variables and sample selection in studies of college-going decisions. In E. P. St. John (Ed.), *Readings on equal education: Vol. 19. Public policy and college access: Investigating the federal and state roles in equalizing postsecondary opportunity* (pp. 65-86). New York: AMS Press.

Breneman, D. W., Finn, C. E., & Nelson, S. (Eds.). (1978). *Public policy and private higher education*. Washington, DC: The Brookings Institution.

Choy, S. P. (2002). *Access & persistence: Findings from 10 years of longitudinal research on students*. Washington, DC: American Council on Education.

College Board. (2002a). *Trends in student aid 2002*. Washington, DC: Author.

College Board. (2002b). *Trends in college pricing 2002*. Washington, DC: Author.

Ellwood, D., & Kane, T. J. (2000). Who is getting a college education: Family background and the growing gaps in enrollment. In S. Danziger & J. Waldfogel (Eds.), *Securing the future: Investing in children from birth to college* (pp. 264-282). New York: Russell Sage Foundation.

Finn, C. E., Jr. (1978). *Scholars, dollars, and bureaucrats: Federal policy toward higher education*. Washington, DC: The Brookings Institution.

Fitzgerald, B. (2004). Federal financial aid and college access. In E. P. St. John (Ed.), *Readings on equal education: Vol. 19. Public policy and college access: Investigating the federal and state roles in equalizing postsecondary opportunity* (pp. 1-28). New York: AMS Press.

Fogel, R. W. (2000). *The fourth great awakening and the future of egalitarianism*. Chicago: University of Chicago Press.

Gladieux, L. E., & Swail, W. S. (1999). Financial aid is not enough: Improving the odds for low-income and minority students. In J. E. King (Ed.), *Financing a college education: How it works, how it is changing* (pp. 177-197). Phoenix, AZ: Oryx Press.

Gladieux, L. E., & Wolanin, T. (1976). *Congress and the colleges: The national politics of higher education*. Lexington, MA: Lexington Books.

Hansen, W. L, & Weisbrod, B. A. (1969). *Benefits, costs, and finance of public higher education*. Chicago: Markham.

Heller, D. E. (1997). Student price response in higher education: An update of Leslie and Brinkman. *Journal of Higher Education, 68*(6), 624-659.

Heller, D. E. (2004). NCES research on college participation: A critical analysis. In E. P. St. John (Ed.), *Readings on equal education: Vol. 19. Public policy and college access: Investigating the federal and state roles in equalizing postsecondary opportunity* (pp. 29-64). New York: AMS Press.

Hossler, D., Schmit, J., & Vesper, N. (1999). *Going to college.* Baltimore: Johns Hopkins University Press.

Jackson, G. A. (1978). Financial aid and student enrollment. *Journal of Higher Education, 49,* 548-574.

Jackson, G. A. (1988). Did college choice change during the seventies? *Economics of Education Review, 7,* 15-27.

King, J. E. (1999). Conclusion. In J. E. King (Ed.), *Financing a college education: How it works, how it's changing* (pp. 198-202). Phoenix, AZ: Oryx Press.

Lee, J. B. (2004). Access revisited: A preliminary reanalysis of NELS. In E. P. St. John (Ed.), *Readings on equal education: Vol. 19. Public policy and college access: Investigating the federal and state roles in equalizing postsecondary opportunity* (pp. 87-96). New York: AMS Press.

Manski, C. F., & Wise, D. A. (1983). *College choice in America.* Cambridge, MA: Harvard University Press.

McPherson, M. S., & Schapiro, M. O. (1991). *Keeping college affordable.* Washington, DC: The Brookings Institution.

McPherson, M. S., & Schapiro, M. O. (1997). *The student aid game.* Princeton, NJ: Princeton University Press.

National Center for Education Statistics. (1996). *National Education Longitudinal Study: 1988-1994, Descriptive summary report with an essay on access and choice in postsecondary education.* NCES 96-175. Washington, DC: Author.

National Center for Education Statistics. (1997a). *Access to higher postsecondary education for the 1992 high school graduates.* NCES 98-195, by L. Berkner & L. Chavez. Project Officer: C. D. Carroll. Washington, DC: Author.

National Center for Education Statistics. (1997b). *Confronting the odds: Students at risk and the pipeline to higher education.* NCES 98-094, by L. J. Horn. Project officer: C. D. Carroll. Washington, DC: Author.

National Center for Education Statistics. (1998). *The condition of education 1998,* by J. Wirt, T. Snyder, J. Sable, S. P. Choy, Y. Bae, J. Stennett, A. Gruner & M. Peire. Washington, DC: Author.

Paulsen, M. B. (2001a). The economics of human capital and investment in higher education. In M. B. Paulsen & J. C. Smart. (Eds.). *The finance of higher education: Theory, research, policy, and practice* (pp. 55-94). New York: Agathon.

Paulsen, M. B. (2001b). The economics of the public sector: The nature and role of public policy in higher education finance. In M. B. Paulsen & J. C. Smart (Eds.), *The finance of higher education: Theory, research, policy, and practice* (pp. 95-132). New York: Agathon.

Paulsen, M. B., St. John, E. P., & Carter, D. F. (2002). *Diversity, college costs, and postsecondary opportunity: An examination of the financial nexus between college choice and persistence.* Policy Research Report No. 02-01. Bloomington, IN: Indiana Education Policy Center.

Pelavin, S. H., & Kane, M. B. (1988). *Minority participation in higher education.* Washington, DC: Pelavin Associates.

Pelavin, S. H., & Kane, M. B. (1990). *Changing the odds: Factors increasing access to college.* New York: The College Board.

Peng, C. Y. J., So, T. H., Stage, F. K., & St. John, E. P. (2002). The use and interpretation of logistic regression in higher education journals: 1988-1999. *Research in Higher Education, 43*(3), 259-294.

Perna, L. W., & Titus, M. (2002). *Understanding the barrier to college access for students with low family income and low socioeconomic status: The role of state context.* Paper presented at the 29th Annual NASSGAP/NCHELP Student Financial Aid Research Network Conference, Denver, CO.

Sedlacek, W. E. (2004.) *Beyond the big test: Noncognitive assessment in higher education.* San Francisco: Jossey-Bass.

St. John, E. P. (1989). The influence of student aid on persistence. *Journal of Student Financial Aid, 19*(3), 52-68.

St. John, E. P. (1990). Price response in enrollment decisions: An analysis of the High School and Beyond sophomore cohort. *Research in Higher Education, 31*(2), 161-176.

St. John, E. P. (1991). A framework for reexamining state resource management strategies in higher education. *Journal of Higher Education, 62*(3), 263-287.

St. John, E. P. (1994). *Prices, productivity, and investment: Assessing financial strategies in higher education.* ASHE/ERIC Higher Education Report No. 3. Washington, DC: George Washington University.

St. John, E. P. (1997). Desegregation at a crossroads: Critical reflections on possible new directions. In D. Hossler & E. P. St. John (Eds.), Special issue: Rethinking college desegregation. *Journal for a Just and Caring Education, 3*(1), 127-134.

St. John, E. P. (2002). *The access challenge: Rethinking the causes of the opportunity gap.* Policy Issue Report No. 2002-1. Bloomington, IN: Indiana Education Policy Center.

St. John, E. P. (2003). *Refinancing the college dream: Access, equal opportunity, and justice for taxpayers.* Baltimore, MD: Johns Hopkins University Press.

St. John, E. P., Chung, C. G, Musoba, G D., Simmons, A. B., Wooden, O. S., & Mendez, J. (2004). *Expanding college access: The impact of state finance strategies.* Indianapolis: The Lumina Foundation for Education.

St. John, E. P., Hu, S., Simmons, A. B., & Musoba, G D. (2001). Aptitude v. merit: What matters in persistence? *Review of Higher Education, 24*(2), 131-152.

St. John, E. P., & Noell, J. (1989). The effects of student financial aid on access to higher education: An analysis of progress with special consideration of minority enrollment. *Research in Higher Education, 30*(6), 563-581.

St. John, E. P., Paulsen, M. B., & Starkey, J. B. (1996). The nexus between college choice and persistence. *Research in Higher Education, 37*(2), 175-220.

CHAPTER 6

THE TRANSITION TO COLLEGE FOR LOW-INCOME STUDENTS: THE IMPACT OF THE GATES MILLENNIUM SCHOLARS PROGRAM

Sylvia Hurtado, Thomas F. Nelson Laird, and Thomas E. Perorazio

First-time college attendance presents both challenges and opportunities as students encounter new people, face higher academic expectations, and achieve new levels of independence. All students typically face varying degrees of difficulty and have different strategies for adjusting financially, academically, socially, and personally/emotionally, but there are fairly unique issues evident among underrepresented racial/ethnic minorities (Hurtado, Carter, & Spuler, 1996; Smedley, Myers, & Harrell,1993). First-year students often seek to establish new affiliations that provide them with a sense of belonging in the college community, which is based on interests, values, and background. These students also begin to renegotiate former relationships (Hurtado & Carter, 1997). However, low-income students typically have fewer financial resources, possess less knowledge about college, and often come from high schools that lack appropriate resources for college-level preparation (e.g., college counseling, AP coursework). The purpose of this study was to determine how low-income students who were selected to be a part of the Gates Millennium Scholars (GMS) program experience the transition to college compared with students who applied but were not selected. The experience of these students provides important insight into the barriers to and facilitators of success in college for low-income students of color. The study is a test to determine whether the GMS program's method of identifying talent and providing financial support has the effect of extending opportunity and ensuring student success during the transition to college and against the odds that typically confront low-income students.

Perspectives from the Literature

College Adjustment
    The first year of college has been identified as the most critical period because it shapes students' chances for later success, with success being defined as positive adjustment to the new academic, social, professional, and personal challenges that accompany enrollment in college (Upcraft & Gardner, 1989). As the demographics of our nation shift to include more minority families, higher education administrators also face a more complex array of challenges in promoting the success of students of color. These challenges involve rethinking traditional ways of identifying student talent and managing retention and persistence strategies to incorporate the particular needs of diverse racial and ethnic groups, thereby increasing their chances of success (Johnson & Ottens, 1996).
    Scholarship on college adjustment has increased our understanding of the student experience in the past quarter century. One prominent area of research on college adjustment has tended to focus on concepts concerning student integration or engagement in college life. Much of this work stems from Tinto's models (1975; 1986; 1993) of student departure that theorize about student transition, proposing that persistence in college is a function of academic and social integration. Similarly, after studying thousands of college students, Astin postulated that student engagement in college (in many contexts) leads to success

manifested in a host of educational outcomes (Astin, 1984, 1993). The concept of integration has prompted scholarship on the experiences students have while enrolled in college, particularly the importance of their behaviors regarding engagement and involvement in all areas of campus life.

For instance, building on Tinto's (1975) concept of academic integration, Donovan (1984) noted that college experiences, particularly academic integration, were more important than their precollege characteristics for the persistence of minority students, suggesting that programmatic interventions could increase persistence. Nora and Cabrera (1996) did not find significant differences in the effects of academic preparation on the persistence of minority and nonminority students, leading to the conclusion that college experiences were more important. This finding was supported in later work (Cabrera, Nora, Terenzini, Pascarella, & Hagedorn, 1999). Academic integration plays a key role in the adjustment to college. It is more important than students' entering ability and contributes greatly to their academic success. One difference between minority and nonminority students is the influence of institutional quality on the intent to persist, with quality being influenced by students' academic and social integration as well as an affinity with the perceived values of faculty and other students (Eimers & Pike, 1997). Such affinity does not develop without acquiring a sense of belonging on campus, which is determined by minority students' activities and engagement on campus (Hurtado & Carter, 1997). Any aspect that hinders students' capacity for becoming involved in college and feeling that they are a part of campus life is likely to become a barrier to adjustment and persistence.

Other theories, looking more specifically at minority students' experiences, focus on psychological stressors and students' coping behaviors. Smedley, Myers, & Harrell (1993) theorized that minority students face unique stresses at predominantly White institutions that should be distinguished from the common strains all students share. These unique stresses increase feelings of isolation that impede their integration into the campus community in both direct and indirect ways. The most subtle effects are the personal sources of stress minority students experience, such as when the environment causes them to have negative feelings about their own preparedness, when there are concerns about family expectations, and when questions arise regarding their legitimacy at a competitive institution (Smedley et al., 1993). While these feelings are generated by a hostile climate, which can have a negative effect on many aspects of minority student adjustment (Hurtado et al., 1996), researchers have concluded that these climate factors can be overcome by interracial contact (Bennett & Okinaka, 1990) and positive interactions with students and faculty (Cabrera et al., 1999; Nora & Cabrera, 1996).

An additional and important factor in college adjustment is support from family, peers, and college authority figures. Specifically, Latinos who were identified as high achievers in high school were asked to identify who helped them the most during their first year of college (Hurtado et al., 1996). They responded overwhelmingly that their peers and, to a lesser but important extent, family members were responsible for easing the transition and helping them adjust to college. They also noted that college personnel were particularly helpful with academic adjustment. Other research has confirmed that personal and family relations can have a positive effect on integration into college, academic performance, and intellectual development (Feenstra, Banyard, Rines, & Hopkins, 2001; Nora & Cabrera, 1996; Terenzini, Rendon, Upcraft, Millar, Allison, Gregg, & Jalomo, 1994). Thus, support from new and old relationships is particularly important to the success of minority students in college.

Low-Income and Minority Students

A recent study concluded that one-quarter of all undergraduates in the U.S. were low-income students (Choy, 2000). Low-income and minority students frequently must overcome challenges posed by social and structural barriers to higher education not experienced by other students. These barriers include, but are not limited to, factors such as parental education attainment, first-generation status, family income, and limited English proficiency (Wolanin, 2003). Understanding the effects of these barriers and how they might be overcome is critical. These barriers have far-reaching implications for all aspects of the students' higher education, including the decision to search for and choose to apply to a particular institution, the transition from high school to college, the experiences they have while enrolled in college, and the benefits they accrue while there (O'Brien & Shedd, 2001).

For instance, the relationship between family income and educational aspirations is not trivial. Students from the lowest quintile of family income are far more likely to have parents with a high school education or less. They also have lower expectations for attending college and attaining a degree (Terenzini, Cabrera, & Bernal, 2001). Presumably, this is due to the realities of having to work to earn income while in high school and college. Also, according to a recent report of the federal Advisory Committee on Student Financial Assistance (ACSFA, 2002), among academically prepared low-income high school graduates, only 70 percent expected to finish college, compared with 95 percent of high-income high school graduates.

With regard to all of the college search and transition processes, low-SES students are at a disadvantage relative to their peers of greater means. Regarding academic preparation, low-SES students often bring fewer academic resources to college. This is often because they are less likely to have been exposed to a rigorous high school curriculum, more likely to have lower scores on admissions tests, have a lower rank in their class, and lower GPAs (Terenzini et al., 2001). In addition, low-SES students more frequently exhibit one or more of the seven risk factors for attrition identified by the National Center for Education Statistics in its study of entering freshmen. The seven risk factors are as follows: 1) delayed enrollment after high school, 2) lacking a high school diploma, 3) enrolling part-time, 4) being financially independent, 5) working full-time, 6) having dependent children, and 7) being a single parent (NCES, 1996). Despite this rather dismal portrait of low-income students derived from national data, it should be noted that those who apply to a national scholarship program such as GMS are a somewhat unique population. Applicants to the program aspire to earn a postsecondary degree, are seeking ways to fund their education, and have done their best to prepare themselves for college despite these risk factors. These low-income students must have the academic self-confidence to compete in such a scholarship program and may have received some counseling/advising to take advantage of these opportunities. In many ways, the program played an initial role in attracting, and subsequently selecting, talented, low-income minority students.

Once in college, however, it is up to both the student and college to make success possible. Financial aid plays no small role in this process. Four factors have been found to be of interest in determining successful adjustment for low-income students: pre-college preparation, financial aid, engagement and feeling connected with their institution, and attendance patterns (O'Brien & Shedd, 2001). The current structure of the financial aid system, although need based, does not readily assist low-income students with college degree aspirations. For example, college prepaid plans seldom benefit low-income students (Olivas, 1999) because their parents do not have the income to take advantage of such investments, nor are low-income families likely to encourage extensive debt in the form of loans. The outcome of current financial aid policies is that low-income students are forced to regularly use funds from work and credit cards to meet their expenses (O'Brien & Shedd, 2001), leaving them with student loan and personal credit card debts whether they complete their degrees or not (Nora, 2001).

For financial aid recipients, unmet need becomes a real hardship. Having the certainty of aid in the future is an important factor in the decision to remain in college (Cunningham, 2002)—a factor built into the GMS program and that often is critical for low-income minority students. Having sufficient funds enhances academic performance, contributes to social integration, and increases the chances of persistence (Nora & Cabrera, 1996). Because some students have unmet need but still must pay their expenses, Choy (2000) theorized that these students could be surviving on less income than their institutions calculate in their budget or are working more than they have reported. This takes a toll on enrollment, and as a result, low-income students were less likely to have persisted or earned a degree than other students (Choy, 2000). This may be because such concerns and time spent working takes time away from studies and the important social networking that students need in order to learn how to negotiate the challenges posed in the transition to college.

The conceptual model for the study takes into account these important factors in order to study the college adjustment of recipients and nonrecipients of GMS support. The model, derived from previous research, includes background characteristics of students and characteristics of the college attended; both are factors that influence students' preparation and the level of challenge experienced in college. Important information about the college experience includes student behaviors, levels of engagement in social and academic activities, and elements of social and academic support in the first year.

Methods

Data Sources

From April to October 2002, the National Opinion Research Center (NORC) at the University of Chicago administered a Web-based survey to Gates Millennium Scholars from the first two years of the program (i.e., academic years 2000-01 and 2001-02). In addition, for each of the first two years, a sample of students was drawn from the pool of program applicants who did not receive a scholarship. The survey focused on gathering information from respondents about their college enrollment, experiences with the GMS program, work and college finances, academic and community engagement, college experience, attitudes, future plans, and background. The data for the current study came primarily from the NORC GMS survey.

Measures of several institutional characteristics were needed for the current study, but were not gathered by NORC. In order to obtain a measure of the selectivity of the institution attended by each respondent, the percentage of applicants admitted to the institution was found in recent college guides. Most selectivity data came from the 2001 edition of *The College Board College Handbook*, but several other college guides (e.g., Peterson's and Barron's) were consulted to obtain data for as many institutions as possible. The admission rate, or number of students who are accepted from the applicant pools, was added to the data file for each college attended by a Scholar and nonrecipient.

Several other institutional measures also are used in the current study. These measures, which include the percentage of students of color, the enrollment size, private or public control, and the location of the college (urban or rural), were obtained from the 1998-99 institutional characteristics and enrollment data contained in the Integrated Postsecondary Education Data System (IPEDS) of the National Center for Education Statistics (NCES). These data also were merged with the student survey data to determine whether our findings hold regardless of the type of college a Scholar or nonrecipient attended.

Sample

The sample for this study comes from the second year of the GMS program (2001-02). Those students who received a GMS award for 2001-02 (Scholars) were included in this study along with a sample of GMS applicants who did not receive awards (nonrecipients). A student is eligible to become a Scholar if she/he is an African American, American Indian/Alaska Native, Asian Pacific Islander American, or Hispanic American. In addition, the program requires each student to meet specific academic requirements (e.g., a high school GPA of 3.3 or higher), to demonstrate financial need (e.g., qualify for a federal Pell Grant), and to have exercised leadership abilities in community-based, extracurricular, or other activities. The award each Scholar receives is based on her/his needs and covers tuition, fees, additional school costs (e.g., books and supplies), and living expenses at the institution attended. The amount of the award, however, is reduced by the value of other grants and scholarships the student receives.

After an initial selection process for the 2001-02 academic year, the GMS program chose 1,000 Scholars from among a group of 4,069 possible recipients. All Scholars and a sample of 1,340 nonrecipients were asked to complete the survey administered by NORC. A total of 831 (83.1%) Scholars and 778 (58.6%) nonrecipients responded to the survey. Of the 1,609 individuals in the sample, 68.3 percent are female, 35.8 percent are African American, 12.4 percent are American Indian/Alaska Native, 20.1 percent are Asian Pacific Islander American, 31.6 percent are Hispanic American, and 51.7 percent were known to be eligible for a Pell Grant.

Measures

Three separate dependent variables are used in the analyses to capture students' adjustment to college (see Table 1). The first, *Academic Adjustment*, is a scale composed of two survey items indicating the amount of difficulty students felt they had keeping up with schoolwork and managing their time. The second, *Paying College Expenses*, is a single item that indicates the amount of difficulty students had meeting college expenses. Although we anticipated participation in the GMS program to predict all three dependent variables, the fact that the main component of the GMS program is a scholarship suggests that its largest impact will be on students' perceptions of the difficulty they have paying college expenses. The final measure, *Social Adjustment*, is a composite of four items that indicate the difficulty students felt they had in the social realm of college (e.g., making friends and getting assistance from others).

The independent variables used in the analysis are described in Table 2. Several measures were used to capture different aspects of the concepts within the conceptual model. Background characteristics include measures for sex, race, and mother's level of education, which research indicates are linked to financial support (King, 1999) and educational outcomes. The amount of money a student borrowed to pay college expenses was included as an indicator of the financial burden the student was taking on to participate in college. The racial profile of students in the respondents' high school courses—students rated their level of

Table 1. Dependent Variables.

Variables	Description/Coding
Academic Adjustment	Scale (range, 1 – 4; α = 0. 80)
Difficulty keeping up w/schoolwork	1 = Very difficult, 4 = Not difficult
Difficulty managing time	1 = Very difficult, 4 = Not difficult
Paying College Expenses	1 = Very difficult, 4 = Not difficult
Social Adjustment	Scale (range, 1 – 4; α = 0.67)
Difficulty getting help w/school work	1 = Very difficult, 4 = Not difficult
Difficulty making new friends	1 = Very difficult, 4 = Not difficult
Difficulty finding comfortable living	1 = Very difficult, 4 = Not difficult
Difficulty learning my way around	1 = Very difficult, 4 = Not difficult

agreement with whether students in their high school classes were mostly of their own racial group—was included as a control for their prior exposure to a diverse group of students. This measure is an adaptation of more commonly used measures that inquire about the racial makeup of a student's high school. It is, however, more specific than most because it captures the segregation that occurs in many high school courses through tracking. The final background characteristic included in the analysis was the student's total SAT score. In instances where a student had an ACT score and not an SAT score, ACT scores were converted to an equivalent SAT score using the conversion table from Dorans (1999).

Institutional characteristics include the undergraduate enrollment of a student's institution, the control (public versus private), and the location (rural or town versus urban). In addition, the admission rate—the percentage of applicants admitted to an institution—was included as a measure of the college's selectivity. Also, the percentage of students of color within the undergraduate student body of a student's institution was included. The inclusion of this measure is based on prior research suggesting that increased representation of students of color on a campus is associated with Hispanic students' adjustment to college (e.g., Hurtado et al., 1996).

Table 2. Independent Variables.

Variables	Description/Coding
Student Background Characteristics	
Sex	Dichotomous: 1 = male, 2 = female
African American	Dichotomous: 1 = no, 2 = yes
American Indian	Dichotomous: 1 = no, 2 = yes
Hispanic American	Dichotomous: 1 = no, 2 = yes
Asian or Pacific Islander [reference]	Dichotomous: 1 = no, 2 = yes
Mother's educational attainment	1 = Less than high school, 6 = Doctorate
Total amount of loans this academic year	Continuous
Race of high school classes[a]	1 = Strongly disagree, 4 = Strongly agree
SAT Total Score[b]	Continuous (range, 400 – 1600)
Institutional Characteristics	
Admission rate	Continuous- High = less selective college
Enrollment size	Continuous- High = large college
Control	Dichotomous: 1 = public, 2 = private
Location	Dichotomous: 1 = rural or town, 2 = urban
Percentage of students of color	Continuous
College Experience	
Hours per week working for pay	Continuous
Living on campus	Dichotomous: 1 = off campus, 2 = on campus
Academic engagement	Scale (range, 1 – 6; α = 0.85)
Frequency working with other students	1 = Less than once a month, 6 = 3+ times per week
Frequency discussing ideas with students	1 = Less than once a month, 6 = 3+ times per week
Frequency discussing ideas with faculty	1 = Less than once a month, 6 = 3+ times per week
Frequency working harder than expected	1 = Less than once a month, 6 = 3+ times per week
Frequency working on creative projects	1 = Less than once a month, 6 = 3+ times per week
Hours per week studying	Continuous
Hours per week extracurricular activities	Continuous
Studied with person of different race	Dichotomous: 1 = no, 2 = yes
Rely on racial group for support	1 = Strongly disagree, 4 = Strongly agree
One professor interested in development	1 = Strongly disagree, 4 = Strongly agree
Received support from resident advisor	1 = Not at all, 4 = A lot
Received support from other students	1 = Not at all, 4 = A lot
Family encouraged me to stay in college	1 = Strongly disagree, 4 = Strongly agree
Commitment to earn degree	1 = Strongly disagree, 4 = Strongly agree

[a] Students indicated agreement that classes they took in high school were mostly with students of their race.

[b] When SAT scores were not available, ACT scores conversions detailed in Dorans (1999) were included.

Measures under the college experience category fall into two subcategories: student behaviors and support. The measures of student behaviors are intended to capture the amount of time, energy, and effort students put into several aspects of college that may affect their adjustment to college, including the amount of time spent working for pay, studying, and participating in extracurricular activities. There is also a general academic engagement scale that was constructed from measures that capture the frequency with which students discussed ideas with other students and faculty as well as the frequency with which they worked harder than they expected. Additionally, a measure of whether or not a student studied with a person of another racial group was included as one way to capture whether students were interacting across racial lines. The amount of support students received during their first year was captured through measures that examined the support they derived from friends, faculty, residence hall staff, and family.

Analyses

Scholars were selected based on financial need, race/ethnicity, academic achievement, and a host of noncognitive measures. As a result, Scholars and nonrecipients should be different on measures that reflect the selection criteria and may be different on additional measures. To explore differences between the groups on the measures included in the study, tests were run comparing the means of Scholars versus nonrecipients. It is interesting to note that although SAT score was not used in the criteria for selection, Scholars and nonrecipients had about the same average scores but differed on other important characteristics. Statistical significance tests (t-tests)[1] conducted on the dependent variables give an initial indication of the effect that participation in the GMS program has on college adjustment. However, for a more complete understanding of the factors that contribute to the academic, financial, and social adjustment of Scholars and nonrecipients, each dependent variable was regressed on the complete set of independent variables. The regression analyses allow for an estimation of the proposed model's fit on each dependent variable.

These analyses allow us to determine the effect of participation in the GMS program on the adjustment to college variables, controlling for the other variables in the model, and allow us to determine the important predictors of each aspect of adjustment for Scholars and nonrecipients.

Limitations

A review of studies suggests that the racial climate on a campus is a critical factor in the adjustment of students of color to college (Hurtado, Milem, Clayton-Pederson, & Allen, 1999). The lack of climate measures in the survey of the GMS program is a limitation of the data collection that has important consequences for anyone studying adjustment using this data. In the future, additional measures of the campus climate will be available for studying the long-term success of low-income students of color. In the current study, the lack of these measures will lower the explanatory power of our proposed model somewhat.

A second limiting factor is that this is a very select sample of students of color—all of them are applicants to a national scholarship program. Therefore, one has to presume that they are more motivated and have taken advantage of opportunities in high school to prepare for college.

Results

Figure 1 shows the differences between Scholars and non-recipients within each racial/ethnic group represented in the student sample for a key measure in the study, *Paying College Expenses.* The graphs indicate that across each racial/ethnic group, the GMS program has made a difference in lowering students' concern about the difficulties associated with paying college expenses. There are particularly significant differences among African American and Asian Pacific Islander American Scholars and nonrecipients. Well over half of the African American and Asian Pacific Islander American nonrecipients reported considerable concern about their ability to finance college and living expenses.

Figure 1. Difficulty Paying College Expenses, by Race and GMS status (N = 1577).

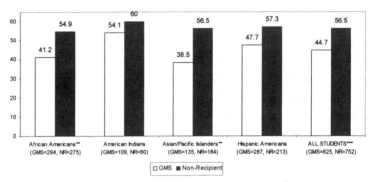

Figure 2 shows that more than one third of all students of color in the study reported difficulty in their academic adjustment to college. In this area of adjustment, however, there was no significant difference between Scholars and nonrecipients in each of the racial/ethnic groups. Given that all of these students were applicants for a national scholarship, it may be that they were also the most confident about their abilities and felt prepared to meet the academic challenge. Additional analyses reveal important distinctions between Scholars and recipients in subsequent results.

The results of the mean comparisons of Scholars and non-recipients are presented in Table 3. The mean values suggest that the academic adjustment of the students and their ability to pay college expenses is between difficult and not difficult, whereas their social adjustment leans toward being less difficult. The significance tests indicate that, on average, Scholars find it less difficult than nonrecipients to pay college expenses. This result is important, but not surprising given that the GMS program's major component is financial assistance. There appears to be no significant difference between the groups on the other two college adjustment measures. However, additional results show that this is an impressive finding because of the differences in the types of colleges and subsequent activities that Scholars and nonrecipients select.

Figure 2. Difficulty with Academic Adjustment, by Race and GMS Status (N = 1581).

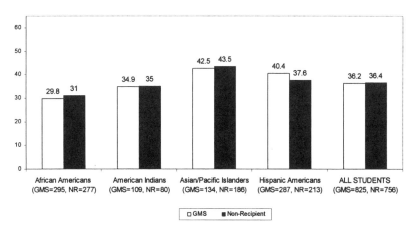

At first blush, it is tempting to suggest that the GMS program may not affect the academic and social adjustment of Scholars compared with nonrecipients. However, examining the differences between Scholars and nonrecipients on the independent variables suggests that perhaps the effects will have substantial long-term consequences (e.g., in a separate study, St. John documents that Scholars are more likely to be retained in college). The results in Table 3 suggest that Scholars are more likely to have overcome the difficulties associated with low levels of parental education; the mothers of nonrecipients are more likely to have achieved higher levels of education. In addition, Scholars are likely to attend more selective institutions (i.e., institutions with lower admissions rates) and private institutions. These results suggest that prior to college entry, Scholars may be disposed to choosing more selective institutions where the competition, income, and academic preparation of peers are high—as the program provides award money that enhances their college choices. In other words, it is not unreasonable, based on these findings, to suggest that Scholars adjust about as well as nonrecipients who attend less demanding colleges and institutions where the background differences among student peers may be less divergent.

Once in college, Scholars are more likely to work fewer hours for pay, live on campus, engage academically, rely on their racial group for support, report that a faculty member has taken interest in their development, and report a commitment to earn a degree. These findings suggest that Scholars are more likely than nonrecipients to exhibit behaviors and receive support that are important to their adjustment to college and long-term academic success.

The results of the multivariate models are reported in Tables 4-6. As expected, there is considerable variability in the important predictors of each aspect of college adjustment. For academic adjustment (Table 4), the model controlling all aspects of background, college characteristics, and aspects of the college experience indicates several key predictors. In terms of student background, only students from families with high mother's educational attainment and students who initially took out fewer loans[2] had relatively higher academic adjustment. These talented racial/ethnic minority students also were better adjusted academically at institutions that admitted a larger proportion of applicants (less selective) and institutions with relatively higher numbers of students of color. The college experience measures are key indicators of successful adjustment, including working fewer hours per week, having a professor interested in the student's development, and having family that encouraged the student to stay in college. In relation to academic adjustment, students who reported receiving support from other students continued to report difficulty with academic adjustment, presumably because these students may not have relied on traditional support services.

Table 3. Comparison of Means Between Scholars and Nonrecipients.

Variables	GMS Scholars (N = 831)		Nonrecipients (N = 778)		
	Mean	SD	Mean	SD	
Dependent Variables					
Academic Adjustment	2.60	0.84	2.58	0.83	
Paying College Expenses	2.63	0.95	2.34	0.98	***
Social Adjustment	3.27	0.57	3.26	0.57	
Independent Variables					
Background					
Gender	1.68	0.47	1.68	0.47	
African American	1.36	0.48	1.36	0.48	
American Indian	1.13	0.34	1.12	0.32	
Hispanic American	1.35	0.48	1.28	0.45	**
Asian or Pacific Islander [reference]	1.16	0.37	1.24	0.43	***
Mother's educational attainment	2.61	1.24	2.89	1.20	***
Total loans this year	1288.48	2594.41	2903.60	5218.12	***
Race of high school classes	2.08	1.08	1.99	1.04	
SAT Total Score	1134.02	168.55	1127.10	177.27	
Institutional Characteristics					
Admission rate (less selective)	59.98	24.40	63.34	23.71	**
Enrollment size	17351.41	13136.24	16919.21	12698.83	
Control (private)	1.43	0.50	1.34	0.48	***
Location (urban)	1.88	0.33	1.84	0.36	*
Percentage of students of color	31.68	22.59	31.80	22.52	
College Experience					
Hours per week working for pay	10.66	13.72	13.82	14.71	***
Living on campus	1.67	0.47	1.62	0.49	*
Academic engagement	4.04	1.04	3.79	1.14	***
Hours per week studying	23.37	15.07	21.67	15.12	*
Hours per week activities	6.70	6.44	6.40	7.38	
Studied with person of other race	1.96	0.19	1.96	0.21	
Rely on racial group for support	2.42	0.86	2.27	0.89	**
Support of a professor	3.22	0.79	3.08	0.85	**
Support from resident advisor	2.01	1.00	1.92	0.97	
Support from other students	3.24	0.84	3.23	0.88	
Family encouraged me to stay	3.81	0.48	3.81	0.49	
Commitment to earn degree	3.84	0.46	3.79	0.54	*

Significant differences in the means for Scholars and nonrecipients, determined using t-tests, are indicated as follows: * p < .05, ** p < .01, *** p < .001.

Previous research confirms that reliance on peers, particularly other first-year students, is less helpful in academic adjustment for some minority groups in college (Hurtado et al., 1996). The results also show that the number of hours per week a student spent studying was negatively related to academic adjustment, perhaps indicating that those students who were spending more time than normal probably were concerned that they were having more difficulty with academic adjustment. It is not unusual for students to work especially hard in the first year to compensate for the inequality in high school preparation, or for even the brightest students to realize that they must work harder to adjust to new levels of academic competition and the expectations of faculty.

After controlling for all other variables, participation in the GMS program does not have a significant *direct* effect on academic adjustment. The results of the t-tests, however, suggest that it may be fruitful to examine the indirect effects of the GMS program through the effects of the amount of time students spend studying, their level of engagement with faculty, and the types of colleges they elect to attend.

The most important student background predictor of the difficulty students have paying for college expenses (Table 5) is the amount of loans a student has taken out in the first year. This finding applies to Scholars and nonrecipients alike. Interestingly enough, those students with the highest SAT total scores were most concerned about their ability to pay for college. Perhaps this is because they are the students who are most likely to think about the long-term expenses of continued education and often desire to attend the most selective and expensive colleges in the country. It is not unusual, however, to find that students attending public (versus private) institutions were significantly less concerned about paying for college.

Table 4. Regression Results—Academic Adjustment (n = 1322).

Variables	r	B	Beta
Background			
Sex	0.06*	0.08	0.04
African American	0.12***	0.10	0.06
American Indian	0.01	-0.05	-0.02
Hispanic American	-0.06*	-0.02	-0.01
Asian or Pacific Islander [reference]			
Mother's educational attainment	0.10***	0.06	0.09***
Total amount of loans this academic year	-0.08**	-0.00	-0.07*
Race of high school classes	0.00	-0.00	-0.00
SAT Total Score	-0.07**	0.00	0.01
Institutional Characteristics			
Admission rate (less selective)	0.17***	0.01	0.16***
Enrollment size	-0.08**	0.00	0.03
Control (private)	-0.03	0.07	0.04
Location (urban)	-0.06*	-0.12	-0.05
Percentage of students of color	0.10***	0.00	0.08**
College Experience			
Gates Millennium Scholar	0.01	0.02	0.01
Hours per week working for pay	-0.01	-0.00	-0.01
Living on campus	-0.01	0.03	0.02
Academic engagement	0.03	0.02	0.03
Hours per week studying	-0.10***	-0.00	-0.08**
Hours per week extracurricular activities	-0.02	-0.00	-0.01
Studied with person of different race	-0.09**	-0.15	-0.04
Rely on racial group for support	-0.04	-0.06	-0.06*
One professor interested in development	0.15***	0.13	0.12***
Received support from resident advisor	-0.00	0.03	0.04
Received support from other students	-0.12***	-0.11	-0.11***
Family encouraged me to stay in college	0.09***	0.13	0.07**
Commitment to earn degree	0.02	0.02	0.01
(constant)		1.51 **	
R squared			0.11
Adjusted R squared			0.10
Standard Error			0.79
F			6.36***

*p <.05, ** p <.01, *** p <.001.

Table 5. Regression Results—Paying College Expenses (n = 1322).

Variables	R	B	Beta
Background			
Sex	-0.00	-0.02	-0.01
African American	0.05*	0.12	0.06
American Indian	-0.04	-0.16	-0.05
Hispanic American	-0.04	-0.03	-0.01
Asian or Pacific Islander [reference]			
Mother's educational attainment	0.05	0.04	0.05
Total amount of loans this academic year	-0.22***	-0.00	-0.19***
Race of high school classes	0.02	0.02	0.03
SAT Total Score	0.07**	0.00	0.11**
Institutional Characteristics			
Admission rate (less selective)	0.00	0.00	0.02
Enrollment size	0.04	-0.00	-0.01
Control (private)	-0.08**	-0.16	-0.08*
Location (urban)	-0.02	-0.12	-0.04
Percentage of students of color	0.05	0.00	0.04
College Experience			
Gates Millennium Scholar	0.14***	0.24	0.12***
Hours per week working for pay	-0.12***	-0.01	-0.11***
Living on campus	-0.02	-0.04	-0.02
Academic engagement	-0.07**	-0.07	-0.07*
Hours per week studying	-0.07*	-0.00	-0.06*
Hours per week extracurricular activities	-0.01	0.00	0.03
Studied with person of different race	-0.01	0.06	0.01
Rely on racial group for support	-0.02	-0.02	-0.02
One professor interested in development	0.01	0.03	0.03
Received support from resident advisor	-0.03	0.01	0.01
Received support from other students	-0.06*	-0.02	-0.02
Family encouraged me to stay in college	-0.02	-0.06	-0.03
Commitment to earn degree	0.04	0.11	0.06*
(constant)		1.97 **	
R squared			0.11
Adjusted R squared			0.09
Standard Error			0.93
F			6.19***

*p <.05, ** p <.01, *** p <.001.

In terms of college experiences, the GMS program participants were significantly less concerned about paying for college in the first year than were nonrecipients. This direct relationship opens the door to a host of opportunities that contribute to important long-term outcomes. Beyond the direct effect of participation in the GMS program, these regression results and the t-test results suggest that the GMS program may have several indirect effects as well. In particular, participation in the GMS program reduces student concern about paying college expenses as well as the number of hours they elect to work per week during college, allowing them to spend more time on academic engagement and studying and enhancing their commitment to earn a degree.

A key college experience that is indicative of a high level of concern about paying for college is the amount of time students spend working during the week while in college. This direct relationship is not unexpected. However, it is interesting to note that those students who are less academically engaged, who spend less time studying during the week, and who are less committed to attaining a degree are those least concerned about paying for college. Overall, this reflects a pattern of a lack of investment in college. Ironically, those most invested, who work long hours in order to pay for college, are least likely to enjoy the benefits of academic and social engagement.

Table 6 shows the strongest predictors of social adjustment in college. It is interesting to note that among the different racial/ethnic groups, African Americans report the most ease in social adjustment. However, during the first year of college, it appears that most students in this sample feel less socially adjusted on the largest campuses, presumably because it takes some time to find a niche and welcoming community. In terms of college experiences, various levels of support and student behaviors play a key role in social adjustment. Specifically, those students who are more academically engaged, spend more time studying, had a professor take an interest in them, spend more time in extracurricular activities, and received support from other students were relatively less concerned about social adjustment. Similarly, those with family encouragement also reported relatively higher social adjustment. Students who relied on their racial group for support also reported being somewhat less socially adjusted. This is the result of a statistical suppressor effect, indicating that other college experience measures in the model qualify this finding. Possibly, the more engaged students are, both academically and socially, the less evident are the negative effects of relying on racial support. This requires further study to understand the complex dynamics of racial interactions on campus—much of which has to do with campus climate (Hurtado et al., 1999).

Table 6. Regression Results—Social Adjustment (n = 1324).

Variables	r	B	Beta
Background			
Sex	0.04	0.06	0.05
African American	0.10***	0.13	0.11**
American Indian	0.02	0.11	0.06
Hispanic American	-0.03	0.08	0.06
Asian or Pacific Islander [reference]			
Mother's educational attainment	0.11***	0.03	0.06
Total amount of loans this academic year	0.02	0.00	0.00
Race of high school classes	0.00	0.01	0.01
SAT Total Score	0.02	0.00	0.05
Institutional Characteristics			
Admission rate (less selective)	-0.02	-0.00	-0.04
Enrollment size	-0.10***	-0.00	-0.07*
Control (private)	0.04	-0.06	-0.05
Location (urban)	-0.05	-0.03	-0.02
Percentage of students of color	0.01	-0.00	-0.01
College Experience			
Gates Millennium Scholar	0.01	0.01	0.01
Hours per week working for pay	-0.02	-0.00	-0.03
Living on campus	0.05	-0.04	-0.03
Academic engagement	0.14***	0.04	0.07*
Hours per week studying	-0.04	-0.00	-0.09**
Hours per week extracurricular activities	0.14***	0.01	0.10***
Studied with person of different race	0.00	-0.01	-0.00
Rely on racial group for support	0.00	-0.05	-0.08**
One professor interested in development	0.18***	0.09	0.13***
Received support from resident advisor	0.10***	0.02	0.04
Received support from other students	0.13***	0.06	0.09**

Table 6. Regression Results—Social Adjustment (n = 1324) (continued).

Variables	r	B	Beta
College Experience			
Family encouraged me to stay in college	0.12***	0.08	0.07*
Commitment to earn degree	0.05	0.03	0.03
(constant)		1.86 **	
R squared		0.10	
Adjusted R squared		0.08	
Standard Error		0.54	
F		5.66***	

* p < .05 ** p < .01, *** p < .001.

As with academic adjustment, participation in the GMS program does not directly influence social adjustment, though again, there may be important indirect effects. In combination with the t-test results, the final regression suggests that participation in the GMS program may influence social adjustment through other forms of engagement (e.g., participation in academic and extracurricular activities).

Discussion

This study shows that the Gates Millennium Scholars program has the direct impact of lowering student concern about paying for college in the first year, which is a major worry for families of college-bound students today. This is particularly important among the lowest-income families, who lack substantial assets to invest in a college education. The scholarship program attracts talent from among the most underrepresented students in higher education—low-income racial/ethnic minorities. The method of GMS selection and the promise of long-term financial support for each student have the effect of extending opportunity, allowing students to focus on college goals and ultimately ensuring success against the odds typical for the majority of college-bound low-income students.

One of the key issues in this study of racial/ethnic minority students is that the elements that detract from engagement in college have a deleterious effect on transition to college in terms of both academic and social adjustment. This confirms much of the previous research on college transition and retention. For example, financial difficulties impede academic adjustment and take time away from engaging in campus life (e.g., taking out large college loans, working long hours to pay for college). Ironically, the least academically engaged are the least concerned about paying for college, while racial/ethnic minority students who are working long hours to pay for college are least likely to experience the full range of college benefits.

When compared with nonrecipients, Scholars were more likely to be engaged in both academic and extracurricular activities. In turn, these engagement activities allow students to develop social networks of peers that increase the probability of their success as they acquire knowledge about college, study skills, and information about additional opportunities while in college. These students probably already were predisposed to take advantage of many of the opportunities college affords, and the scholarship program allows them to proceed in furthering their success.

It is important to note that Scholars reported about the same level of ease with academic and social adjustment as nonrecipients, and yet more of the Scholars selected challenging college environments and defied the odds of having relatively low parental education levels (i.e., their learning about college was done through their own resources). The study shows that family encouragement and support, regardless of education level, remains important for racial/ethnic minority students, but identifying a faculty member who will take a special interest in the student's development is even more important during the first year of college. The implications are that providing the right combination of support services is important, particularly if one of the key goals is to have students become engaged with faculty. Concerning social adjustment, students who relied only on peers may be less likely to receive the support they need for successful academic adjustment.

Other research on the GMS program attests to the additional factors of success for low-income racial/ethnic minority students. The story of the Scholars is one of success, a bright hope in the dismal portrait of low-income students that most educational research portrays. Too often this research has focused on family background as the determining factor—blaming the students for lack of success because of the social and structural circumstances into which they were born. The research here suggests that there are support structures facilitated by institutions (e.g., colleges, foundations, and programs) that can help to identify and develop talent in the most unlikely places in our communities. Further research is needed on the opportunity structures, support networks, turning points, and stories of resilience that these low-income racial/ethnic minorities can tell about their experiences prior to and during college. It is both individual behavior and the structure of opportunity that influences success in a society where the gaps between racial and economic groups continue to widen. We have much to learn from these students.

Notes

1. Significance tests are used to compare the average scores of two groups—Scholars and nonrecipients, in this case—taking into account variability among individuals in the groups (standard deviations) and sample size. A t-test is a formula that generates a number, which is used to determine the probability level of rejecting the null hypothesis (i.e., that there is no difference between the comparison groups). For more information see J. H. McMillan & S. Schumacher (1984), *Research in education: A conceptual introduction.* Boston: Little, Brown, and Company.
2. Scholars generally took out significantly lower amounts of loans than nonrecipients due to the financial support provided by GMS, but the relationship between loan debt and academic adjustment held as a finding regardless of scholarship status.

References

Advisory Committee on Student Financial Assistance (ACSFA). (2002). *Empty promises: The myth of college access in America.* Washington, DC: Author.

Astin, A. W. (1984). Student involvement: A developmental theory for higher education. *Journal of College Student Personnel, 25,* 297-308.

Astin, A. W. (1993). *What matters in college: Four critical years revisited.* San Francisco: Jossey-Bass.

Cabrera, A. F., Nora, A., Terenzini, P. T., Pascarella, E., & Hagedorn, L. S. (1999). Campus climate and the adjustment of student to college: A comparison between White students and African-American students. *Journal of Higher Education, 70* (2), 134-160.

Choy, S. P. (2000). *Low income students: Who they are and how they pay for their education* (Statistical Analysis Report NCES 2000-169). Washington, DC: National Center for Education Statistics.

Cunningham, A. F. (2002). *The policy of choice: Expanding student options in higher education.* Washington, DC: The Institute for Higher Education Policy.

Donovan, R. (1984). Path analysis of a theoretical model of persistence in higher education among low-income black youth. *Research in Higher Education, 21,* 243-259.

Dorans, N. J. (1999). *Correspondences between ACT and SAT I scores,* College Board Report No. 99-1. New York: The College Board.

Eimers, M. T., & Pike, G. R. (1997). Minority and nonminority adjustment to college: Differences or similarities? *Research in Higher Education, 38* (1), 77-97.

Feenstra, J. S., Banyard, V. L., Rines, E. N., & Hopkins, K. R. (2001). First-year students' adaptation to college: The role of family variables and individual coping. *Journal of College Student Development, 42* (2), 106-113.

Hurtado, S., & Carter, D. F. (1997). Effects of college transition and perceptions of campus racial climate on Latinos' sense of belonging. *Sociology of Education, 70* (4), 324 –345.

Hurtado, S., Carter, D. F., & Spuler, A. (1996). Latino student transition to college: Assessing difficulties and factors in successful college adjustment. *Research in Higher Education, 37* (2), 135-157.

Hurtado, S., Milem, J., Clayton-Pedersen, A., & Allen, W. (1999). Enacting diverse learning environments: Improving the climate for racial/ethnic diversity in higher education. *ASHE-ERIC Higher Education Report, 26* (8). San Francisco: Jossey-Bass.

Johnson, I. H., & Ottens, A. J. (Eds.). (1996). *Leveling the playing field: Promoting academic success for students of color.* San Francisco: Jossey-Bass.

King, J. E. (1999). *Money matters: The impact of race/ethnicity and gender on how students pay for college.* Washington, DC: American Council on Education.

NCES. (1996). *Beginning postsecondary students* (NCES 96-136). Washington, DC: Author.

Nora, A. (2001). *How minority students finance their higher education.* (ERIC Digest 171). New York: Eric Clearinghouse on Urban Education.

Nora, A., & Cabrera, A. F. (1996). The role of perceptions in prejudice and discrimination and the adjustment of minority students to college. *Journal of Higher Education, 67* (2), 119-148.

O'Brien, C., & Shedd, J. (2001). *Getting through college: Voices of low-income and minority students in New England.* Washington, DC: The Institute for Higher Education Policy.

Olivas, M. A. (1999). *College prepaid savings plans: Third generation progress and problems.* Houston, TX: The Institute for Higher Education Law and Governance.

Smedley, B. D., Myers, H. F., & Harrell, S. P. (1993). Minority-status stresses and the college adjustment of ethnic minority freshmen. *Journal of Higher Education, 64* (4), 434-452.

Terenzini, P. T., Cabrera, A. F., & Bernal, E. M. (2001). *Swimming against the tide: The poor in American higher education* (Research Report 2001-01). New York: The College Board.

Terenzini, P. T., Rendon, L., Upcraft, M. L., Millar, S., Allison, K., Gregg, P., & Jalomo, R. (1994). The transition to college: Diverse students, diverse stories. *Research in Higher Education, 35*, 57-73.

Tinto, V. (1975). Dropout from higher education: A theoretical synthesis of recent research. *Review of Educational Research, 45*, 89-125.

Tinto, V. (1986). Theories of student departure revisited. In J. C. Smart (Ed.), *Higher education: Handbook of theory and research* (vol. II, pp. 359-384). New York: Agathon Press.

Tinto, V. (1993). *Rethinking the causes and cures of student attrition*. Chicago, IL: The University of Chicago Press.

Upcraft, M. L., & Gardner, J. N. (Eds.). (1989). *The freshman year experience*. San Francisco: Jossey-Bass.

Wolanin, T. R. (2003). *Reauthorizing the Higher Education Act: Issues and options*. Washington, DC: The Institute for Higher Education Policy.

CHAPTER 7

ACADEMIC SUCCESS OF GATES MILLENNIUM SCHOLARS

William E. Sedlacek and Hung-Bin Sheu

Understanding the success in higher education of the Gates Millennium Scholars is critical to the success of the entire program. The Scholars were chosen for their academic potential, but that potential likely was shown in ways other than test scores and grades because of the experiences they have had based on their race and culture. Those ways that Scholars have shown their potential were investigated in this study. The academic activities of Scholars in higher education were studied and comparisons to Non-Scholars were made. Results of this study will help choose future Gates Millennium Scholars in the best way possible and also will document their pathways through higher education. In addition, the results will allow educators to plan retention and student service programs while Scholars are in school to maximize their chances of having a positive experience and graduating.

Alternatives to standardized tests and prior grades as predictors of success have been studied for many years. A system of noncognitive variables that measures a wider range of attributes than more traditional methods, and is more equitable for students of color, has been developed (Sedlacek, 1998; 2003; 2004a; 2004b).

The noncognitive variables were positive self-concept, realistic self-appraisal, negotiating the system, long-range goals, strong support person, leadership, community service, and nontraditional knowledge.

The noncognitive variables noted above were used to select the Gates Millennium Scholars, along with assessments of the academic rigor of their high school curriculum, their high school academic achievement, and their ability to write a good essay explaining their interests in becoming a Scholar. The goals of the selection process were to judge the academic potential of students of color, who tend to show their abilities in ways other than the more traditional standardized tests and prior grades.

Two methods of determining applicant potential on the noncognitive variables have been utilized in the Program. In the first year, applications were scored on the noncognitive variables based on materials provided in personal statements, letters of recommendation, and other parts of the application that provided information. Raters were trained to identify and consider this information in scoring each of the eight noncognitive variables. The raters were educators of color, familiar with multicultural issues in education and in working with the kinds of students that were applying. Interjudge reliability was estimated at .83 for judgments from a sample of raters in the first year. In the first year of the program, awards were given to new entering first-year students, returning students, and graduate students.

In the second and third years of the program, the GMS application was redesigned to include short-answer questions focused on each of the noncognitive variables. Again, raters of color were trained to interpret the new items, along with the other information on the application, in order to develop scores for each noncognitive variable. While in the first year raters judged candidates from all racial groups, in the second and third years they evaluated candidates from their own racial group only. No reliability estimates were made for the second or third year ratings. Interjudge reliability information for applicants in the second year of the program is provided in the current study. Following is an analysis of students from the second year of the program who began their postsecondary studies as first-year students in 2001.

Method

Participants

The sample size was 1,609 and included Gates Millennium Scholars (Scholars) and a comparison group of individuals who applied for scholarships but were not selected (Non-Scholars). Table 1 provides information regarding their gender and racial backgrounds. The sample consisted of African Americans (36%), American Indians (12%), Asian Pacific Islander Americans (20%), and Hispanic Americans (32%). Thirty-two percent of the participants were males and 68 percent were females. At the time of data collection, 27 percent were freshmen, 70 percent were sophomores, and 3 percent were juniors or above. Return rates were 83 percent for Scholars and 59 percent for Non-Scholars.

Table 1. Race and Gender of Participants.

	African Americans		American Indians		Asian Pacific Islanders		Hispanic Americans		Total
	M	F	M	F	M	F	M	F	
Scholars	78	218	38	71	45	92	100	189	831
Non-Scholars	79	201	27	64	57	130	80	140	778
Total	576		200		324		509		1609

Note. M: Male; F: Female

Instrument

A 120-item instrument was administered to participants in the spring and summer of 2002 by the National Opinion Research Center (NORC). The instrument contained a variety of items on student activities, adjustments, and attitudes (see Appendix).

Data Analyses

Chi square tests were conducted to examine group differences (race, gender, Scholar/Non-Scholar) on participants' intention of retention, commitment to graduate from their current institutions, and educational aspirations. Univariate General Linear Models were computed to investigate group differences (race, gender, Scholar/Non-Scholar) on several continuous variables, including difficulties with schoolwork, time management, studying time, and

GPA. Finally, Pearson Product-moment correlation and multiple regression analyses were used to explore relationships between noncognitive variables and continuous variables. All tests were conducted at the .05 level of significance. Where appropriate, effect sizes (η^2) also were reported.

Results

Academic Activities of Scholars

Retention and Educational Aspirations. Nearly all Scholars indicated that they were very unlikely to drop out of school and were strongly committed to earn a degree at their current institutions. Ninety percent or more of the male Scholars from each racial group indicated that they were very unlikely to drop out. Less than 2 percent of male Scholars from each racial group indicated that they were very likely or somewhat likely to drop out. A similar pattern was observed for female Scholars, with 90 percent or more from each racial group indicating that they were very unlikely to drop out. Additionally, over 95 percent of the Scholars were committed to earning a degree at their current school. There were no differences by race or gender.

Table 2 provides information regarding educational aspirations across race and gender for Scholars. The majority of Scholars expected to complete an advanced degree (master's degree or above). There were no differences on highest degree expected by race for male Scholars ($\chi^2 = 17.58$, p = .285). However, for female Scholars, the four racial groups had different educational aspirations ($\chi^2 = 67.76$, p < .0001), with more African Americans interested in receiving a doctoral degree and more American Indians, Asian Pacific Islander Americans, and Hispanic Americans expecting to get a master's degree.

Table 2. Percentages of Highest Degree Expected for Scholars.

	African Americans			American Indians			Asian/Pacific Islanders			Hispanic Americans		
	M	F	Total	M	F	Total	M	F	Total	M	F	Total
Less than two years college	0	0	0	0	0	0	0	0	0	0	0	0
Two or more years college	0	0	0	3	3	3	0	0	0	0	0	0
Bachelor's degree	10	3	5	17	18	18	10	4	6	9	14	12.4
Post-baccalaureate certificate	0	0	0	3	0	1	0	0	0	0	1	.4
Master's degree	37	28	30	29	44	38	46	36	39	36	35	35.2
Professional degree	17	26	24	17	21	20	17	33	28	14	14	14
Doctoral degree	36	43	41	31	14	20	27	27	27	41	36	38
Total	100%	100%	100%	100%	100%	100%	100%	100%	100%	100%	100%	100%

Note. M: Male; F: Female

Studying Time and Difficulties with Schoolwork. Table 3 contains information regarding difficulties with schoolwork and time management experienced by Scholars. In terms of difficulty in keeping up with schoolwork, differences by gender or the interaction of race and gender were not significant. However, there were significant differences among racial groups ($F = .5.79$, $p = .001$, $\eta^2 = .021$). Significant post hoc analyses (LSD) indicated that Asian Pacific Islander Americans (2.60) and Hispanic Americans (2.63) experienced more difficulties with schoolwork than African Americans (2.95). There were no differences by race or gender or their interactions on time management.

In terms of study time per week for Scholars, there were no differences by gender or the interaction of race and gender, while there were significant differences by race ($F = 7.71$, $p < .0001$, $\eta^2 = .028$). American Indians spent significantly less time studying per week (17.89 hours) than African Americans (23.26 hours), Asian Pacific Islander Americans (27.58 hours), or Hispanic Americans (23.55 hours).

Table 3. Difficulty with Schoolwork and Time Management by Race and Gender for Scholars.

		African Americans		American Indians		Asian/Pacific Islanders		Hispanic Americans	
		M	**SD**	**M**	**SD**	**M**	**SD**	**M**	**SD**
Schoolwork	Male	2.81	.89	2.82	.73	2.58	.96	2.51	.89
	Female	3.00	.86	2.75	.87	2.62	.94	2.69	.87
Time Mgmt.	Male	2.42	.98	2.37	.75	2.30	1.02	2.25	.97
	Female	2.58	.94	2.45	.92	2.43	.93	2.41	.98

Note: Higher scores indicate fewer difficulties (1 = difficult; 4= not difficult).

Academic Engagement and GPA of Scholars. There were five items assessing academic engagement: (a) how often they worked with other students; (b) how often they discussed ideas from their readings with students; (c) how often they discussed ideas with faculty; (d) how often they worked harder than expected; (e) and how often they worked on creative projects. Since internal consistency reliability of scores from these five items was acceptable (.75), a score on the 1-6 scale was derived from obtaining the mean of the five items to represent Scholars' academic engagement, with higher scores indicating more engagement. Results of a univariate General Linear Model indicated that there were no differences by gender or the interaction of race and gender for Scholars. However, significant differences by race ($F = 3.51$, $p = .015$, $\eta^2 = .013$) indicated that American Indian Scholars (3.82) were less engaged in academic activities than their African American (4.09) and Hispanic American (4.11) counterparts.

Finally, the mean cumulative GPA of Scholars was 3.25 on a four point system with a standard deviation of .56 ($N = 755$). The interaction of race and gender on GPA was not significant. While GPA did not vary by gender, there were racial differences on this variable ($F = 11.20$, $p < .0001$, $\eta^2 = .043$). Post hoc analyses (LSD) indicated that the GPAs of Asian Pacific Islander American Scholars (3.38) and Hispanic American Scholars (3.34) were significantly higher than those of African American Scholars (3.18) and American Indian Scholars (3.00). African American Scholars also had significantly higher GPAs than American Indian Scholars.

Comparing Academic Activities of Scholars and Non-Scholars
    Retention and Educational Aspirations of Scholars and Non-Scholars. Most Scholars and Non-Scholars indicated that they were very unlikely to drop out (93% or more), with the exception of American Indian Non-Scholars (see Table 4). While nearly all African American Scholars (97%) indicated that they were very unlikely to drop out, a significantly (χ^2 = 6.68, p = .036) smaller percentage of Non-Scholars (94%) from this group indicated the same intention to stay in school. However, this small but significant difference in percentage (3%) for African Americans might not be practically meaningful. Also, it is noteworthy that more American Indian Scholars (94%) showed an intention to stay in school than their Non-Scholar counterparts (87%), although the χ^2 test was not significant, probably because of the smaller sample size for this group.
    Most of the Scholars and Non-Scholars had high educational aspirations (see Table 5). Results of a χ^2 test indicated that for African Americans, Scholars and Non-Scholars had different educational aspirations (χ^2 = 12.38, p = .015).
    Studying Time and Difficulties with Schoolwork of Scholars and Non-Scholars. In terms of difficulties in keeping up with schoolwork and time management, there were no differences by gender or Scholar/Non-Scholar or their interaction. However, there were differences by race (F = 8.67, p < .0001, η^2 = .016) for difficulty in keeping up with schoolwork, indicating that Asian Pacific Islander Americans (2.59) and Hispanic Americans (2.65) perceived more difficulties with schoolwork than African Americans (2.92). There were no significant differences by race, gender, Scholar/Non-Scholar, or their interactions on difficulties with time management.

Table 4. Percentages of Likelihood of Dropping Out for Scholars and Non-Scholars.

	African Americans			American Indians			Asian/Pacific Islanders			Hispanic Americans		
	S	N-S	Total	S	N-S	Total	S	N-S	Total	S	N-S	Total
Very likely	0	0	0	0	0	0	0	.5	.4	.4	0	.2
Somewhat likely	1	.3	1	0	1	.5	2	.5	1	.7	1	1
Somewhat unlikely	2	5	4	6	12	9	2	6	4	4	6	4.6
Very unlikely	97	94	95	94	87	90.5	96	93	94.6	95	93	94.2
Total	100%	100%	100%	100%	100%	100%	100%	100%	100%	100%	100%	100%

Note: S: Scholars; N-S: Non-Scholars

Table 5. Percentages of Highest Degree Expected for Scholars and Non-Scholars.

	African Americans			American Indians			Asian/Pacific Islanders			Hispanic Americans		
	S	N-S	Total	S	N-S	Total	S	N-S	Total	S	N-S	Total
Less than two years college	0	0	0	0	1	.5	0	0	0	0	0	0
Two or more years of college	0	2	.7	3	2	2.7	0	.6	.3	0	0	0
Bachelor's degree	5	9	7	18	21	19.2	6	8	7.2	12	16	13.8
Post-baccalaureate certificate	0	0	0	1	1	1	0	1.7	1	.4	0	.2
Master's degree	30	36	33	39	42	40	39	38	38.7	35	43	38.7
Professional degree	24	20	22	20	7	14.3	28	26	26.4	14	15	14.4
Doctoral degree	41	33	37.3	20	25	22	27	26	26.4	38	26	32.9
Total	100%	100%	100%	100%	100%	99.7%	100%	100%	100%	100%	100%	100%

Note: S: Scholars; N-S: Non-Scholars

For time spent studying, the three-way interaction of Scholar/Non-Scholar by race by gender and the main effect of gender were not significant, while the two-way interaction of Scholar/Non-Scholar and race was significant (F = 3.06, p = .027, η^2 = .006). Further analyses indicated that for Scholars, Asian Pacific Islander Americans (27.58 hours) spent more time studying than their American Indian (17.89 hours) counterparts. This difference did not occur for Non-Scholars. On the other hand, Asian Pacific Islander American Scholars (27.58 hours) spent more time studying than Non-Scholars (23.22 hours). Studying time did not vary between Scholars and Non-Scholars for the other three racial groups.

Academic Engagement of Scholars and Non-Scholars. In terms of academic engagement, there were differences by Scholar/Non-Scholar (F = 12.12, p = .001, η^2 = .008), race (F = 5.47, p = .001, η^2 = .010), and gender (F = 9.98, p = .002, η^2 = .006), but there were no interactions. Specifically, Scholars (4.04) were more academically engaged than Non-Scholars (3.79); African Americans (4.02) and Hispanic Americans (3.95) were more academically engaged than American Indians (3.68); and males (4.05) were involved in more academic activities than females (3.86).

Noncognitive Variables and Academic Performance
      Table 6 provides information regarding how consistent two judges were in rating the 11 GMS selection variables, which consisted of 8 noncognitive variables (V3-10) and 3 other variables (V1, V2, and V11). The two judges agreed 90 percent or more of the time within a 1-point difference and were significantly consistent in evaluating these variables. The internal consistency (Coefficient Alpha) reliability estimate for scores on the eight noncognitive variables (V3-10) was .92 (N = 1608). The Coefficient Alpha reliability estimate for scores on all eleven selection variables, including curriculum rigor (V1), academic achievement (V2), and use of language in essays (V11), was also .92 (N = 1608).

190   *Academic Success of GMS Scholars*

Table 6. Inter-rater Reliability of Scores on Variables Used in GMS Selection.

	Kappa	Contingency Coefficient	% [a]	% [b]
V1: Curriculum Rigor	.223	.300	59	94
V2: Academic Achievement	.307	.362	62	94
V3: Positive Self-Concept	.101	.275	49	94
V4: Realistic Self-Appraisal	.059	.265	44	94
V5: Understanding/Navigation of Social System	.094	.240	42	90
V6: Preference for Long-Term Goals	.121	.246	48	93
V7: Leadership Experiences	- [c]	.213	44	93
V8: Community Service	.118	.243	46	92
V9: Nontraditional Acquisition of Knowledge	.096	.219	43	90
V10: Strong Support Person	.168	.166	64	100
V11: Use of Language in Essays	.151	.319	48	93

Note: N = 1608. All Kappa coefficients were significant at α = .01 level. All contingency coefficients were significant at α = .001 level. [a] Percentage of identical ratings from raters 1 and 2. [b] Percentage of ratings from raters 1 and 2 that were within a 1-point difference. [c] Unable to compute.

The eight noncognitive variables were moderately to highly intercorrelated (r ranged from .34 to .82; see Table 7). They also correlated highly with the composite selection score. A Principal Axis factor analysis of the eight noncognitive variables, using squared multiple correlations as communality estimates, indicated a single factor structure that explained 58 percent of the common variance. All noncognitive variables loaded highly on the factor (ranging from .71 to .86), with the exception of the Strong Support Person scale (.48). The Strong Support Person scale also had the lowest correlations with the other noncognitive scales and the composite score. The scale intercorrelations and the single factor structure of the eight noncognitive variables were consistent with high internal consistency reliability of their scores. For Scholars only, Positive Self-Concept, Realistic Self-Appraisal, Understanding/Navigation of Social Systems, and Community Service were correlated with their GPAs.

Table 7. Intercorrelations of Noncognitive Variables.

Noncognitive Variables	1	2	3	4	5	6	7	8	9	10
1. Positive Self-Concept	-									
2. Realistic Self-Appraisal	.82	-								
3. Understanding/Navigation of Social Systems	.69	.67	-							
4. Preference for Long-Term Goals	.70	.72	.66	-						
5. Successful Leadership Experiences	.65	.61	.62	.62	-					
6. Community Services	.57	.55	.55	.55	.67	-				
7. Nontraditional Acquisition of Knowledge	.63	.62	.62	.63	.58	.55	-			
8. Strong Support Person	.42	.41	.41	.37	.35	.34	.39	-		
9. Composite Selection Score	.77	.77	.74	.74	.71	.68	.72	.47	-	
10. College GPA [a]	.12	.11	.09	.07	.06	.09	.07	.01	.19	-

Note. Sample sizes vary from 1,573 to 1,608 due to missing values. All correlation coefficients in **bold** are significant at p < .0001 level. [a] Correlation coefficients involving college GPA are derived only from Scholars (N varies from 755 to 830). Underlined coefficients are significant at p < .05 level.

Multiple regression analyses indicated that Community Service ($\beta = .160$, p < .0001) was positively predictive of academic engagement. While Positive Self-Concept ($\beta = -.134$, p = .006) was negatively predictive of difficulty keeping up with schoolwork, no noncognitive variables predicted difficulty with time management. In other words, Scholars and Non-Scholars who had more positive self-concepts experienced fewer difficulties with schoolwork. Also, Realistic Self-Appraisal ($\beta = .114$, p = .017) positively predicted hours studied per week.

Discussion

Gates Millennium Scholars seem to be doing very well academically. Their grades in college were high, their aspirations to pursue advanced degrees were high, they intended to complete their degrees at their current institutions, and they seemed to be engaged in successful academic activities. This was true regardless of race or gender. They were selected for their potential and they are showing it. This serves as a reminder that this is a highly successful, relatively homogeneous group. So overall, the GMS program seems to be working well.

Research has shown that having high aspirations is associated with academic success for all students, but it is a particularly strong correlate for students of color (Sedlacek, 2004). If students feel they will succeed, their self-concepts are positive and they tend to do well in school. The Scholars were specifically selected for their positive self-concepts. Another of the noncognitive variables employed in selecting Scholars was having long-term goals. That over 90 percent of the Scholars were interested in pursuing advanced degrees is a testament to the success of the selection process. Though such goals may evolve or change over time, the fact that the Scholars are future oriented bodes well for their continued success in school and in life.

Another finding worthy of comment is that Scholars were committed to completing their degrees at their current institutions. This demonstrates a tenacity in interpreting the system and making it work for them, and is another of the noncognitive variables used in their selection. Often higher education environments are difficult for students of color to negotiate (Allen, 1992; Ancis, Sedlacek & Mohr, 2000; Fries-Britt & Turner, 2002; Helm, Sedlacek & Prieto, 1998), due to institutional barriers, prejudice, and racism (Ancis, Bennett-Choney, & Sedlacek, 1996; Leong & Schneller, 1997; Sedlacek, 1996, 2004a). Sometimes transferring may involve avoiding issues that students of color must learn to handle to be successful (Wawrzynski & Sedlacek, 2003).

Because of skewed distributions of criterion variables, the noncognitive variables did not show statistically significant relationships in many cases, or those relationships were significant but not strong. Some variance is required to be able to generate statistically significant differences. In other words, since so many Scholars are doing so well, and they have such high ambitions, there is not sufficient variability to have statistically significant findings or large effect sizes. Despite the restriction of range limitations, for Scholars, Positive Self-Concept, Realistic Self-

Appraisal, Understanding/Navigation of Social Systems, and Community Service were correlated with their GPAs. Also, Community Service predicted academic engagement. In addition, Scholars and Non-Scholars who had more positive self-concepts experienced fewer difficulties with schoolwork, and Realistic Self-Appraisal predicted studying hours per week. All these relationships were in the expected direction, indicating the utility of noncognitive variables in relating to positive academic experiences.

GPA suffers from some serious problems as a measure of success (Sedlacek, 2004). Because of "grade inflation" at all levels of education (Rojstraczer, 2003), GPA has lost much variability, so the attempt to distinguish among people with high GPAs may be illogical (Sedlacek, 2004). Nonetheless, there were racial differences on GPA among Scholars. Specifically, Asian Pacific Islander and Hispanic American Scholars had higher GPAs than their African American and American Indian counterparts. Scholars appear to be engaging in the activities that will see them be retained and graduate, a criterion that may be more important to their success than GPA. Future studies will examine predictors of the retention and graduation of Scholars.

American Indians studied less, had lower GPAs, and were less engaged in academic activities than the other groups. These findings need to be investigated further. It may be that American Indians are attending different kinds of institutions or have different majors compared with the other racial groups. Additionally, it may be that American Indians do not see some activities as academic in the same way that other groups do. Also, American Indians may be more reluctant to call something academic, which may seem to be boasting of their accomplishments. These issues were discussed in Garrod and Larimore (1997) in conversations with Native American college graduates, and in Sedlacek and Sheu (2003) regarding leadership among American Indian Scholars.

It should be noted that data were not available on all variables for Non-Scholars, including GPA. However, where differences were found, Scholars were doing better than Non-Scholars. For example, Scholars were more likely to be engaged in academic activities than Non-Scholars. Among American Indians, more Scholars than Non-Scholars felt they were unlikely to drop out of school. Also, among Asian Pacific Islander Americans, Scholars studied more than Non-Scholars, and among African Americans, Scholars had higher educational aspirations than Non-Scholars.

Although they had higher GPAs, Asian Pacific Islander and Hispanic Americans also reported experiencing more difficulties with schoolwork than African Americans. These perceptions should be monitored carefully in future studies. For example, it could be that Asian Pacific Islander Americans feel more pressure to get high grades than the other groups. Liang and Sedlacek (2003) documented the so-called "Model Minority Myth" when they found that student service personnel had positive stereotypes of Asian Pacific Islander Americans in a number of situations. While apparently positive, any stereotype places students in a situation where it may be difficult to express their needs or form relationships with faculty, staff, or other students.

Asian Pacific Islander Americans may be expected to be better than others, which increases the pressure on them to be "perfect" and denies them the right to need advising and student services as do other students. For example, Sheu and Sedlacek (2002) and Liang and Sedlacek (2003) found that Asian American students sought counseling less often than other students. Use of student services is correlated with academic success for students of color, and the pressure on Asian Pacific Islander American students to avoid such services is a form of racism that they need to learn to handle to be successful in higher education (Sedlacek, 2004).

On the other hand, Hispanic American students often feel that they are getting mixed messages about their accomplishments and are not sure how "Latino" they should be to successfully negotiate the system of higher education (Ancis, Sedlacek & Mohr, 2000; Fuertes & Sedlacek, 1993; Helm Sedlacek & Prieto, 1998; Sedlacek, 2004).

This study was the first of many that will follow the progress of Gates Millennium Scholars through their educational experiences and beyond. It has provided some ideas for further thought and analysis, and it has documented the significant positive accomplishments and activities of some Scholars thus far.

References

Allen, W. R. (1992). The color of success: African American college student outcomes at predominantly White and historically Black public colleges and universities. *Harvard Educational Review, 62* (1), 26-44.

Ancis, J. R., Bennett-Choney, S. K., & Sedlacek, W. E. (1996). University student attitudes toward American Indians. *Journal of Multicultural Counseling and Development, 24*, 26-36.

Ancis, J. R., Sedlacek, W. E., & Mohr, J. J. (2000). Student perceptions of the campus cultural climate by race. *Journal of Counseling and Development, 78* (2), 180-185.

Fries-Britt, S. & Turner, B. (2002). Uneven stories: Successful Black collegians at a Black and a White campus. *Review of Higher Education, 25*, 315-330.

Fuertes, J. N., & Sedlacek, W. E. (1993). Barriers to the leadership development of Hispanics in higher education. *National Association of Student Personnel Administrators Journal, 30*, 277-283.

Garrod, A., & Larimore, C. (Eds.) (1997). *First person, first peoples: Native American college graduates tell their stories.* Ithaca, NY: Cornell University Press.

Helm, E. G., Sedlacek, W. E., & Prieto, D. O. (1998). The relationship between attitudes toward diversity and overall satisfaction of university students by race. *Journal of College Counseling, 1*, 111-120.

Liang, C. T. H., & Sedlacek, W. E. (2003). Utilizing factor analysis to understand the needs of Asian American students. *Journal of College Student Development, 44* (2), 260-266.

Leong, F. T. L. & Schneller, G. (1997). White Americans' attitudes toward Asian Americans in social situations: An empirical examination of potential stereotypes, bias and prejudice. *Journal of Multicultural Counseling and Development, 25*, 68-78.

Rojstraczer, S. (2003). *Where all grades are above average.* http://www.gradeinflation.com.

Sedlacek, W. E. (1996). An empirical method of determining nontraditional group status. *Measurement and Evaluation in Counseling and Development, 28*, 200-210.

Sedlacek, W. E. (1998). Admissions in higher education: Measuring cognitive and noncognitive variables. In D. J. Wilds & R. Wilson (Eds.), *Minorities in higher education 1997-98: Sixteenth annual status report* (pp. 47-71). Washington, DC: American Council on Education.

Sedlacek, W. E. (2003). Alternative measures in admissions and scholarship selection. *Measurement and Evaluation in Counseling and Development, 35*, 263-272.

Sedlacek, W. E. (2004a). *Beyond the big test: Noncognitive assessment in higher education.* San Francisco: Jossey-Bass.

Sedlacek, W. E. (2004b). The case for noncognitive measures. In W. J. Camara & E. W. Kimmel (Eds.), *Choosing students: Higher education admissions tools for the 21st century.* Mahwah, NJ: Lawrence Erlbaum.

Sedlacek, W. E., & Sheu, H. B. (2003, April). *Correlates of leadership activities of Gates Millennium Scholars.* Paper presented at the American Educational Research Association Convention, Chicago, IL.

Sheu, H. B., & W. E. Sedlacek. (2002). Help-seeking attitudes and coping strategies among college students by race. *Counseling Center Research Report #7-02.* University of Maryland College Park.

Wawrzynski, M. R., & Sedlacek, W. E. (2003). Race and gender differences in the transfer student experience. *Journal of College Student Development, 44* (4), 489-501.

APPENDIX

Complete Items and Response Modes

Intention of retention and educational aspirations
- How likely is it that you will drop out before graduation? [a]
- I am committed to earning a degree at my current college or university [b]
- What is the highest degree you expect to receive? [c]

Difficulties with schoolwork and studying time
- How difficult did you find keeping up with your schoolwork? [d]
- How difficult did you find managing your time effectively? [d]
- In a typical week, how much time do you spend studying (hours)?

Academic engagement items [e]
- How often do you work with other students on schoolwork outside of class?
- How often do you discuss ideas from your readings or classes with students outside of class?
- How often do you discuss ideas from your readings or classes with faculty outside of class?
- How often do you work harder than you thought you could to meet an instructor's expectatic
- How often do you work on creative projects that you help design (research or artistic)?

Response modes:
[a] 1: Very likely
  2: Somewhat likely
  3: Somewhat unlikely
  4: Very unlikely
[b] 1: Strongly disagree
  2: Disagree
  3: Agree
  4: Strongly agree
[c] 1: Less than two years of college
  2: Two or more years of college
  3: Bachelor's degree
  4: Post-baccalaureate certificate
  5: Master's degree (M.A., M.S., M.B.A., etc.)
  6: First professional degree (M.D., J.D., D.D.S., O.D.)
  7: Doctoral degree (Ph.D., ED.D., D.P.H., etc.)
[d] 1: Very difficult
  2: Difficult
  3: Not very difficult
  4: Not difficult
[e] 1: Three or more times a week
  2: Two or three times a week
  3: Once a week
  4: Two or three times a month
  5: Once a month
  6: Less than once a month

CHAPTER 8

HOW DO COLLEGE CHOICE AND PERSISTENCE FOR GMS RECIPIENTS COMPARE TO MINORITY STUDENTS WHO RECEIVED PELL?

John B. Lee and Suzanne B. Clery

Students who receive awards through the Gates Millennium Scholars (GMS) Program are high-achieving minority Pell Grant recipients. Since the National Opinion Research Center (NORC) comparison group included students who were not Pell-eligible (St. John & Chung, chapter 5), it is important to consider how GMS recipients compare to other high-achieving minorities receiving Pell Grants.

This chapter compares the GMS recipients to appropriate national comparison groups. The purpose of these comparisons is to identify how the Scholars differ from other students of similar backgrounds. Three questions are addressed:

- Does the GMS award add to the resources available to students or simply replace funds from other sources?
- Do GMS students attend different types of colleges than other minority students who receive Pell Grants?
- Do GMS students persist at rates similar to those of comparable groups who do not receive the GMS Grant?

These analyses are important not only because the comparison group used in the previous GMS analyses resembles the overall applicant population rather than Pell recipients, but also because we cannot understand the impact of GMS by considering only students who applied for the program. This analysis examines the types of colleges attended and the aid packages students received.

Methodology

The analysis in this chapter provides a different vantage point on the role of GMS than is evident in the comparisons in preceding chapters in this volume. Comparisons are made herein between GMS recipients and comparable students from national samples.

Different datasets were utilized for the ensuing comparisons. This was necessary due to the types of data available for GMS recipients and the national samples.

- Different data regarding the GMS recipients were used for the analyses of college choice and aid amounts, and the persistence analysis. The actual recipient data collected by the United Negro College Fund (UNCF) were used to examine attendance and aid packages. However, this file does not track students through college. St. John and Chung's analysis for persistence rates (chapter 5) was used to determine GMS persistence for the persistence section of this analysis.
- Different national samples were also utilized to create the comparative groups. NPSAS, the National Postsecondary Student Aid Study, which is collected by the U.S. Department of Education, includes data for one academic year (1999-2000). NPSAS was utilized for the aid and attendance patterns analyses. BPS (Beginning Postsecondary Students), also collected by the U.S. Department of Education, provides a longitudinal look at students who began their academic careers in 1995-96, following up on the cohort in 1998 and 2001. BPS provides the ability to analyze the persistence of a comparative group.

Students included in the analysis of the national samples are minority Pell Grant recipients who attended full-time. The BPS data also reflect students with GPAs of 3.0 or higher in their first academic year.

Due to the many cuts and subsettings necessary on the NPSAS sample, the resulting groups were too small to analyze; therefore, we could not limit this sample only to students with high GPAs in college, a group that would be more directly comparable to GMS recipients. On the other hand, statistical tests were completed on the NPSAS sample between students with high GPAs and all students regarding attendance and aid variables; results indicated differences between the groups were small in the NPSAS sample (for example, there was an overall 5.8 percent difference in the average price of attendance between students with GPAs of 3.0 or higher and students with any GPA). However, including only students with GPAs of 3.0 or higher drastically reduced the number of records in the analysis group, which limited the number of possible comparisons. Therefore, the NPSAS group includes all minority Pell Grant recipients attending on a full-time basis.

The following analysis describes how, demographically, the GMS recipients are similar in some ways and different in others when matched with the nationally-representative samples of students who are minority Pell Grant recipients attending colleges and universities on a full-time basis.

Aid Packages for Undergraduate Students

GMS recipients attended different types of colleges and universities than did undergraduates in the NPSAS group. Sixty-two percent of GMS recipients attended public or private universities, compared with 36 percent of the NPSAS group (derived from Table 1). Only 3 percent of GMS recipients attended community colleges, while 23 percent of the NPSAS group attended community colleges. Too few undergraduates attended private for-profit and private two-year institutions to support statistical analysis, and they are not included in this report.

Table 1. Percentage distribution of NPSAS sample and GMS recipients, by institution type.

	Percent of NPSAS Sample	Percent of GMS Recipients	Average Price of Attendance
Total	100.0	100.0	$18,368
Institution type			
Public universities	27.4	40.5	13,691
Public baccalaureate/masters	17.4	15.0	11,685
Public 2-year	22.9	3.4	9,611
Private universities	8.4	21.5	31,681
Private baccalaureate/masters	13.4	19.0	24,281
Private not-for-profit, less-than-4-year	1.4	0.1	--
Private for-profit	9.0	0.4	--
--Sample size too small to yield reliable results.			

Source: NCES, NPSAS:2000 Undergraduate Students 10/12/01; GMS recipient data from UNCF.

These distributions are similar to the analyses in chapter 5 with respect to enrollment in private colleges. The combination of findings illustrates that GMS improves the odds of enrolling in four-year colleges. The analyses in the prior chapters also indicate that GMS recipients are less likely to enroll in two-year colleges, controlling for other factors. Additionally, indicated in both sets of analyses are the differences in opportunities to enroll in private colleges.

There were also some demographic differences between the two groups. A larger share of the GMS recipients was female compared with the NPSAS group, 69 compared with 62 percent (Table 2). The GMS recipients include a higher concentration of Asian/Pacific Islander (24 compared with 15%) and American Indian/Alaskan Native (10 compared with 3%) students than the NPSAS group (Table 3). However, the percentages of Black, non-Hispanic and Hispanic students were slightly lower in the GMS recipients group compared with the NPSAS group (36 and 30% compared with 42 and 41%).

Table 2. Percentage distribution of NPSAS sample and GMS recipients, according to gender, by institution type.

	NPSAS Distribution		GMS Distribution	
	Male	Female	Male	Female
Total	37.8	62.2	30.6	69.4
Institution type				
Public universities	41.5	58.5	32.6	67.4
Public baccalaureate/masters	38.9	61.1	27.2	72.8
Public 2-year	31.8	68.2	28.0	72.0
Private universities	46.1	53.9	35.1	64.9
Private baccalaureate/masters	41.1	58.9	24.7	75.3
Private not-for-profit, less-than -4-year	49.8	50.2	--	--
Private for-profit	25.7	74.3	--	--
--Sample size too small to yield reliable results.				

Source: NCES, NPSAS:2000 Undergraduate Students 10/12/01; GMS recipient data from UNCF.

Ninety-seven percent of GMS recipients[1] were dependent students (Table 4). This compares with the 57 percent of the NPSAS group that were dependent students. Overall, the average age of the GMS recipients is relatively close to that of the NPSAS group, 22 compared with 23 years of age (table 5). However, 11 percent of the GMS recipients were older than 24 compared with 26 percent of the NPSAS group.

Table 3. Percentage distribution of NPSAS sample and GMS recipients according to race/ethnicity, by institution type.

	Black, non-Hispanic	Hispanic	Asian/Pacific Islander	American Indian/Alaskan Native
NPSAS Distribution				
Total	41.5	40.6	15.3	2.6
Institution type				
Public universities	44.2	30.9	23.3	1.6
Public baccalaureate/masters	42.2	41.4	15.1	1.4
Public 2-year	48.6	33.3	12.6	5.6
Private universities	37.4	42.6	20	0
Private baccalaureate/masters	26.4	63	7.3	3.2
Private not-for-profit, less-than-4-year	41.5	50.6	7.3	0.6
Private for-profit	40.1	50.1	7.5	2.3
GMS Distribution				
Total	36	30.3	23.8	9.9
Institution type				
Public universities	30.2	29.1	30.7	10.1
Public baccalaureate/masters	42.3	34.1	7.5	16
Public 2-year	26.7	32.2	10.5	30.8
Private universities	33.2	32.2	30.9	3.7
Private baccalaureate/masters	47.8	27.1	18.5	6.7
Private not-for-profit, less-than-4-year	--	--	--	--
Private for-profit	--	--	--	--
--Sample size too small to yield reliable results.				

Source: NCES, NPSAS:2000 Undergraduate Students 10/12/01; GMS recipient data from UNCF.

Table 4. Percentage distribution of NPSAS sample and GMS recipients[1] according to dependency status, by institution type.

	NPSAS Distribution		GMS Distribution	
	Dependent	Independent	Dependent	Independent
Total	57.1	42.9	97.3	2.7
Institution type				
Public universities	65.6	34.4	98.7	1.3
Public baccalaureate/masters	59.4	40.6	94.1	5.9
Public 2-year	48.6	51.4	97.1	2.9
Private universities	79.1	20.9	97.1	2.9
Private baccalaureate/masters	55.8	44.2	96.9	3.1
Private not-for-profit, less-than 4-year	49	51	--	--
Private for-profit	32.6	67.4	--	--
--Sample size too small to yield reliable results.				
[1]For GMS recipients that were freshmen only.				

Source: NCES, NPSAS:2000 Undergraduate Students 10/12/01; GMS Recipient data from UNCF.

Table 5. Average age of NPSAS sample and GMS recipients by institution type.

	NPSAS Students		GMS Students	
	Age, 12/31/1999	Percent older than 24	Age	Percent older than 24
Total	23	25.8	22	11.1
Institution type				
Public universities	22	17.1	22	9.5
Public baccalaureate/masters	23	22.9	23	19.7
Public 2-year	25	35.7	26	39.9
Private universities	21	8.3	21	4.2
Private baccalaureate/masters	24	26.9	22	10.1
Private not-for-profit, less-than-4-year	24	33.7	--	--
Private for-profit	25	45	--	--
--Sample size too small to yield reliable results.				

Source: NCES, NPSAS:2000 Undergraduate Students 10/12/01; GMS recipient data from UNCF.

The GMS recipients are geographically mobile. Twenty-four percent of the GMS recipients attended college in a state other than where they lived compared with 9 percent of those in the NPSAS group (Table 6). Although GMS recipients who attended public institutions were more likely to attend college in another state than were those in the NPSAS group, the biggest difference was for those who attended private colleges and universities. Fifty-three percent of GMS recipients who attended private universities attended out-of-state compared with 31 percent of the NPSAS group. Further, 11 percent of the undergraduates in the NPSAS group attended private baccalaureate/masters colleges in another state compared with 39 percent of the GMS recipients.

Table 6. Percentage distribution of NPSAS sample and GMS recipients according to out-of-state attendance status, by institution type.

	NPSAS Distribution		GMS Distribution	
	Out-of-state	In-state	Out-of-state	In-state
Total	9.2	90.8	24.3	75.7
Institution type				
Public universities	7.3	92.8	9.4	90.6
Public baccalaureate/masters	8.3	91.7	9.8	90.2
Public 2-year	3.3	96.7	2.8	97.2
Private universities	30.5	69.5	53	47
Private baccalaureate/masters	11.4	88.6	38.8	61.2
Private not-for-profit, less-than-4-year	11	89	–	–
Private for-profit	9.6	90.4	–	–
–Sample size too small to yield reliable results.				

Source: NCES, NPSAS:2000 Undergraduate Students 10/12/01; GMS recipient data from UNCF.

Even though the GMS recipients were low-income, they were slightly better off than were those in the comparison group. Dependent GMS recipients came from families with average incomes of $25,790 compared with $19,858 for those in the NPSAS group. Independent GMS recipients had incomes approximately $3,600 less than did those in the NPSAS group (Table 7).[2] Only three percent of the GMS recipients were independent of their parents' incomes.

Table 7. Average income[1] of NPSAS sample and GMS recipients, by institution type.

	NPSAS Students		GMS Recipients	
	Income: independent students 1998	Family income: dependent students 1998	Income: independent students	Family income: dependent students
Total	$10,836	$19,858	$7,198	$25,790
Institution type				
Public universities	8,233	21,553	3,242	25,606
Public baccalaureate/masters	10,300	20,836	4,866	25,361
Public 2-year	12,516	16,922	--	13,814
Private universities	8,083	21,546	10,003	26,395
Private baccalaureate/masters	11,768	18,868	9,514	26,038
Private not-for-profit, less-than-4-year	13,479	20,593	--	--
Private for-profit	11,667	16,284	--	--
--Sample size too small to yield reliable results.				
[1]For GMS recipients that were freshmen only.				

Source: NCES, NPSAS:2000 Undergraduate Students 10/12/01; GMS recipient data from UNCF.

The income differences between the two groups are in the same direction and magnitude within types of institutions, with the exception of those undergraduates attending community colleges. In community colleges, the average family income for the GMS recipients was $13,814, compared with $16,922 for those in the NPSAS group.

By region of postsecondary attendance, the GMS recipients were distributed differently than the NPSAS comparative group. The differences were larger by sector rather than overall. For example, in the private, not-for-profit sector, much higher proportions of the GMS recipients went to institutions in the New England and Mid-Atlantic regions (15 and 25%) than those in the NPSAS group (4 and 15%, respectively) (Table 8); costs tend to be higher in these two regions than the others. On the other hand, GMS recipients attended public institutions in the Mid-Atlantic and Southeast regions (8 and 23%) with less frequency than those in the NPSAS group (17 and 29%, respectively). Yet, the attendance of GMS recipients in public institutions in the Southwest and Far West regions (21 and 30%) was greater than for those in the NPSAS group (16 and 21%).

Table 8. Percentage distribution of GMS recipients and NPSAS comparative group according to institutional control, by region.

	NPSAS Distribution			GMS Distribution		
	Total	Public	Private not-for-profit	Total	Public	Private not-for-profit
New England	2.3	1.7	4.2	6.4	0.9	14.5
Mid Atlantic	16.1	16.5	15.2	14.9	7.9	25.1
Great Lakes	7.9	7.6	9.3	7.7	6.8	9
Plains	2.2	1.8	4	4.6	5.3	3.7
Southeast	25	29.2	15.6	22.1	22.7	21.1
Southwest	12.8	15.5	3.2	15.6	21.1	7.4
Rocky Mountains	1.4	1.6	1.2	3.3	4.4	1.7
Far West	18.2	20.8	9.4	24.7	30.2	16.8
Outlying Areas	14.1	5.5	38	0.7	0.8	0.7

Source: NCES, NPSAS: 2000 Undergraduate Students 10/12/01; GMS recipient data from UNCF.

In summary, when compared with the NPSAS group, the GMS recipients were more likely to possess the following characteristics:

- attend universities
- be female
- be Asian/Pacific Islander or American Indian
- be dependent

- attend college in another state, especially in the private sector
- if dependent, have a higher family income
- in the private sector, attend in the New England or Mid Atlantic regions; in the public sector, attend in the Southwest or Far West regions.

Student Finances

A key concern for the GMS program is whether the Scholarship is adding to students' resources or replacing aid that might have been available to the Scholars from other sources. The evidence suggests that colleges and universities did not reduce aid to the GMS recipients, at least during the first year. Rather, the program allowed low-income students to attend more expensive colleges and universities, and do so without extra borrowing. It is possible that institutions reduced their aid awards for GMS students more after the first year than they do for other students. This practice, commonly referred to as 'front loading,' is fairly common. Since the NORC surveys can collect only self-reported information on student aid, more follow-up analyses of the UNCF databases would need to be done to determine if there was large scale reduction.

The following section displays information about student finances, including the price of attendance, unmet financial need, and aid packages received by the GMS recipients and the NPSAS group.

The GMS awards allow recipients to attend higher-priced colleges and universities than would otherwise be the case. The average price of attendance was $19,562 for GMS recipients[3] compared with $12,772 for the NPSAS group (Table 9).

The price of attendance varied between the two groups by institutional type. The price of attendance difference was smaller between the GMS recipients and the NPSAS group for those attending public institutions than for those attending private institutions. In the public sector, the difference ranged from $1,332 in universities to $909 in community colleges. In the private sector, the difference was much larger—$10,298 in the universities and $10,417 in the baccalaureate/masters colleges.

Table 9. Average cost and aid variables for GMS recipients a NPSAS comparative group, by institutional type.

	Cost of attendance	Unmet need	Total aid	Grants	Loans (incl. PLUS)	Work-study	GM awa
	NPSAS Sample						
Total	$12,772	$4,058	$8,247	$4,818	$2,988	$301	
Institution type							
Public universities	12,738	2,567	9,699	5,201	3,983	368	
Public baccalaureate/masters	10,267	2,840	6,958	3,871	2,630	319	
Public 2-year	8,780	4,121	4,332	3,297	750	166	
Private universities	22,024	4,361	17,154	10,948	5,289	733	
Private baccalaureate/masters	14,369	5,216	8,724	5,288	3,006	242	
Private not-for-profit, less-than-4-year	14,726	6,250	7,947	4,736	2,887	123	
Private for-profit	16,519	8,432	7,866	3,217	4,456	143	
	GMS Recipients						
Total	19,562	3,737	13,922	9,619	3,446	857	6,8
Institution type							
Public universities	14,070	2,901	9,997	5,987	3,239	771	5,8
Public baccalaureate/masters	11,520	3,418	6,787	4,370	2,035	382	5,0
Public 2-year	9,689	3,484	4,203	3,148	627	428	3,9
Private universities	32,322	4,402	24,715	18,947	4,339	1,429	8,2
Private baccalaureate/masters	24,786	4,892	17,565	12,217	4,478	869	8,9
Private not-for-profit, less-than-4-year	--	--	--	--	--	--	--
Private for-profit	--	--	--	--	--	--	--
--Sample size too small to yield reliable results.							

Source: NCES, NPSAS: 2000 Undergraduate Students 10/12/01; GMS recipient data fro UNCF.

Unmet Need

The first measure is unmet need, which is calculated by subtracting the sum of expected family contribution and all student aid from the price of attendance. A $321 difference existed between the average unmet need of GMS recipients and students in the NPSAS group (GMS recipients' unmet need was $3,737, while that of the NPSAS group was $4,058). By institutional type, the differences between the two groups varied only slightly from $41 to $637.

Total Aid

Overall, the GMS recipients received an average financial aid package totaling $13,922, not including their GMS award. GMS added another $6,834 to the package, summing to a total of $20,756.

The results indicate that the GMS recipients received larger aid packages than did those in the comparison group. The GMS recipients had larger aid packages than did the students in the NPSAS group in all types of institutions, with the exception of public baccalaureate/masters colleges and community colleges. This difference was calculated without including the GMS award.

The difference between the two groups in the public universities was $298. The GMS recipients received $171 less than did those in the NPSAS group attending public baccalaureate/masters colleges and $129 less than did those in community colleges. On the other hand, GMS recipients in private universities received $7,561 more in total aid than did students in the NPSAS group. The GMS recipients attending private baccalaureate/masters colleges received $8,841 more aid than did those in the NPSAS group.

The second key measure is the average amounts of grant and loan aid received by students. One of the goals of the GMS program is to reduce students' dependency on loans. By this measure, the Scholars received significantly more aid in the form of grants than did those in the NPSAS group. At the same time, the Scholars received smaller loans on average in each of the institutional sectors than did those in the NPSAS group, with the exception of private baccalaureate/masters colleges.

The differences are easier to see using the type of aid as a percent of total aid (Table 10). The GMS recipients received 69 percent of their aid as grants and 25 percent as loans compared with 58 percent in grants and 36 percent as loans for the NPSAS group. The GMS Program succeeded in reducing recipients' dependency on loans.

The Scholars covered a larger share of their price of attendance with grant aid, even though they attended higher-priced colleges and universities than did those in the NPSAS group.

By all measures, the GMS recipients program has achieved its objective of increasing student choice. It has allowed students to attend more expensive colleges and universities than would otherwise be possible. It has also allowed students to exercise their choice without undue dependence on loans.

Persistence Rates

The second analysis considered whether persistence rates were different for the GMS sample than for a comparable national sample (Table 11). Persistence over two years was examined to determine differences between students nationally and GMS recipients. The analyses revealed GMS recipients persisted at much higher rates than the comparison group.

For the national comparison sample in Table 11, a persisting student was defined as one who either attained and was enrolled during two consecutive academic years, or did not attain and was enrolled at least eight months during each of the two consecutive academic years. A nonpersistor was one who did not attain and was enrolled less than eight months or not at all during at least one of the two consecutive academic years. The persistence rate for GMS recipients in Table 11 indicates the percentage of students who enrolled each term during, excluding summer, for the two years after they enrolled in college.

Table 11 displays the persistence of the GMS recipients and students from the national sample: GMS recipients were more likely to persist through two consecutive academic years than those in the comparative sample, 99 compared with 69 percent.

Table 10. Average cost of attendance, total aid awarded and aid as a percentage of cost of attendance and total aid, by type of aid, for GMS recipients and NPSAS comparative group, by institutional type.

	Attendance cost	Grants %of total aid	Loans %of total aid	Work-study: %of total aid	Total aid	Grants %of attendance cost	Loans %of attendance cost	Work-study: %of attendance cost
				NPSAS Sample[1]				
Total	$12,772	58.4	36.2	3.7	$8,247	37.7	23.4	2.4
Institution type								
Public universities	12,738	53.6	41.1	3.8	9,699	40.8	31.3	2.9
Public baccalaureate/masters	10,267	55.6	37.8	4.6	6,958	37.7	25.6	3.1
Public 2-year	8,780	76.1	17.3	3.8	4,332	37.6	8.5	1.9
Private universities	22,024	63.8	30.8	4.3	17,154	49.7	24	3.3
Private baccalaureate/masters	14,369	60.6	34.5	2.8	8,724	36.8	20.9	1.7
Private not-for-profit, less-than-4-year	14,726	59.6	36.3	1.5	7,947	32.2	19.6	0.8
Private for-profit	16,519	40.9	56.7	1.8	7,866	19.5	27	0.9
				GMS Recipients				
Total	19,562	69.1	24.8	6.2	13,922	49.2	17.6	4.4
Institution type								
Public universities	14,070	59.9	32.4	7.7	9,997	42.6	23	5.5
Public baccalaureate/masters	11,520	64.4	30	5.6	6,787	37.9	17.7	3.3
Public 2-year	9,689	74.9	14.9	10.2	4,203	32.5	6.5	4.4
Private universities	32,322	76.7	17.6	5.8	24,715	58.6	13.4	4.4
Private baccalaureate/masters	24,786	69.6	25.5	4.9	17,565	49.3	18.1	3.5
Private not-for-profit, less than 4-year	-	—	—	—	—	—	—	—
Private for-profit	--	--	--	--	--	--	--	--

[1]The total for grants, aid and work study does not sum to 100% in the NPSAS sample due to the exclusion of the "other" category which appears in the NPSAS sample but not in the GMS recipients Program sample.
--Sample size too small to yield reliable results.
Source: NCES, NPSAS: 2000 Undergraduate Students 10/12/01; GMS recipient data from UNCF.

Table 11. Two-year persistence of GMS recipients and BPS comparative group.

	GMS Scholars	BPS Group
Persisted	98.6	68.5
Did not persist	1.4	31.5

Source: NCES, BPS; GMS data from UNCF.

This comparison reveals that GMS students persisted at a higher rate than similarly high achieving students of color in a comparable national sample. Since the purchasing power of Pell Grants has declined since the middle 1990s (chapter 5), the comparison group would have had a more favorable financial situation than a similar group in 2000. However, as the analyses in the preceding chapters illustrate (Trent et al., chapter 3, St. John & Chung, chapter 5), students who took the steps to apply for the GMS grant, and who met the noncognitive criteria were exceptionally well prepared and probably highly motivated. Nevertheless, we can conclude that GMS recipients persist at a higher rate than similarly prepared students of color across the U. S.

Conclusions

Most of the analyses in this chapter have compared the financial aid awards and college choices by GMS recipients to a comparison group generated using data from the National Postsecondary Student Aid Study (NPSAS). This is a nationally-representative sample of students attending accredited postsecondary institutions in the 1999-2000 academic year. The comparison group was limited to ethnic and racial minority students who attended college full-time and received a Pell Grant. Four conclusions were evident about enrollment patterns from this comparison.

First, this analysis leads to the conclusion that the GMS Program allows undergraduate recipients to attend more expensive colleges and universities than would otherwise be possible. GMS recipients attended colleges and universities that cost $19,562 on average, compared with $12,772 for a comparison group.

Second, the GMS recipients attended universities at a higher rate than did those in the comparison group, or, the corollary, they attended community colleges at a lower rate. Sixty-two percent of the GMS recipients attended universities compared with 36 percent of those in the comparison group. On the other hand, only three percent of the GMS recipients attended community colleges compared with 23 percent of those in the comparison group. These comparisons are confirmatory of the findings on college choice in this volume (St. John & Chung, chapter 5)

Third, GMS recipients attended more expensive institutions, but received less loan aid and more grant support than did those in the comparison group. The GMS recipients received grants that covered one-half of their cost of attendance before the GMS award. The students in the comparison group received grant aid that covered 38 percent of their costs. GMS recipients used loans to pay 18 percent of their costs compared with 23 percent for those in the comparison group. These results suggest that the GMS Program did not displace other aid.

Finally, by comparing GMS recipients with a comparison group from the BPS, it was evident that students who received the GMS awards persisted at a much higher rate than the average high-achieving minority Pell recipient in the national sample. Nearly all (99%) of GMS recipients persisted through the first two years of their academic studies compared with 69 percent in the national sample. This suggests that the GMS Program is alleviating financial pressure on students, and allowing them to focus on and persist through their education.

Notes

1. These data are available only for freshmen on the GMS recipients data.
2. These data are only available for freshmen on the GMS recipients data.
3. The GMS recipients' price of attendance was computed in one of three ways: 1. as provided to JBL Associates, Inc., by UNCF in the GMS datafiles; 2. imputed, if possible, based on the average student aid reported in the GMS data within the same institution, same level of education (graduate vs. undergraduate), and attendance status (in- or out-of-state); 3. If neither one nor two were available, the costs were computed using the IPEDS data.

Price of attendance was based on the respective in- or out-of-state tuition for the student's level and room and board costs for 1999-2000.

Reference

Lee, J. B. (2004). Access revisited: A preliminary reanalysis of NELS. In E. P. St. John (Ed.), *Readings on equal education: Vol. 19. Public policy and college access: Investigating the federal and state roles in equalizing postsecondary opportunity.* New York: AMS Press.

CHAPTER 9

STUDENT AID AND MAJOR CHOICE: A STUDY OF HIGH-ACHIEVING STUDENTS OF COLOR

Edward P. St. John and Choong-Geun Chung

The Gates Millennium Scholars (GMS) Program promises undergraduates that they will receive support through graduate school if they pursue graduate degrees in library/information sciences, engineering, education, mathematics, and science (including computer science). This promise is intended to encourage minorities to go into fields in which they are underrepresented and to which they can make contributions. While the major fields of undergraduate students are not considered in the selection process for potential GMS awardees, receiving the award may influence students to choose a major that is related to one of the fields that receives long-term support. Thus, the GMS Program provides the opportunity to examine how grant subsidies and debt reduction influence major choice.

There are three logical bases for assuming that GMS might influence choices about education programs. First, for many decades the federal government has provided specially directed

217

financial aid for students enrolling in health sciences and other high-demand fields. And while these programs were seldom considered in economic research on student aid, there was evidence that the decline in federal need-based grants was associated with the growing opportunity gap for minorities compared with Whites in the U.S. after 1980 (St. John, 2003). Second, debt forgiveness has been used to encourage students to enter teaching or the medical professions, especially if they locate in geographic areas experiencing shortages. However, the influence of targeted debt forgiveness has seldom been evaluated systematically. Recent research on debt forgiveness for public service is not encouraging (Schrag, 2001). It is not clear whether debt forgiveness influences students to enter fields or merely rewards students who would have entered these fields anyway. Third, the idea that student aid might influence major choice gained momentum in the 1980s, when some educational leaders began to speculate about the consequences of growing levels of student debt (Kramer & Van Dusen, 1986; Newman, 1985). The initial test of this proposition found that debt burden was not associated with choosing majors with high expected earnings (St. John, 1994), but this issue merits further study.

Not only does GMS provide recipients of grant aid with the opportunity to secure more support for graduate studies, providing a clear incentive for major choice, but it also reduces student debt. So the major choices by students could, in theory at least, be related to the amounts of both debt and grants received. Using a national sample of qualified applicants for GMS (recipients and nonrecipients), this paper examines the impact of student aid (GMS and amounts of scholarships and debt). To test whether GMS influenced major choice, we used both versions of our model, one that considered the impact of GMS only and another that considered GMS and the amounts of grants and debt burden, controlling for other forces that could influence major choice. The analyses are restricted to the 2000 freshmen and continuing student samples because these students were enrolled long enough to have declared a major. Often, freshmen (e.g., the 2001 freshman cohort) do not declare majors during their freshman year.

Logical Approach

Logically, we assumed that student background, aspirations, college choice, achievement, and educational experiences influence major choice, along with student aid. Prior studies have established a basis for examining the linkage between debt and choosing majors with higher expected earnings (St. John, 1994). However, this logic does not exactly fit the GMS program, which provides the promise of funding for graduate education in specified fields. Since earnings vary significantly in these major fields, the old logic does not hold. Instead, the incentive for choice of field in GMS is future grant aid, rather than future earnings. GMS would reduce debt, which could make some low-earning fields—like library science and education—appear to be more attractive options than they would be without the financial inducement. Fortunately, the choice construct provides a more complete basis for conceptualizing the linkages between financial variables and major choice. After discussing below the theoretical foundations for a new major choice model, we describe the new model.

The logic of the student choice construct is informed by social theory on attainment, economic theory on human capital and price response, and education research with an explicit focus on the student choice process. The models used in this volume to examine educational choices by high-achieving minority students integrate an understanding of distinct choices informed by the continuity of choice. Specifically, consideration of the situated contexts in which students make educational choices guided the logical development of the analytic models. Each of these elements of the major choice process is examined below.

First, the situated contexts that are crucial in this study are the lived experiences of minority students. The notion that major choices could be constructed differently within different ethnic communities has some roots in educational research. For example, Gail Thomas (1985) found that African Americans were attracted to majors in math and science, but had special developmental needs. A more recent study found that African Americans choosing majors in education, health, and other applied fields were more likely to persist than other African Americans (St. John, Hu,

Simmons, Carter, & Weber, in press). However, a similar pattern was not evident for Whites.

Ethnic differences in major choice could be related to educational background, aspirations, and/or culture. It also is possible that such differences are related to financial considerations and will change in significance once variables are considered. Thus there is a tension between the social/economic and academic aspects of situated contexts, at least at a conceptual level. Therefore, to build an understanding of the role and influence of situated contexts in major choice, we need to consider ethnic differences.

Second, social theory of educational attainment periodically needs reinterpretation to contend with the complexities of educational choices by diverse groups. Specifically, in the case of major choice, social attainment theory argues that social class and the professions are linked, that fathers' occupational status influences choices across generations (Blau & Duncan, 1967). This notion of major choice is constraining for groups that have faced historic discrimination in education or the labor market. Accordingly, the role of GMS could be to enable students from disadvantaged backgrounds to overcome these barriers to access.

The concept of racial uplift, a logic that is compatible with attainment theory, has some relevance to the reinterpretation process. There is compelling and growing evidence that the concept of cross-generation uplift remains salient among African Americans (Kaltenbaugh, St. John, & Starkey, 1999; St. John, Musoba, Simmons, & Chung, 2002; Paulsen, St. John, & Carter, 2002). These tensions between cultural reproduction and uplift are manifest in research on major choices, as they are in research on college choice and enrollment.

Third, theory and research on student engagement (Kuh & Love, 2000) and learning communities (Tinto, 2000) can inform the study of major choice as well. It is possible that student engagement with community groups could influence the choices of particular fields, like education, that are socially oriented. It also is possible that engagement with faculty—working on research with faculty or having the opportunity to get to know faculty—might influence the choice of majors in which the individuals' ethnic group is underrepresented. For example, working with faculty on research will illuminate the prospect that scientific research is interesting, feasible, and worthwhile. Therefore, we examine the influence of variables related to student engagement on major choice.

Fourth, economic theory on human capital assumes that people make educational choices based on consideration of costs and benefits (Becker, 1964). Prior analyses of the role of major choice in persistence indicate important differences between Whites and African Americans in this regard (St. John, Hu, Simmons, Carter, & Weber, in press). In theory, debt burden can influence students to choose majors with higher earning potential. By constraining debt in both graduate and undergraduate school, GMS could influence students to choose majors that have lower expected earnings, like education and library science, than business or other fields with high expected earnings.

It is possible that the prospect of long-term support from GMS could influence students to choose all of the majors that are eligible for support through graduate school. While it is possible to enter graduate school in education from almost any undergraduate field, it is more difficult to go on in the sciences and engineering without preparation in these fields. Further, receiving teaching credentials might help students secure admission to graduate school in the field. Therefore, it is reasonable to examine the influence of GMS awards on the choice of majors in math, science (including computer science), engineering, education, and library science/information.

Fifth, continuity of choice also can play a substantial role in major choice (St. John, Asker, & Hu, 2001; St. John, Cabrera, Nora, & Asker, 2000). It is logical that financial reasons for choosing a college also could have an influence on the choice of major. For example, if students were concerned about living at home, they might want a major that enabled them to find a local job. In contrast, choosing a major because of scholarships might open students to broader horizons academically, since the additional funding brings a new freedom to learn, to pursue new interests, and to discover that which is compelling. Similarly, it is possible that choosing a college because of a strong reputation could be related to choosing majors that are more prestigious, such as science or engineering. Therefore, there is reason to consider whether the financial and educational reasons for choosing a college also have an influence on major choice. Thus, a variation on the financial nexus (Paulsen & St. John, 2002; Paulsen, St. John, & Carter, in review; St. John, Paulsen, & Starkey, 1996) could function as an integral part of the major choice process. It is possible that choosing a college because of low expenses, high scholarships, proximity to home, and reputation are related to aid amounts in the major choice process. These relationships merit exploration.

Based on these considerations, we developed a logical model for the analysis of major choice that considered the influence of social background (including ethnicity), preferences in college choice, type of college, student engagement, achievement, GMS, and the amounts of financial aid.

Research Approach

The paper uses surveys of two cohorts of GMS recipients and nonrecipients to examine the influence of student financial aid on major choices by high-achieving students of color. One cohort consists of freshmen who applied for GMS as high school seniors expecting to enroll in college in 2000. The other cohort is made up of continuing undergraduates—students who already were enrolled in college—and who were qualified to receive awards in fall 2000. This section describes the surveys, model specifications, statistical methods, and limitations of the study.

The NORC Surveys

The National Opinion Research Center at the University of Chicago (NORC) developed surveys of two cohorts of students who applied for GMS in 2000 (freshmen and continuing students). NORC conducted surveys of samples of students who met the academic qualifications and of all recipients in the two cohorts. Students' majors or preferred majors were not a factor considered in their selection for GMS. After it was determined that students met the academic criteria (e.g., the right types of preparatory courses and grade point averages above 3.3), the students were reviewed by different groups using noncognitive criteria (Sedlacek, in press) and they were reviewed for financial eligibility.

The result was a quasi-random distribution of awards during the first year for qualified students (St. John & Chung, chapter 5).

Although the survey instruments varied somewhat across the two groups, both the continuing and freshman cohorts were asked about family background, college choices, involvement in college, college majors, and other variables used to examine major choice, consistent with the logical model described above. NORC used a Web survey for the study and had reasonable response rates (see chapter 2). In addition, NORC added sample weights for each group, adjusting for the probability of selection. The analyses presented here use the NORC weights.

Model Specifications

The dependent variables compared students choosing majors in math, science (including computer science), engineering, education, and library/information sciences with students making other major choices. The model included independent variables related to:

- GMS (students who received GMS compared with others)
- Student characteristics
    - Male (compared with female)
    - Ethnicity (African Americans, American Indians,[1] and Hispanics were compared with Asian Americans)
- Reasons for choosing a college
    - Choosing a college because of low expense (students rating this as a "5" were compared with others)
    - Choosing a college because of grant/scholarship (students rating this as a "5" were compared with others)
    - Choosing a college close to home (students rating this as a "5" were compared with others)
    - Choosing a college for a strong reputation (students rating this as a "5" were compared with others)

- Family ability to pay (parents contributed to college finances; affirmative responses compared with negative responses)
- Involvement
    - Cultural group (students who participated in events put on by a cultural group were compared with students who did not)
    - Tutoring (students who participated were compared with students who did not)
    - Community service (students who participated in community service were compared with students who did not)
    - Assisted faculty on research (students responding affirmatively were compared with others)
    - Supported by one or more faculty (students responding affirmatively were compared with others)
- Type of institution (students enrolled in private colleges and public two-year colleges were compared with students enrolled in public four-year colleges)
- Finances
    - Loan debt $/1,000 (second step only)
    - Grant/Scholarship $/1,000 (second step only)

Five of these variables were related to student involvement in college. The variables for community service and cultural groups indicate frequent involvement in student social and civic activities. Involvement in faculty research and support by faculty indicate measure of academic involvement. Students who are more involved in the academic life of their campuses are more likely to feel supported by faculty than students who are less involved. The question of faculty support asked whether students perceived that they had the support of one or more faculty. The variable for involvement in tutoring served as an indicator of perceived need for academic support.

A two-step analysis procedure was used as a means of untangling the monetary effects of the GMS program from the effects of other program features (i.e., leadership training, the halo effect of being a GMS recipient, and the criteria used for selection). The first step considered the full model excluding aid amounts; the second step added the amounts of scholarships and debt burden.

Statistical Methods

Logistic regression is an appropriate method for examining educational choices and other qualitative outcomes (Aldrich & Nelson, 1986; Peng, So, Stage, & St. John, 2002). Multinomial logistic regression, the statistical method used in this study, is appropriate when multiple choices are being compared, as in the model specified above.

Odds ratios are presented for the independent variables. An odds ratio below one (1) indicates a negative association, while an odds ratio above one (1) indicates a positive association. For dichotomous variables, which are the primary type of independent variable used here, a significant ratio can be interpreted as raising the odds if positive and lowering the odds if negative. For example, an odds ratio of .9 should be interpreted to mean that students with this characteristic have .9 times the odds of the outcome.

For continuous variables (i.e., grant/scholarship amounts and debt burden) the odds ratios can be applied to increments (i.e., 1,000 dollar increments since these variables are divided by 1,000). However, we use a cautious approach in interpreting the effects of continuous variables and, thus, focus on whether the associations are positive (above zero) or negative (below zero) if they are significant.

The analyses present three levels of statistical significance for independent variables. Two levels (.01 and .05) provide indicators of significant difference. The third level (.1) provides a measure of moderate association that we interpret more cautiously. Since our analyses use a two-step process aimed at understanding the monetary impact of GMS, we considered changes in significance across two steps for each cohort.

Limitations

While this study uses an appropriate logical model and statistical method, the study does have a few limitations that merit consideration by readers.

First, this study represents the initial test of a new logical model for research on major choice. Only a few prior studies have treated major choice as an outcome. The proposed model builds on the logic of this prior research, consistent with the logic of the student choice construct (St. John, Asker, & Hu, 2001). This study tests the logic of the new model on cohorts of lower division and upper division undergraduates, examining the influence of finances on educational choices.

Second, regression analysis does not "prove" causality. Rather, logic should guide the selection of independent variables. When variables are included that should have a logical linkage to the outcome, then it is generally acceptable to interpret significance as having an influence on the outcome. However, caution should be used when assuming causality from a single analysis. By using two cohorts in this study, we can build a better understanding of effects by comparing the analyses for the two cohorts.

While the GMS program was not designed as an experiment, the 2000 award year had quasi-experimental distribution of aid for the qualified group (St. John & Chung, 2003). First, students were selected as eligible based on GPA and noncognitive variables. Then, students were contacted to see if they met the financial criteria (i.e., Pell eligibility). In addition, some students who were Pell eligible were excluded to ensure racial balance or were not contacted. Thus, both the award and nonaward groups the met the noncognitive award criteria and there was variation in financial need within both groups. As long as proper statistical controls are used in appropriate statistical models, this was an appropriate database for examining the impact of student aid on major choices by college-qualified students.

2000 Freshmen

Students in the 2000 freshman cohort had been enrolled in college for nearly two years when they responded to the survey, sufficient time to make an initial major choice. The GMS award process did not explicitly consider major preferences. Further, if GMS attracted students predisposed toward specified majors, then all applicants would have a probability of having this predisposition. Therefore, the awards decisions and major choices are appropriately viewed as independent of each other. However, it is possible that the financial commitments for support in graduate school could have induced more GMS recipients to choose high-priority majors than did nonrecipients.

Student Characteristics

The distribution of major choices was similar across the two groups (Table 1). There were a few differences in background characteristics. There was a slightly higher percentage of Hispanics in the recipient group and a slightly higher percentage of Asian Americans in the nonrecipient group.

The differences in reasons for choosing a college were not substantial for the two groups. Scholarship/grant aid was very important for both groups. However, there were more Pell recipients (low-income students) in the GMS recipient populations. Thus, financial aid was important to most qualified applicants, but the GMS students had lower family incomes.

The patterns of major choice were very similar for the two groups, further indicating major preferences were not a factor in selection. About half of both groups chose other majors (50% of GMS recipients compared with 49% of others). Approximately 28 percent of both groups chose majors in math and science. The percentage of nonrecipients who chose engineering was slightly higher (18%, compared with 15% of GMS recipients), while the percentages of students choosing education and library/information science were nearly equal. Given the modest differences in major choices, we would not expect GMS to have had much influence.

There were differences in student engagement between the two groups. A higher percentage of GMS recipients participated in events conducted by cultural groups (47%, compared with 40%). GMS recipients also were somewhat more likely to participate in tutoring sessions (30%, compared with 24%), a difference that could be attributable to variations in student achievement and preparation[2] (St. John & Chung, 2003). Further, GMS recipients also were more likely to participate in community activities (30%, compared with 24%). However, similar percentages of the two groups had been involved in faculty research.

Table 1. 2000 Freshman Students: Descriptive Statistics for Variables in the Multinomial Logistic Regression for Choice of Major.

| Variable | Value | Gates Scholarship | | | |
| | | Recipient | | Nonrecipient | |
		Count	Col%	Count	Col%
Field of Declared Major	Mathematics & Sciences	170	28.9	250	28.2
	Engineering	88	15.0	162	18.2
	Education	29	5.0	36	4.1
	Library/Information Sci.	5	0.9	6	0.7
	All Other	294	50.1	432	48.7
Gender	Male	176	29.9	296	33.4
	Female	411	70.1	590	66.6
Ethnicity	African Americans	202	34.3	319	36.0
	American Indians	35	5.9	47	5.3
	Hispanic Americans	174	29.5	189	21.4
	Asian/Pacific Islanders	178	30.3	331	37.4
Reason expenses	Very important	258	44.0	409	46.2
	Other	329	56.0	477	53.8
Reason Scholarship/grant	Very important	515	87.7	653	73.7
	Other	72	12.3	233	26.3
Reason live at home	Very important	45	7.6	82	9.3
	Other	543	92.4	804	90.7
Received Pell Grant	Yes	520	89.3	232	26.4
	No	63	10.7	646	73.6
Parents contributed	Yes	222	37.8	568	64.1
	No	365	62.2	318	35.9
Cultural group	Very often or often	275	46.8	356	40.1
	Other	312	53.2	531	59.9
Tutoring sessions	Very often or often	177	30.2	209	23.6
	Other	410	69.8	677	76.4
Comm. service activity	Very often or often	282	48.1	383	43.2
	Other	305	51.9	504	56.8
Assisted on faculty research	Yes	129	22.0	195	22.0
	No	458	78.0	691	78.0
Support of one or more faculty	A lot	115	19.5	139	15.7
	Other	473	80.5	747	84.3

Table 1. 2000 Freshman Students: Descriptive Statistics for Variables in the Multinomial Logistic Regression for Choice of Major (continued).

Variable	Value	Gates Scholarship			
		Recipient		Nonrecipient	
		Count	Col %	Count	Col %
	Private	260	44.2	366	41.3
Institution Type in 2000 Fall	Public 2-year	8	1.3	25	2.8
	Public, 4-year or above	320	54.5	495	55.9
Debt (in $1,000)		2.409		6.736	
Grant (in 1,000)		13.745		8.504	
Valid cases		1,474			
Cases with missing values		355			
Total number of cases with relative weight		1,829			

Impact of GMS

Both gender and ethnicity were associated with major choices (Table 2). Male students were more likely than females to choose majors in math, science, engineering, and library/information sciences. However, females were more likely to choose majors in education. Hispanics were less likely than Asian Americans to choose majors in math, science, and engineering. African Americans also were less likely to choose majors in engineering, but more likely to choose majors in education.

The college choice variables were not associated with the major choices by students in the 2000 freshman cohort, raising the possibility that the two types of choices are not linked.

Student involvement variables were associated with major choice. Students choosing both math and science majors and engineering were more likely to participate in tutoring, possibly because these majors are more demanding academically.[3] Participation in activities organized by cultural groups was positively associated with choosing math and science majors, but negatively associated with choosing engineering majors.

Being involved with faculty on research was positively associated with choosing majors in math and science, but being supported by faculty was negatively associated with this major choice. In combination, these findings indicate a different mode of interaction between faculty and students in math and science than in other fields.

Table 2. The Impact of GMS on Major Choice for 2000 Freshman Students: Multinomial Logistic Regression Results.

Variable		Mathematics and Sciences		Engineering		Education		Library/Infor. Science	
		Odds Ratio	Sig.	Odds Ratio	Sig.	Odds Ratio	Sig.	Odds Ratio	Sig.
GMS	Recipient	1.0359		0.8289		1.1384		1.3675	
Gender	Male	1.4766	***	4.6898	***	0.4014	**	4.8269	**
Ethnicity	African Am.	0.9213		0.7287	*	1.7964	*	1.0721	
	Hispanic	0.6052	***	0.6569	**	1.6647		0.4259	
Low expenses	Very important	1.0608		0.9229		1.2144		0.8666	
Scholarship/grant	Very important	0.8169		0.9359		1.4377		4.0155	
Live at home	Very important	0.9762		0.9202		1.8467		2.3895	
Parents	Contributed	0.9633		0.9259		0.9640		1.0783	
Cultural group	Often	0.8804		0.9395		0.8777		0.9397	
Tutoring sessions	Often	1.7017	***	1.9898	***	0.6157		2.0791	
Comm. service	Often	1.4275	***	0.7268	*	1.3539		1.9016	
Assist on research	Yes	1.5453	***	0.9083		1.0034		0.2320	
Faculty support	A lot	0.7236	*	0.8237		0.6363		1.8572	
Institution Type Fall 2000	Private	0.8921		0.6893	**	0.6915		0.3615	
	Public 2-year	1.0011		0.5002		0.7326		6.2555	*
No. of cases w/relative weight =		1,474							
Model χ^2 =		229.016							
-2 Log Likelihood =		2,775.968							
Cox & Snell Pseudo R^2 =		0.144							

***<0.01, **<0.05, *<0.1

Minority students in private colleges were less likely to choose majors in engineering than students in public four-year colleges. Since private colleges frequently are liberal arts institutions, many do not offer engineering majors, a contextual factor that could explain this finding. In contrast, students in public two-year colleges were substantially more likely to major in library/information sciences.

GMS awards were not significantly associated with major choices for the freshman cohort, at least before aid amounts were considered. This finding was expected, given the major distributions reported above.

These findings raise the possibility that involvement enables students to acquire cultural capital. Specifically, the ability to choose some of the preferred majors was related to student engagement, including the time to work with faculty. Since GMS students were more engaged, it is logical that GMS could influence the process of building cultural capital.

The Impact of Aid Amounts

When the amounts of aid were considered, GMS recipients were less likely to choose engineering majors (Table 3). Scholarship/grant amounts were positively associated with the choice of engineering majors. In combination, it appears that the prospect of receiving the additional financial support GMS provides through graduate school may have influenced some students to choose engineering majors, but these effects were confounded with the effects of GMS (compare Tables 2 and 3).

The confounding relationship between GMS and scholarship is revealing. It is apparent that the positive effects of receiving scholarship dollars through GMS were offset by other program features. From the statistics comparing the two groups, it is evident that more low-income (Pell) students were included in the recipient population. Further, low-income students generally are less likely than middle-income students to aspire to engineering degrees because of differences in cultural capital (i.e., prior educational and cultural experiences associated with high education attainment). Therefore, it is possible that the funding through GMS helps the recipients overcome some of these differences.

Loan amounts were negatively associated with the choices of majors in math and science and in education. Education majors typically earn less than students in other majors, which could explain the influence of debt burden on the choices of education majors. However, the finding on debt and math and science majors is somewhat of a surprise. While math and science majors might earn more, they may have to get a graduate degree to do so.

Thus, it is possible that debt burden diminishes the choice of math and science majors among minority students because of the prospect of long-term debt. It is alarming that the educational choices of minority students have been negatively influenced by debt burden. Ironically, this finding further supports the linkage between grant funding for students and the formation of cultural capital.

Table 3. Impact of Aid Amount on Major Choices by 2000 Freshm Students: Multinomial Logistic Regression Results.

Variable		Mathematics/Sciences		Engineering		Education		Library/Infor. S	
		Odds Ratio	Sig.	Odds Ratio	Sig.	Odds Ratio	Sig.	Odds Ratio	Si
GMS	Recipient	0.9636		0.6975	**	1.0728		1.7828	
Gender	Male	1.4608	***	4.5285	***	0.4033	**	5.1016	*
Ethnicity	African Am.	0.9009		0.6955	*	1.7418	*	1.2255	
	Hispanic	0.5994	***	0.6459	**	1.6302		0.4410	
Low expenses	Very important	1.0494		0.9603		1.1194		0.7474	
Scholarship/ grant	Very important	0.8223		0.8484		1.5936		4.8292	
Live at home	Very important	0.9435		0.9325		1.6561		2.2898	
Parents	Contributed	0.9544		0.9428		0.9306		0.9904	
Cultural group	Often	0.8842		0.9588		0.9041		0.8731	
Tutoring	Often	1.7037	***	1.9867	***	0.6116		1.9614	
Comm. service	Often	1.4312	***	0.7220	*	1.3534		2.0099	
Research project	Yes	1.5399	***	0.8740		1.0249		0.2392	
Faculty support	A lot	0.7185	*	0.8329		0.6242		2.0029	
Institution Type in 2000 Fall	Private	0.9583		0.5745	***	1.0393		0.5143	
	Public 2-year	0.9635		0.5258		0.6233		4.5429	
Debt (in $1000)		0.9848	**	0.9834		0.9612	*	1.0283	
Grant (in $1000)		0.9992		1.0228	**	0.9701	*	0.9212	
No. of cases w/relative weight =		1,474							
Model χ^2 =		251.202							
-2 Log Likelihood =		3,232.038							
Cox & Snell Pseudo R^2 =		0.157							

***<0.01, **<0.05, *<0.1

In addition to having a positive association with the choice of engineering majors, scholarships had a negative association with the choice of education majors. There are two possible explanations for the findings about education and scholarship aid. Students choosing education majors may not be as likely to be influenced by monetary considerations as students in other fields. Further analyses would be needed to untangle these underlying relationships.

Only one other independent variable (in addition to GMS awards for engineering majors) changed in significance in the analysis of aid amounts. Being enrolled in two-year colleges was no longer significant, but the odds ratio remained high. Students in two-year colleges generally received less grant aid than students enrolled in four-year colleges, partially because of lower tuition. Therefore, it is not surprising that this change in significance was observed.

Continuing Students

Continuing students received GMS awards initially in fall 2000. Most still were enrolled or had graduated when they responded to the survey. The models used to examine major choice by continuing students were identical to those specified above for the 2000 freshman cohort.

Student Characteristics
There were slight differences in the major choices by GMS recipients compared with nonrecipients (Table 4). A slightly higher percentage of the nonrecipients were in majors outside the select group, while slightly more of the GMS recipients were in majors that would receive long-term funding.

The background characteristics and reasons for choosing college were similar for the two populations. There were more African Americans than other racial and ethnic groups among both recipients and nonrecipients. Most students in both groups considered scholarship grant aid to be very important in their college choice.

There were substantial differences in educational engagement between the two groups. More GMS recipients were involved in events organized by cultural groups. Higher percentages of GMS awardees were involved in tutoring sessions and community activities, assisted on research projects, and were supported by one or more faculty. This reinforces the finding that GMS recipients had more opportunities to engage in college life than did nonrecipients (Allen, 2003; Hurtado, 2003; Sedlacek, 2003).

Table 4. 2000 Continuing Students: Descriptive Statistics for Variables in the Multinomial Logistic Regression for Choice of Major.

| Variable | Value | Gates Scholarship | | | |
| | | Recipient | | Nonrecipient | |
		Count	Col%	Count	Col%
Declared Major Field	Mathematics and Sciences	220	30.1	190	27.8
	Engineering	102	13.9	99	14.5
	Education	70	9.6	48	7.1
	Library/Information Science	15	2.0	7	1.0
	All Other	325	44.4	338	49.5
Gender	Male	234	32.1	185	27.1
	Female	497	67.9	498	72.9
Ethnicity	African Americans	296	40.5	295	43.2
	American Indians	66	9.0	37	5.4
	Hispanic Americans	202	27.6	169	24.7
	Asian/Pacific Islanders	167	22.9	183	26.8
Reason expenses	Very important	384	52.5	345	50.4
	Other	348	47.5	339	49.6
Scholarship/grant	Very important	644	88.1	538	78.7
	Other	87	11.9	145	21.3
Could live at home	Very important	169	23.2	129	18.9
	Other	562	76.8	554	81.1
Strong reputation	Very important	555	75.8	532	77.9
	Other	177	24.2	151	22.1
Received Pell Grant	Yes	551	75.8	168	24.7
	No	176	24.2	512	75.3
Parents contributed	Yes	153	20.9	367	53.6
	No	579	79.1	317	46.4
Cultural group	Very often or often	329	44.9	234	34.2
	Other	403	55.1	450	65.8
Tutoring sessions	Very often or often	159	21.8	95	13.9
	Other	572	78.2	589	86.1
Comm. service	Very often or often	370	50.5	283	41.5
	Other	362	49.5	400	58.5

Table 4. 2000 Continuing Students: Descriptive Statistics for Variables in the Multinomial Logistic Regression for Choice of Major (continued).

Variable	Value	Gates Scholarship			
		Recipient		Nonrecipient	
		Count	Col%	Count	Col%
Research project	Yes	261	35.7	217	31.8
	No	470	64.3	466	68.2
Support of faculty	A lot	256	35.0	204	29.9
	Other	476	65.0	479	70.1
	Private	284	38.8	319	46.7
	Public 2-year	38	5.2	22	3.2
	Public, 4-year or above	409	56.0	342	50.1
Debt (in $1,000)		7.660		12.300	
Grant (in $1,000)		11.778		7.698	
Valid cases		1,415			
Cases with missing values		751			
Total number of cases with relative weight		2,166			

The Impact of GMS

GMS awards were positively associated with the choice of education majors, but not with the other majors (Table 5). However, most of the other variables in the model had a more substantial influence on major choices.

Gender and ethnicity were associated with major choice. Males were more likely to choose science and math, engineering, and library/information science majors, consistent with the analyses of the freshman cohort. Once again, African Americans and Hispanics were less likely to choose engineering majors. American Indians and Hispanics, along with African Americans, were more likely to choose education majors.

Students who chose a major because of a scholarship or grant were less likely to choose education majors, providing a further indicator that the choice of education was not related to finances per se. It is entirely possible that the positive effects of GMS on education major choice are attributable to the long-term financial commitment, which enables students to attain their goals without acquiring high levels of debt. Debt can be problematic for education majors because of their lower expected earnings.

Table 5. The Impact of GMS on Major Choice for 2000 Continuing Students: Multinomial Logistic Regression Results.

Variable		Mathematics and Sciences		Engineering		Education		Library and Infor. Science	
		Odds Ratio	Sig.	Odds Ratio	Sig.	Odds Ratio	Sig.	Odds Ratio	Sig.
GMS	Recipient	1.2046		0.8903		1.5429	*	1.7131	
Gender	Male	1.3810	**	4.6644	***	0.7417		3.8044	***
Ethnicity	African Am.	0.8115		0.6440	**	2.1954	**	0.8351	
	Am. Indian	0.8528		0.6280		3.7390	***	1.4901	
	Hispanic Am.	0.7997		0.4957	***	2.1798	**	0.8823	
Low expenses	Very important	0.9391		0.7745		1.3006		0.7422	
Scholarship/grant	Very important	1.2251		0.9176		0.5316	**	0.9807	
Live at home	Very important	1.0842		0.5485	**	1.4154		1.1265	
Reputation	Very important	0.8931		1.3429		1.2115		0.7578	
Parents	Contributed	1.2830	*	0.7584		0.9288		1.0169	
Cultural group	Often	0.8512		0.8604		0.9577		1.8513	
Tutoring	Often	2.1556	***	2.2107	***	0.8015		1.4522	
Comm. service	Often	0.9514		0.5192	***	0.8536		1.6079	
Research project	Yes	1.6892	***	2.0338	***	0.6695		0.5734	
Faculty support	A lot	0.7814	*	0.6901	*	1.0285		0.5833	
Institution Type in 2000 Fall	Private	0.9785		0.4707	***	1.2125		0.6533	
	Public 2-year	1.0461		0.5396		2.1093	*	0.6119	
N. cases w/relative weight =		1,415							
Model χ^2 =		277.502							
-2 Log Likelihood =		3,093.843							
Cox & Snell Pseudo R^2 =		0.178							

***<0.01, **<0.05, *<0.1

Choosing colleges because they were close to home was negatively associated with being engineering majors. This finding is illuminating when juxtaposed with others in this study. It already is evident that choosing a college close to home was closely related to finances (e.g., St. John & Chung, 2003) and that Hispanics were more likely to have made this choice. Engineering programs are not as widely disbursed across state systems of higher education as are most other education programs, an artifact of the higher costs associated with engineering programs (Halstead, 1974). For the continuing students, GMS awards were made later than for the freshman groups. Awardees were not able to adjust their college choices like some freshman GMS recipients who received awards in the midst of making these decisions. Therefore, the analysis reveals the logical relationship between these choice phenomena.

Choosing a college because of a strong reputation was not associated with major choice in either analysis (i.e., for neither freshmen nor continuing students). Thus, while a sustained link exists between financial choices (i.e., recurrence of the financial nexus phenomena), the academic nexus is not as visible. Students choosing colleges because of their reputations were not more likely to choose higher prestige science or engineering majors.

Parental contributions were positively associated with decisions to pursue majors in math and science. Parents with "high" incomes generally can afford to contribute more. It is possible that the prospects of long-term enrollment and high debt burden are mitigating factors in the choice of science and math majors because of the negative effects of debt (see analyses of aid amounts above and below).

Again, a relationship was seen between tutoring and the selection of majors in both math and science and engineering. The two sets of analyses provide compelling evidence that many minority students who pursue technical majors must seek additional tutoring support. It is possible that GMS enabled more students to major in these areas as an artifact of the higher percentage of GMS students being involved in tutoring. Apparently, money buys the time needed to find the support necessary to pursue highly demanding courses in math, science, and engineering.

Being involved in community service activities was negatively associated with majoring in engineering by continuing students (Table 5), consistent with the analysis of the 2000 freshman cohort. This could be an artifact of the time required to complete engineering majors or the culture of these majors, a topic that merits further exploration.

Assisting faculty with research was positively associated with choosing majors in math and science and engineering, consistent with the analysis of the 2000 freshman cohort. However, being supported by one or more faculty was negatively associated with majoring in both math and science and engineering, another finding that was consistent across the two cohorts. These patterns may be related to the nature of scholarship in these fields, especially in advanced courses. Nevertheless, these findings merit further exploration by researchers and policymakers interested in encouraging more minority students to enroll in these fields. If the lack of faculty support is an inhibiting factor for minorities, as is abundantly evident here, but not for Whites, then faculty support is seriously problematic.

Minority students choosing engineering majors were less likely to be enrolled in private colleges, while students enrolled in public two-year colleges were more likely to choose education majors.[4] It is entirely possible that this finding is an artifact of the distribution of major programs across different types of institutions.

The Impact of Aid Amounts

The impact of GMS awards was even more substantial after aid amounts were considered (Table 6). The size of the odds ratio increased and the level of significance increased. Further, the amount of grant/scholarship awards was negatively associated with this major choice. Thus, the effects of GMS awards on the decision to major in education is distinct from the increase in the amount of aid received, a finding consistent for both groups. We explore the meaning of this finding in the conclusion below.

The amount of grant aid awarded was positively associated with choosing majors in math and science and engineering. Thus, finances have a clear link to the education choice process for minority students.

Loan burden was negatively associated with the choice of math and science majors, consistent with the analysis above. It is possible that GMS had an indirect association with the major choice process because it reduced debt burden. However, the fact that debt burden is negatively associated with major choices in both analyses is troubling. It is apparent that debt burden has intruded into the educational choice process for minority students.

Table 6. The Impact of Aid Amount on Major Choices by 2000 Continuing Students: Multinomial Logistic Regression Results.

Variable		Mathematics / Sciences		Engineering		Education		Library/Infor. Science	
		Odds Ratio	Sig.	Odds Ratio	Sig.	Odds Ratio	Sig.	Odds Ratio	Sig.
GMS	Recipient	1.0858		0.7960		1.7346	**	1.9072	
Gender	Male	1.4022	**	4.7365	***	0.7378		3.7527	***
Ethnicity	African Am.	0.8244		0.6523	**	2.2264	**	0.8571	
	Am. Indians	0.8339		0.6130		3.7224	***	1.6104	
	Hispanic Am.	0.7987		0.5017	***	2.1659	**	0.9344	
Low expenses	Very important	0.9582		0.8026		1.1487		0.7385	
Scholarship/grant	Very important	1.1877		0.8771		0.5545	**	1.0113	
Live at home	Very important	1.1440		0.5847	**	1.2931		1.1389	
Reputation	Very important	0.9111		1.3833		1.2261		0.7299	
Parents	Yes	1.2818	*	0.7624		0.8479		1.1029	
Cultural group	Often	0.8718		0.8662		0.9942		1.8669	
Tutoring	Often	2.1090	***	2.1588	***	0.7857		1.4933	
Comm. service	Often	0.9562		0.5246	***	0.8464		1.5964	
Research project	Yes	1.6453	***	1.9527	***	0.6984		0.5572	
Faculty support	A lot	0.7731	*	0.6876	*	1.0513		0.5839	
Institution Type	Private	0.9423		0.4273	***	1.5861	*	0.5621	
in 2000 Fall	Public 2-year	1.0230		0.5237		2.1362	*	0.6366	
Debt (in $1,000)		0.9898	*	0.9896		0.9898		1.0153	
Grant (in $1,000)		1.0133	**	1.0187	**	0.9530	***	1.0011	
Number of cases w/ relative weight =		1,415							
Model χ^2 =		308.873							
-2 Log Likelihood =		3,264.567							
Cox & Snell Pseudo R^2 =		0.196							

***<0.01, **<0.05, *<0.1

Only one variable changed in significance when the amount of aid was considered. Attending private colleges was positively associated with the decision to major in education after the amount of aid was considered. While private colleges are less likely to offer engineering programs, they frequently offer education programs. The reasons students in private colleges choose education merit exploration in future studies.

Conclusions

Research on major choice by minority students is scant, and the current study adds substantially to the research base in this area. Three of the findings from this study provide information that confirms the design features of the GMS Program.

First, GMS awards had a direct effect on some educational choices. GMS appeared to enable some recipients in the 2000 freshman cohort to choose majors in engineering. It is reasonable that GMS awards would influence freshmen but not continuing students to major in engineering. The potential for receiving support during college apparently had an influence on this choice. However, continuing students were not as directly responsive because the decision to change to an engineering major often means more years of undergraduate study, given the extensive prerequisites in engineering. The immediate monetary aspect was evident because this variable was significant only after the amount of aid was considered, that is, after the positive effect of the additional aid was considered.

It also is important to recognize that engineering is a highly structured major that is easier to complete if students begin their studies in that field. Therefore, it is not surprising that there was no relationship for continuing students between choosing an engineering major and receiving a GMS. Further, engineering is a field with a high attrition rate, given the demanding nature of the courses. Studies of subsequent surveys of the 2000 freshmen should consider whether GMS mitigates transfer to other fields from engineering. It is possible that the additional time for study afforded by GMS awards could reduce attrition from engineering by low-income minority students.

GMS also had a direct influence on decisions by continuing students to choose majors in education. This effect was not related to the amount of aid provided by GMS because the effect size and significance increased after the amounts of aid were added to the model. Rather, it appears that GMS enables students to choose education in spite of the lower earnings associated with this major. It is possible that this is an intrinsic choice—for example, that GMS students chose education out of personal interests and commitment. It also is possible that they chose the major because of the potential for receiving aid during graduate school. In addition, it is apparent that the decision to choose a major in education is related to the type of college attended. Students in community colleges and private colleges were more likely to choose education than were students in public four-year colleges.

In combination, these findings provide evidence that GMS is achieving at least one of its goals. GMS awards enable students to choose undergraduate majors in fields that are preferred by the program designers and that are thought to be in the public interest. This finding has substantial implications for education policy, some of which are explored below.

Second, the amount of debt burden was negatively associated with some major choices. Evidence from prior research has shown that minorities are more likely to choose majors with linkages to employment (St. John, Hu, Simmons, Carter, & Weber, in press). However, this is the first study to provide evidence that debt burden inhibits major choices by high-achieving minority students. It has long been speculated that debt could discourage students from choosing majors for educational reasons (Kramer & Van Dusen, 1986; Newman, 1985), but this hypothesis has not previously been confirmed for either majority or minority students (St. John, 1994).

It is possible that growth in student debt has influenced many low-income minority students to avoid education careers. There is evidence that minorities have more debt than Whites because they are from low-income families (Kaltenbaugh et al., 1999; Paulsen, St. John, & Carter, 2002). High debt is problematic in the field of education because salaries are lower than in business and many other applied fields. Thus, the growth in debt contributes to the problems facing education reform in the U.S., given that debt inhibits students from choosing education as a major and career.

But the problem with debt is not limited to education. Indeed, debt was also negatively associated with majoring in science and math. Advanced degrees are needed to gain opportunity for higher earning in the sciences. Yet, from this study, it is apparent that some minorities lack sufficient support from faculty to go on academically. Debt burden adds to the problem, but it is not the only source of the problem facing minority students who seek opportunities in math and science.

The finding that debt was negatively associated with the choice of majors in math and science is the most important finding on the impact of debt. Not only was this finding evident for both populations, but representation of people of color among the nation's scientists remains an important social and policy issue. Apparently, high levels of debt, coupled with the prospect of long years of study and modest earnings (compared with business, law, and medicine) dissuade some minorities from choosing majors in the sciences.

Third, receiving a GMS award enabled students to become more engaged in college (Allen, et al., chapter 4; Hurtado, et al., chapter 6; Sedlacek & Sheu, chapter 7), and this engagement was associated with educational choice. Thus, GMS has an indirect effect on education choices by minority students because it provides the opportunity to become engaged in student life and to work more directly with faculty. This serves as a validation of the design concept behind the GMS program.

Thus, there is strong, compelling evidence that the design of the GMS program not only facilitates students' college choices and enables them to persist better (St. John & Chung, chapter 5), but that it also encourages students to choose majors fields that need more minority professionals. In the process of investigating the effects of GMS, we also documented fundamental problems with the current system of federal student aid.

Implications

This examination of the impact of financial aid on major choices adds substantially to the knowledge base regarding this issue. For the past two decades, there has been repeated speculation that the overemphasis on federal loans was having an influence on education choices, including the choice of academic majors. To untangle the meaning of these findings for education policy, it is important to situate the results in an understanding of the government role in labor force development.

Before the 1960s, the primary federal role in supporting college students was to fund those who pursued a college education in fields that were in high demand (Finn, 1978; Halstead, 1974). Even after the Higher Education Act (HEA) of 1965 created generally available student aid programs,[5] the specially directed programs were substantially larger than the need-based programs. The impact of specially directed programs in health and other areas seldom was evaluated. Over time, specially directed aid was replaced by generally available aid. Some federal programs targeted labor in specific fields, other programs provided aid to specific groups (e.g., veterans, healthcare workers, children of deceased workers). The movement toward generally available aid since 1965[6] made aid more accessible and in this sense was more just, but reductions in grant aid after 1980 caused problems for low-income students (St. John, 2003).

The GMS program has features related to generally available need-based grant aid and features related to the earlier specially directed programs. Our other paper on GMS documents how the need-based features of the program—especially the explicit focus on meeting financial need—enable high-achieving, low-income students to maintain continuous enrollment. It also reveals that the opportunity for high-achieving, low-income minority students to attend four-year colleges has been constrained by finances. Providing GMS awards improves the odds for low-income minority students to enroll in private colleges and attend public four-year colleges. In addition, providing adequate grant aid improves the odds that funded students will persist. In combination, these findings illustrate the inadequacy of federal aid.

This paper examines the specially directed aspect of GMS. The GMS program makes a commitment to provide continued funding through graduate school for students choosing to continue their education in selected high-demand fields in which minorities are underrepresented. This study confirms that this long-term commitment, along with the additional resources provided in the short term, influences students' choice of major in some fields. However, the study also reveals that debt burden is a crucial cause of the shortage of minority representation in education, engineering, and scientific fields. This provides clear evidence that debt burden has entered the domain of education choice in a problematic way.

The reasons debt constrains students' choices to pursue majors in education and science and math are different, revealing the complex and destructive ways debt invades the educational choice process. Students in math and science were more likely to work with faculty on research and to become engaged in their major fields. The negative influence of debt on choosing majors in science may be related to the prospect of the large levels of debt necessary to attain the advanced degrees needed in these fields. GMS helps mitigate this worry about debt by providing more opportunity for students to work with faculty and gain their support (St. John, in preparation). Through this indirect process, the GMS program is enabling more minority students to follow interests in the fields of science and math.

The education story is different but not less revealing. Education majors were not as likely to be persuaded by scholarship aid. Their major choices apparently were intrinsic, related to interest rather than to the amount of grant aid. However, debt dissuaded potential education majors from following their interests because it may be problematic relative to earnings.

These findings further confirm the inadequacy of the current federal student aid programs. They also show that financial aid provides a mechanism for states to influence labor force development. Two possibilities merit consideration: targeting grant aid to undergraduates in select high-demand fields and forgiving loans for students who pursue education or choose careers in high-demand fields. While loan forgiveness has been tried in the past (e.g., for teacher education), it has seldom been studied and remains a little-understood policy instrument. Given the negative effect of debt, it is probable that targeted debt relief would have an influence on labor force development.

Notes

1. American Indians were not considered in the 2000 freshman cohort because of the small number of American Indians in the sample.
2. We did not carry forward the measures of achievement in this model, but tutoring could be a proxy for lower achievement (or test scores) before college.
3. In previous research, having high grades was associated with choosing higher-earning majors like engineering (St. John, 1994a). Therefore, it is possible that tutoring is a proxy measure of needing

to make up for deficiencies in prior preparation, a situation that could relate to the difficulty of some majors as well as the quality of schools attended.

4. In the analysis of the freshman cohort, above, attending two-year colleges was positively associated with choosing a library/information science major. Programs in education and library/information science may be major options for many community colleges.

5. The National Defense Education Act of 1958 actually created the National Defense Student Loan Program (now called the Federal Perkins Loan Program), the first generally available federal student aid program. The HEA of 1965 reauthorized this program and College Work-Study while creating the first generally available grant program, Educational Opportunity Grants, renamed Supplemental Educational Opportunity Grants in 1972.

6. Before the Higher Education Act, federal student grants were directed to special populations, such as veterans. The HEA provided need-based grants that were "generally available" based on financial need and were not directed toward special populations.

References

Aldrich, J. H., & Nelson, F. D. (1986). *Linear probability, logit and probit models*. Beverly Hills, CA: Sage.

Allen, W. (2003). *Who goes to college? High school context, academic preparation, the college choice process, and college attendance.* Prepared for the Bill & Melinda Gates Foundation, Seattle, WA.

Becker, G. S. (1964). *Human capital: A theoretical and empirical analysis with special reference to education*. New York: Columbia University Press.

Blau, P., & Duncan, O. D. (1967). *The American occupational structure*. New York: Wiley.

Finn, C. E., Jr. (1978). *Scholars, dollars and bureaucrats*. Washington, DC: The Brookings Institution.

Halstead, D. K. (1974). *Statewide planning in higher education*. Washington, DC: U.S. Government Printing Office.

Hurtado, S. (2003). *The transition to college for low-income students: The impact of the Gates Millennium Scholars Program.* Prepared for the Bill & Melinda Gates Foundation, Seattle, WA.

Kaltenbaugh, L. S., St. John, E. P., & Starkey, J. B. (1999). What difference does tuition make? An analysis of ethnic differences in persistence. *Journal of Student Financial Aid, 29* (2), 21-32.

Kramer, M. A., & Van Dusen, W. D. (1986). Living on credit. *Change,* May/June, 10-19.

Kuh, G. D., & Love, P. G. (2000). A cultural perspective on student departure. In J. Braxton (Ed.), *Reworking the student departure puzzle.* Nashville: Vanderbilt University Press.

Newman, F. 1985. *Higher education and the American resurgence.* A Carnegie Foundation special report. Lawrenceville, NJ: Princeton University Press.

Paulsen, M. B., & St. John, E. P. (2002). Social class and college costs: Examining the financial nexus between college choice and persistence. *Journal of Higher Education, 73* (2), 189-236.

Paulsen, M. B., St. John, E. P., & Carter, D. F. (2002). Diversity, college costs, and postsecondary opportunity: An examination of the financial nexus between college choice and persistence. *Policy Research Report # 02-1.* Bloomington, IN: Indiana Education Policy Center.

Peng, C. Y. J., So, T. H. S., Stage, F. K., & St. John, E. P. (2002). The use and interpretation of logistic regression in higher education: 1988-1999. *Research in Higher Education, 43,* 259-294.

Schrag, P. G. (2002). *Repay as you earn: The flawed government program to help students have public service careers.* Westport, CT: Greenwood Publishing Group.

Sedlacek, W. E. (2003). *Correlates of leadership activities of Gates Millennium Scholars.* Prepared for the Bill & Melinda Gates Foundation, Seattle, WA.

Sedlacek, W. E. (in press). *Measurement and evaluation in counseling and development.* San Francisco: Jossey-Bass.

St. John, E. P. (1994). The influence of debt on choice of major. *Journal of Student Financial Aid, 24* (1), 5-12.

St. John, E. P. (2003). *Refinancing the college dream: Access, equal opportunity, and justice for taxpayers.* Baltimore: Johns Hopkins University Press.

St. John, E. P. (in preparation). *Diverse pathways.* A report being prepared for the Bill & Melinda Gates Foundation, Seattle, WA.

St. John, E. P., Asker, E. H., & Hu, S. (2001). College choice and student persistence behavior: The role of financial policies. In M. B. Paulsen & J. C. Smart (Eds.), *The finance of higher education: Theory, research, policy & practice* (pp. 419-436). New York: Agathon.

St. John, E. P., Cabrera, A. F., Nora, A., & Asker, E. H. (2000). Economic influences on persistence reconsidered: How can finance research inform the reconceptualization of persistence models? In J. M. Braxton (Ed.), *Rethinking the student departure puzzle: New theory and research on college student retention* (pp. 29-47). Nashville: Vanderbilt University Press.

St. John, E. P., & Chung, C. G. (2003). *The impact of GMS on financial access: Analyses of the 2000 freshman cohort.* Prepared for the Bill & Melinda Gates Foundation, Seattle, WA.

St. John, E. P., Hu, S., Simmons, A. B., Carter, D. F., & Weber, J. (in press). What difference does a major make? The influence of college major field on persistence by African American and white students. *Review of Higher Education.*

St. John, E. P., Musoba, G. D., Simmons, A. B., & Chung, C. G. (2002). *Meeting the access challenge: Indiana's Twenty-first Century Scholars Program.* New Agenda Series, vol. 4, no. 4. Indianapolis: Lumina Foundation for Education.

St. John, E. P., Paulsen, M. B., &. Starkey, J. B. (1996). The nexus between college choice and persistence. *Research in Higher Education, 37* (2), 175-220.

Thomas, G. E. (1985). College major and career inequality: Implications for Black students. *Journal of Negro Education, 54,* 537-547.

Tinto, V. (2000). Linking leaving and learning: Exploring the role of the college classroom in student departure. In J. M. Braxton (Ed.), *Reworking the student departure puzzle* (pp. 81-94). Nashville: Vanderbilt University Press.

CHAPTER 10

CORRELATES OF LEADERSHIP ACTIVITIES OF GATES MILLENNIUM SCHOLARS

William E. Sedlacek and Hung-Bin Sheu

A major goal of the Gates Millennium Scholars (GMS) program is to develop future leaders of color. The program promotes leadership through its annual Leadership Conferences for Scholars after they matriculate into higher education. What is the leadership potential of the Scholars and how can this potential best be developed? By examining items that have been shown to correlate with leadership development, we can help Scholars achieve their potential in school and beyond.

Bowen and Bok (1998) found that African American students who attended highly selective institutions made important contributions to their communities as leaders after they left school. This current study is part of a larger 20-year longitudinal study of GMS recipients and a comparison group of GMS nominees who did not receive awards. The GMS longitudinal study provides an opportunity to investigate a much larger and more diverse group of students of color than the group studied by Bowen and Bok. GMS recipients were chosen on the basis of a number of noncognitive variables, including their leadership abilities (Sedlacek, 1998; 2003a; 2004; in press).

Students of color who show evidence of leadership prior to matriculation into college are more likely to be successful students than those without such leadership experience. Leadership ability is an important asset to any student but may take on different forms in students of color. Further, because many White students have more support built into the system, leadership ability is not as critical an attribute for them to demonstrate for admission to college.

Students of color who are most successful in higher education have shown an ability to influence and organize others. Obtaining nontraditional evidence of the student's ability to lead is what seems to be important. Application forms and interviews typically yield less useful information about the backgrounds of nontraditional students. Many White applicants know how to "play the game" and will have held a wide variety of offices in traditional school organizations. However, many students of color will not have had the time or inclination to get involved in such activities because they may be occupied with family or work responsibilities (Allen, 1992). The GMS application was carefully designed to cover many aspects of leadership, both traditional and nontraditional.

The most promising students of color may have shown their leadership in less typical ways, such as working in their communities, through religious organizations, or even as street gang leaders (Allen, 1992). It is important to pursue the cultural and gender-relevant activities of the applicants rather than to treat them all as if they come from similar environments. For example, Liu and Sedlacek (1999) found that Asian American students showed leadership in ways that were unique and culture related, such as through their family and organizations related to their culture. Fuertes and Sedlacek (1993) concluded that the major barriers to Latino leadership development were institutional racism, encouraged assimilation, and a lack of knowledge about Hispanic values. If an applicant succeeds in his or her culture and is ready to "take on" college, there is evidence that the student has the potential to succeed.

Assertiveness is an important component in leadership as a predictor of success (Sedlacek, 1998, 1996a,b, 2003a, 2004, in press). For students of color, a passive style of relating to others will result in their being denied many opportunities in a system that is not optimally designed for them. Seeking out resources, both human and environmental, is correlated with success for students of color. While such activities are positive for any student, they are particularly important for students of color.

Tracey and Sedlacek (1984a,b, 1985, 1987, 1988, 1989) and White and Shelley (1996) showed evidence of the value of leadership in retaining Hispanic American and American Indian/Alaska Native students in higher education. They also found that leadership is predictive of success in school for African American undergraduate students, just as Webb, et al. (1997) found for female African American medical students.

Method

Participants

Gates Millennium Scholars who received an award in 2000 as first-year baccalaureate students were included in the study. In addition, a group of GMS applicants who did not receive a GMS award (Non-Scholars), but were attending a college or university as first-year baccalaureate students, was included for purposes of comparison.

To be eligible for a GMS award, individuals must be African American, American Indian/Alaska Native, Asian Pacific Islander American, or Hispanic American. American Indian/Alaska Native applicants must show a certificate of tribal enrollment or proof of descendency to be considered. Additional eligibility requirements include having a secondary school GPA of 3.3 on a 4-point scale, having significant financial need (i.e., meeting the Federal Pell Grant eligibility criteria), and having demonstrated leadership abilities through participation in community service, extracurricular, or other activities. Awards are based on student need and cover the costs of tuition, fees, books, and living expenses at the institution of higher education the student attends. Applicants must submit an application, a nominator form, and a recommender form.

The sample consisted of 1,829 participants (1,087 Scholars and 742 Non-Scholars), 65 percent of whom were juniors or above and 35 percent sophomores or first-year students. The sample consisted of the following groups: African Americans (31%),

Asian Pacific Islander Americans (33%), Hispanic Americans (31%), and American Indians/Alaska Natives (5%). Seventy percent of the participants were female and 30 percent were male. While 48 percent of the participants held some kind of campus leadership position, 52 percent did not.

Instrument

A 120-item instrument was administered to participants in the spring and summer of 2002 by the National Opinion Research Center (NORC). The instrument contained a variety of items on student activities, adjustments, and attitudes. (See Appendix for items and response modes.)

Data Analyses

Independent variables included participation in campus leadership activities (yes/no), receipt of GMS award (Scholar/Non-Scholar), and gender (male/female). Dependent variables included the following: (a) internal locus of control, 5 items; (b) self-esteem, 7 items; (c) academic esteem, 4 items; (d) academic engagement, 5 items; and (e) community engagement, 6 items. Chi-square tests were conducted to test the independence among three independent variables (participation in leadership activities, Scholar/Non-Scholar, and gender). Also, because of different cell sizes, five 2 (participation/nonparticipation) × 2 (Scholar/Non-Scholar) × 2 (male/female) three-way multivariate General Linear Models were performed on five sets of dependent variables (internal locus of control, self-esteem, academic self-esteem, academic engagement, and community engagement). All tests were conducted at the .05 level of significance. Where appropriate, effect sizes (η^2) were also reported.

Results

Leadership Positions

As seen in Table 1, descriptive statistics show that there tended to be more Non-Scholars than Scholars within African American, American Indian/Alaska Native, and Asian Pacific Islander American groups who held a campus leadership position. However, Chi-square tests indicated that these differences were not significant. There was no gender difference on the probability of holding campus leadership positions. Overall, there tended to be more Non-Scholars (721, 50%) than Scholars (1,061, 47%) who were involved in campus leadership activities, although the differences were not significant.

Table 1. Chi-Square Tests of Scholar/Non-Scholar and Participation in in a Campus Leadership Position for Each Racial Group.

		African Americans N = 555 (52%)		American Indians/Alaska Natives N = 94 (33%)		Asian Pacific Islander Americans N = 584 (49%)		Hispanic Americans N = 549 (46%)	
		S	N-S	S	N-S	S	N-S	S	N-S
Leadership position	Yes	169	118	12	19	166	122	149	101
	No	174	94	37	26	178	118	176	123
Subtotal		343 (49%)	212 (56%)	49 (24%)	45 (42%)	344 (48%)	240 (51%)	325 (46%)	224 (45%)
		$\chi^2 = 2.14$		$\chi^2 = 3.34$		$\chi^2 = .38$		$\chi^2 = .03$	

Note. S: Scholar; N-S: Non-Scholar. Chi-square tests were conducted using two-tailed critical values. None was significant at the .05 level. Numbers in parentheses are percentages of students who held a campus leadership position within the cell.

Leadership and Internal Locus of Control

There were no three-way or two-way interactions. Those who participated in campus leadership activities had higher internal locus of control than those who did not ($\lambda = .984$; $p < .0001$; $\eta^2 = .016$), while Scholars had higher internal locus of control than Non-Scholars ($\lambda = .986$; $p < .0001$; $\eta^2 = .014$). Females had higher internal locus of control than males ($\lambda = .990$; $p = .003$; $\eta^2 = .010$). See Table 2 for descriptive statistics and results of univariate significance tests, and Appendix for complete items and response modes.

Table 2. Group Differences by Leadership Position, Scholar/Non-Scholar, and Gender on Internal Locus of Control.

	Campus Leadership Position							
	Yes			No				
	M	N	SD	M	N	SD	F	η^2
Enough control	3.20	851	.74	3.04	922	.82	18.34**	.010
Importance of luck	3.44	852	.67	3.40	918	.69	1.54	.001
Control to get ahead	3.12	853	.68	3.05	913	.69	3.94*	.002
Planning	3.37	852	.64	3.23	919	.67	18.62**	.011
Make plans work[a]	3.19	848	.68	3.12	920	.67	4.85*	.003
	Scholars			Non-Scholars				
	M	N	SD	M	N	SD	F	η^2
Enough Control	3.14	1076	.78	3.09	722	.78	2.55	.001
Importance of luck	3.47	1072	.65	3.33	723	.73	16.40**	.011
Control to get ahead	3.10	1070	.68	3.06	720	.70	.77	.001
Planning	3.30	1075	.65	3.28	722	.68	.44	0
Make plans work[a]	3.19	1074	.65	3.10	719	.70	5.53*	.003
	Male			Female				
	M	N	SD	M	N	SD	F	η^2
Enough control	3.10	547	.76	3.13	1251	.80	1.15	.001
Importance of luck	3.32	546	.72	3.46	1249	.67	12.16**	.008
Control to get ahead	3.07	546	.67	3.09	1244	.69	.09	0
Planning	3.27	546	.64	3.31	1251	.68	1.16	.001
Make plans work[a]	3.18	545	.63	3.14	1248	.68	.90	.001

Note. [a] Item is reflected as stated in the survey. * $p < .05$; ** $p < .01$. Total N may not be equal to 1,829 due to incomplete data.

Leadership and Self-Esteem

There were no three-way or two-way interactions and no main effect of Scholar/Non-Scholar. Those who participated in campus leadership activities had higher self-esteem than those who did not (λ = .982; p < .0001; $\eta 2$ = .018). Males tended to have higher self-esteem than females, as measured by seven self-esteem items as a whole (λ = .987; p = .002; $\eta 2$ = .013). See Table 3 for descriptive statistics and results of univariate significance tests.

Leadership and Academic Esteem

There were no three-way or two-way interactions and no main effect of Scholar/Non-Scholar on academic self-esteem. Those who were involved in campus leadership activities had higher academic self-esteem than those who were not (λ = .985; p < .0001; η^2 = .015), whereas females had higher academic self-esteem than males (λ = .991; p = .003; η^2 = .009). See Table 4 for descriptive statistics and results of univariate significance tests.

Table 3. Group Differences by Leadership Position and Gender on Self-Esteem.

| | Campus Leadership Position | | | | | | | |
| | Yes | | | No | | | | |
	M	N	SD	M	N	SD	F	η^2
Feel good about self [a]	3.43	853	.68	3.31	920	.67	14.64**	.008
A person of worth [a]	3.54	850	.60	3.46	919	.61	7.46**	.004
Do things well [a]	3.42	853	.68	3.41	922	.61	.06	0
Satisfied w/self [a]	3.39	852	.69	3.28	922	.69	11.46**	.007
Feel useless at times	3.03	852	.86	2.91	916	.84	10.06**	.006
Feel no good at all	3.06	849	.89	2.98	916	.87	3.87*	.002
Nothing to be proud of	3.52	853	.69	3.39	920	.73	14.69**	.008
	Male			Female				
	M	N	SD	M	N	SD	F	η^2
Feel good about self [a]	3.41	547	.67	3.35	1252	.68	2.79	.002
A person of worth [a]	3.49	545	.61	3.50	1248	.61	.39	0
Do things well [a]	3.47	547	.64	3.39	1254	.65	5.44*	.003
Satisfied w/self [a]	3.33	546	.71	3.33	1254	.69	.01	0
Feel useless at times	2.99	546	.85	2.96	1248	.86	.50	0
Feel no good at all	3.04	545	.87	3.00	1245	.88	.98	.001
Nothing to be proud of	3.41	548	.74	3.47	1250	.70	2.31	.001

Note: [a] Items are stated in reverse in the survey. * p < .05; ** p < .01. Total N may not be equal to 1,829 due to incomplete data.

Table 4. Group Differences by Leadership Position and Gender on Academic Self-Esteem.

| | Campus Leadership Position | | | | | | | |
| | Yes | | | No | | | | |
	M	N	SD	M	N	SD	F	η^2
Don't do well in school	3.32	849	.74	3.30	907	.71	.06	0
Be an honor student[a]	3.82	844	.86	2.95	913	.85	17.08**	.010
Get higher grades[a]	2.19	832	.87	2.26	895	.88	1.66	.001
Not make it through	3.50	851	.71	3.36	920	.75	12.55**	.007
	Male			Female				
	M	N	SD	M	N	SD	F	η^2
Don't do well in school	3.21	543	.75	3.35	1239	.71	14.00**	.008
Be an honor student[a]	3.02	539	.86	3.04	1241	.86	.49	0
Get higher grades[a]	2.25	531	.88	2.22	1220	.87	.18	0
Not make it through	3.42	547	.72	3.43	1249	.73	.01	0

Note. [a] Items are reflected as stated in the survey. * p < .05; ** p < .01. Total N may not be equal to 1,829 due to incomplete data.

Leadership and Academic Engagement

There was a two-way interaction ($\lambda = .992$; $p = .016$; $\eta^2 = .008$) between participation in leadership activities and Scholar/Non-Scholar. The main effect of gender ($\lambda = .973$; $p < .0001$; $\eta^2 = .027$) was significant, with males being more academically engaged than females. The results of simple main effect analyses indicated that those students who held a campus leadership position were more academically engaged than those who did not, which was true for both Scholars and Non-Scholars. However, only among those students who did not participate in leadership activities were Scholars found to be more academically engaged than were Non-Scholars. Table 5 shows descriptive statistics and results of univariate significance tests for simple main effects.

Table 5. Main Effects of Scholar/Non-Scholar by Campus Leadership on Academic Engagement.

How Often Do You Engage in the Following Activities?[a]	Held campus leadership position						No campus leadership position					
	Scholar[b]		Non-Scholar[c]				Scholar[d]		Non-Scholar[e]			
	M	SD	M	SD	F	η^2	M	SD	M	SD	F	η^2
Work with students on school work	4.69	1.28	4.54	1.49	5.44*	.003	4.25	1.50	3.88	1.56	6.58*	.004
Discuss ideas with other students	4.69	1.23	4.57	1.42	3.81	.002	4.36	1.39	3.95	1.56	10.49**	.006
Discuss ideas with faculty	3.54	1.46	3.38	1.57	4.94*	.003	3.22	1.49	2.72	1.51	14.39**	.008
Study harder than expected	4.52	1.48	4.47	1.46	.60	0	4.50	1.42	4.06	1.54	15.75**	.009
Work on creative projects	3.35	1.79	3.37	1.76	.24	0	2.99	1.79	2.73	1.68	1.74	.001

Note. [a] All five items are reflected as stated in the survey. [b] N = 496. [c] N = 360. [d] N = 565. [e] N = 361. * p < .05; ** p < .01. Total N may not be equal to 1,829 due to incomplete data.

Leadership and Community Engagement

There were no three-way or two-way interactions. In terms of main effects, those who held a campus leadership position were involved more in community activities than those who did not (λ = .797; p < .0001; η^2 = .203), while Scholars were more likely to engage in community activities than Non-Scholars (λ = .968; p < .0001; η^2 = .032). Finally, females were more likely to participate in community activities than males (λ = .982; p < .0001; η^2 = .018). See Table 6 for descriptive statistics and results of univariate significance tests.

Table 6. Group Differences by Leadership Position, Scholar/Non-Scholar, and Gender on Community Engagement.

How Often Have You Participated in the Following Activities?	Campus Leadership Position							
	Yes			No				
	M	N	SD	M	N	SD	F	η^2
Fraternity/sorority events	2.68	848	1.49	1.94	919	1.17	136.68**	.072
Residence hall activities	3.17	854	1.27	2.39	919	1.19	185.95**	.096
Cultural group activities	3.71	855	1.23	2.85	925	1.29	207.73**	.106
Tutoring sessions	2.84	853	1.26	2.70	925	1.32	4.61*	.003
Community service activities	3.76	855	1.08	3.03	923	1.19	180.76**	.094
Religious/spiritual activities	3.24	855	1.44	2.86	925	1.45	30.17**	.017
	Scholars			Nonscholars				
	M	N	SD	M	N	SD	F	η^2
Fraternity/sorority events	2.26	1072	1.35	2.35	720	1.43	1.65	.001
Residence hall activities	2.79	1077	1.26	2.73	721	1.33	.88	0
Cultural group activities	3.40	1081	1.27	3.06	725	1.40	28.32**	.016
Tutoring sessions	2.90	1077	1.29	2.57	725	1.27	29.37**	.016
Community service activities	3.46	1076	1.16	3.27	727	1.23	11.67**	.007
Religious/spiritual activities	3.09	1079	1.44	2.98	727	1.48	3.17	.002
	Male			Female				
	M	N	SD	M	N	SD	F	η^2
Fraternity/sorority events	2.27	547	1.38	2.31	1245	1.38	.33	0
Residence hall activities	2.77	548	1.28	2.76	1250	1.29	.08	0
Cultural group activities	3.15	550	1.34	3.31	1256	1.33	6.47*	.004
Tutoring sessions	2.61	548	1.26	2.84	1254	1.30	11.69**	.007
Community service activities	3.21	548	1.20	3.46	1255	1.18	17.12**	.010
Religious/spiritual activities	2.87	551	1.47	3.13	1255	1.44	12.85**	.007

Note. * p < .05; ** p < .01. Total N may not be equal to 1,829 due to incomplete data.

Conclusions

There were no gender differences in the probability of receiving a GMS award. Furthermore, Scholars/Non-Scholars and females/males were equally likely to hold a campus leadership position.

There were no interactions among participation in campus leadership activities, Scholar/Non-Scholar, and gender on five sets of dependent variables except academic engagement. Concerning academic engagement, Scholars who did not hold a leadership position were more academically engaged than Non-Scholars who also did not hold such a position. First, in terms of internal locus of control, those who held a campus leadership position were more likely than those who did not to believe that they had control over their lives and that they could make their plans work. Scholars were more likely to believe that they could make things work as planned than Non-Scholars, and were less likely to believe in the importance of good luck. Males were more likely than females to believe that good luck was important in their lives.

Second, those who were involved in campus leadership activities had higher self-esteem than those who were not. Third, in terms of academic self-esteem, those who held a campus leadership position were more likely than those who did not to believe that they would become honor students and could make it through college. Females were more likely than males to believe that they could do well in college. Fourth, there was a two-way (participation in campus leadership activities × Scholar/Non-Scholar) interaction on academic engagement. Only among those who did not hold a campus leadership position were Scholars more academically engaged than were Non-Scholars. Those Scholars who were not involved in leadership activities discussed ideas from readings with faculty and fellow students more often and were more likely to work harder than Non-Scholars who did not hold a campus leadership position. Finally, main effects of participation in campus leadership activities, Scholar/Non-Scholar, and gender suggested that those students who held leadership positions, Scholars, and females were all more likely to engage in community activities.

Implications

Academic Focus

Some Gates Millennium Scholars appear to be off to a positive start in their academic careers, in that they are engaged in academic activities. The analyses revealed that among those students who did not hold campus leadership positions, Scholars are more academically engaged than are Non-Scholars. However, among those students who held campus leadership positions, there are no differences between Scholars and Non-Scholars concerning academic engagement. Scholars who were not engaged in leadership activities were more likely to discuss readings with fellow students and faculty and were more likely to work harder than Non-Scholars who were not involved in leadership activities.

These findings suggest that Scholars who may be strong in some areas may not be so in all areas. Therefore, it may be useful to find ways to help those Scholars not involved in leadership to become involved and encourage those Scholars focused on leadership to work harder and engage more in discussions with others. Strength in a range of noncognitive variables is the best way to ensure success in college and beyond.

This is a theme that can be addressed and further reinforced in the Leadership Conferences held for Scholars where academic leadership opportunities can be stressed. A focus on academic leadership and an emphasis on creating one's own opportunities can be a positive approach to working with the Scholars.

One opportunity is to help Scholars develop skills that will be useful to them in graduate and professional school (Sedlacek, 2003b). Negotiating the academic environment has been shown to correlate with the retention and graduation of students of color (Sedlacek, 1998, 2003a, 2004, in press). Another possibility is to help Scholars develop relationships with faculty through the academic orientation, because many students of color have a difficult time developing these supportive relationships that are so important to their success (Sedlacek, 1998, 2004, in press). Relationships with faculty can be encouraged around research and other scholarly activities that may interest both students and faculty. Male Scholars were more likely to believe in luck than female Scholars, indicating that more specific work with males is required to help them develop their ability to initiate the contacts they need.

Academic and Self-Esteem

Students who held leadership positions, females, and Scholars all had a greater tendency to feel that they would do well in higher education than their counterparts. This positive focus should be reinforced in the Leadership Conferences, with particular attention paid to males who are not as sure of their ability to be successful in school. Male Scholars present an interesting challenge; while they are academically focused, they are not as confident as female Scholars that they will do well in school. A positive self-concept has been shown to correlate with success for students of color in higher education (Sedlacek, 1998, 2003a, 2004, in press). Helping males to work with their strengths and academic interests should prove to be particularly fruitful programming for Scholars.

About half of all Scholars and Non-Scholars were engaged in leadership activities, suggesting that there are many Scholars who may need to develop some opportunities for leadership. Reasons for this could be that some Scholars do not see particular activities as ones of leadership, or are reluctant to say they are "leaders" in a culture where humility may be a strong value.

For example, only about one third of all American Indian/Alaska Native study participants were engaged in leadership activities, and only 24% of American Indian/Alaska Native Scholars reported being involved in leadership activities. This finding should be explored further. Perhaps the American Indian/Alaska Native students are engaged in tribal or community activities that they do not perceive as relevant to the context of the questionnaire, or they may not be inclined to report such activities. Many American Indian/Alaska Native applicants may not see calling attention to one's leadership activities as appropriate. Garrod and Larimore (1997) presented some evidence supporting this position based on reports of American Indian/Alaska Native college graduates. Of course, it also could be that many American Indian/Alaska Native students are not engaged in leadership activities.

Because leadership development is a goal of the GMS program, and leadership is a strong correlate of success for students of color, this finding should be explored further in the Leadership Conferences and in future studies. More questions on the forms of leadership in surveys or explorations through focus groups also would seem to be useful.

Community Involvement

Scholars, those students involved in leadership activities, and females were all more likely to be involved in community activities. Involvement in a community has been shown to correlate highly with the success of students of color in higher education. A major goal of the GMS program is to help develop persons of color who will be involved in their communities after leaving school. The finding that leadership activities were correlated with community involvement is particularly interesting. The Leadership Conferences for Scholars can emphasize this link and provide assistance to students who need to make that connection. Because females are more likely to be engaged in community activities, males may need some focused attention in the Leadership Conferences to link their leadership to community activities as well.

References

Allen, W. R. (1992). The color of success: African American college student outcomes at predominantly White and historically Black public colleges and universities. *Harvard Educational Review, 62* (1), 26-44.

Bowen, W. G., & Bok, D. (1998). *The shape of the river: Long-term consequences of considering race in college and university admissions.* Princeton: Princeton University Press.

Fuertes, J. N., & Sedlacek, W. E. (1993). Barriers to the leadership development of Hispanics in higher education. *National Association of Student Personnel Administrators Journal, 30,* 277-283.

Garrod, A., & Larimore, C. (Eds.). (1997). *First person, first peoples: Native American college graduates tell their stories.* Ithaca, NY: Cornell University Press.

Liu, W. M., & Sedlacek, W. E. (1999). Differences in leadership and co-curricular perception among male and female

Asian Pacific American college students. *Journal of The Freshman Year Experience, 11*, 93-114.

Sedlacek, W. E. (1996a). An empirical method of determining nontraditional group status. *Measurement and Evaluation in Counseling and Development, 28*, 200-210.

Sedlacek, W. E. (1996b). Employing noncognitive variables in admitting students of color. In I. H. Johnson & A. J. Ottens (Eds.), *Leveling the playing field: Promoting academic success for students of color* (pp. 79-91). San Francisco: Jossey-Bass.

Sedlacek, W. E. (1998). Admissions in higher education: Measuring cognitive and noncognitive variables. In D. J. Wilds & R. Wilson (Eds.), *Minorities in higher education 1997-98: Sixteenth annual status report* (pp. 47-71). Washington, DC: American Council on Education.

Sedlacek, W. E. (2003a). Alternative admissions and scholarship selection measures in higher education. *Measurement and Evaluation in Counseling and Development, 35*, 263-272.

Sedlacek, W. E. (2003b). Negotiating admissions to graduate and professional schools. In Farmer, V. L. (Ed.), *The Black student's guide to graduate and professional school success* (pp. 13-22). Westport, CT: Greenwood Publishing Group.

Sedlacek, W. E. (2004). *Beyond the big test: Noncognitive assessment in higher education*. San Francisco: Jossey-Bass.

Sedlacek, W. E. (in press). The case for noncognitive measures. In W. Camara & E. Kimmel (Eds.), *Choosing students: Higher education admission tools for the 21st century*. Mahwah, NJ: Lawrence Erlbaum.

Tracey, T. J., & Sedlacek, W. E. (1984a). Noncognitive variables in predicting academic success by race. *Measurement and Evaluation in Guidance, 16*, 172-178.

Tracey, T. J., & Sedlacek, W. E. (1984b). Using ridge regression with noncognitive variables by race in admissions. *College and University, 50*, 345-350.

Tracey, T. J., & Sedlacek, W. E. (1985). The relationship of noncognitive variables to academic success: A longitudinal comparison by race. *Journal of College Student Personnel, 26*, 405-410.

Tracey, T. J., & Sedlacek, W. E. (1987). Prediction of college graduation using noncognitive variables by race. *Measurement and Evaluation in Counseling and Development, 19,* 177-184.

Tracey, T. J., & Sedlacek, W. E. (1988). A comparison of White and Black student academic success using noncognitive variables: A LISREL analysis. *Research in Higher Education, 27,* 333-348.

Tracey, T. J., & Sedlacek, W. E. (1989). Factor structure of the Noncognitive Questionnaire-Revised across samples of Black and White college students. *Educational and Psychological Measurement, 49,* 637-648.

Webb, C. T., Sedlacek, W. E., Cohen, D., Shields, P., Gracely, E., Hawkins, M., & Nieman, L. (1997). The impact of nonacademic variables on performance at two medical schools. *Journal of the National Medical Association, 89* (3), 173-180.

White, C. J., & Shelley, C. (1996). Telling stories: Students and administrators talk about retention. In I. H. Johnson & A. J. Ottens (Eds.), *Leveling the playing field: Promoting academic success for students of color* (pp.15-34). San Francisco: Jossey-Bass.

CHAPTER 11

CONCLUSIONS AND IMPLICATIONS

Edward P. St. John

The Gates Millennium Scholars program is a major social experiment in providing supplemental financial support to high-achieving students of color. In the short term, research on this program can inform the policy discourse about student financial aid. During a period when federal student financial aid has fallen short of meeting financial need for low-income students who are prepared to enroll in higher education, these studies provide evidence about the effects of meeting financial need. GMS guarantees scholarship and grant aid sufficient to meet financial need, replacing the need to borrow and work excessively for thousands of college-qualified, low-income students of color. Over the longer term, the program aims to support emergence of a new generation of leadership as well as to encourage more students of color to enter fields in which they are currently and historically under-represented.

These studies in this volume provide a comprehensive overview of the GMS program and the early impact on educational opportunity during the first two years of operation. These early studies of the first two GMS cohorts provide a comprehensive view of the effects of the program that have substantial implications for public policy on student financial aid and college admissions.

265

This chapter reviews the findings to build an understanding of the program and its impact, considers how this research informs us relative to the three critical challenges facing research on equal opportunity, and considers the implications for education and public finance policy.

Understanding the Impact of GMS

In chapter 1, Merkowitz argues that these studies of the GMS program answer the critics of equal opportunity by demonstrating there is a large pool of prepared students of color who lack the financial resources needed to be successful in the academic domain. The fact that such a pool of students exists is demonstrated in this volume. However, critics of research on equal education might argue that since random assignment of treatment was not used to make awards within this population, the research falls short of meeting the new standard for education policy research.

Federal legislation has emphasized using experimental research with random assignment as a means of informing public policy on education policy, creating a new scientific standard for education research. Since the GMS program did not use random assignment with matched comparison groups, critics who believe in the primacy of this scientific approach to educational research might argue that GMS has fallen short of demonstrating the impact of meeting financial need. Indeed, critics could claim that since GMS was a natural experiment—and not a true experiment—that the results are not conclusive. However, before these findings are dismissed because of the devaluing of natural experiments, it is necessary to reconsider the comparability of the two groups—the nonawardees and the awardees.

The analyses in this volume used statistical methods appropriate for natural experimental design. The first stage of selection—requiring a minimum GPA and evidence of leadership—yielded a large group of academically eligible students who were largely comparable. The selected group had higher financial need (St. John & Chung, chapter 5), but this difference would only further demonstrate the importance of meeting financial need. The critical basis of comparability would be the academic criterion used in the first round of selection and the noncognitive measure used to select among eligible applicants. Before summarizing the findings on the impact of GMS, the comparability of the recipient and nonrecipient populations is examined below.

The Comparability of the Recipients and Nonrecipients

Most of the chapters in this volume analyzed the survey data collected for the 2000 and 2001 cohorts of GMS recipients, collected by the National Opinion Research Center (NORC). NORC surveyed all recipients and selected random samples of eligible nonrecipients (Nichols, Zimowski, Lodato, & Ghadialy, chapter 2). NORC surveyed two freshman cohorts (for 2000 and 2001), plus a cohort of continuing students, and a small group of graduate students, both for 2000. Sample weights were provided to correct for differences in the selection probabilities of the nonrecipients and for nonresponse to the survey on the part of recipients and nonrecipients. As long as sample weights and appropriate statistical controls are used, it should not matter that there were minor differences in the second round of selection (i.e., the application of the noncognitive criteria and the proof of Pell eligibility). These surveys meet the standards necessary for rigorous statistical research using the logic of quasi-experimental research.

The studies in this volume used the NORC surveys with appropriate statistical methods, but these adjustments do not completely overcome the lack of randomization. Five of these studies used the 2001 freshman cohort exclusively (Allen et al., chapter 4[1]; Trent et al., chapter 3; Hurtado et al., chapter 6, and Sedlacek & Sheu, chapters 7 and 10), one used the 2000 freshman cohort exclusively (St. John & Chung, chapter 5[2]), and one used the two freshman cohorts (2000 and 2001) and the continuing students in the 2001 cohort (St. John & Chung, chapter 9). A review of the key findings from the analyses that examined freshman cohorts reveals substantial comparability between the populations of GMS recipients and nonrecipients. Two of the findings merit particular note.

First, Trent et al. (chapter 3) compared the curriculum offered at the high schools attended by applicants in the 2001 cohort to the average offerings at the average high school in the U.S. They found that the applicants (i.e., GMS recipients and nonrecipients) attended high schools that had higher levels of curricular offerings than the average American high school. Not only did these findings indicate that applicants had more opportunity to prepare than the average U. S. student in the typical high school, but these analyses also indicated a high level of similarity within the sample. In other words, the applicants were somewhat advantaged academically, compared to the typical American high school students, because of the high schools they attended. They had attended better quality high schools, at least as measured by curricular offerings—indicating that the GMS recipients and nonrecipients differed from the majority of the U.S. high school students.

Second, the findings on Pell eligibility help reconcile these findings with what is known about the intent of the selection process. It is important to note that the GMS recipients had a higher rate of poverty (as indicated by percentage with Pell awards) than did the eligible nonrecipients (St. John & Chung, chapter 5) and other indicators of socioeconomic status (SES) (Hurtado et al., chapter 6). Thus there was a difference between GMS recipients and nonrecipients. However, this difference would not bias the results in favor of GMS—quite the opposite.

Given the substantial pool of qualified students of color, the awarding of aid based on noncognitive variables was a reasonable approach. The noncognitive variables emphasize racial justice rather than racial specific interest, as well as realistic views of self and a predisposition toward academic success (Sedlacek, 2004). Using these criteria to select awardees from among a group of highly qualified students had little in its real effect of differences between groups, as was similar to random assignment with respect to differences in academic qualification. In particular, the applicants (a group that included recipients and nonrecipients) were similar with respect to the high schools they attended (Trent et al., chapter 3) and their predisposition toward academic success (Sedlacek & Sheu, chapter 7).

The analyses in this volume do not assume a random experiment. The authors have used statistical methods that control for other factors influencing outcomes in carefully designed studies. However, there was no possible way to adjust fully for the lack of randomization. Instead, the program was designed to optimize opportunity rather than to conduct research. The program administration had the advantage of using a proven methodology for selection. They did not treat applicants as experimental subjects, an inherent design flaw in experiments using random assignment.

Lee and Clery (chapter 8) examined aid packages for a comparable population of Pell recipients. They concluded that GMS students attended private colleges and four-year colleges at higher rates that other Pell recipients, a pattern that was also evident when recipients and nonrecipients were compared (St. John & Chung, chapter 5). They also found substantial differences in student aid packages, clearly indicating that GMS reduced debt burden. This further verifies that GMS altered the relative use of loans and grants in the aid packages of recipients, a change that could help explain the program effects.

Impact on Academic Success

The overarching goal of the GMS program is "to increase access to higher education for outstanding African American, American Indian/Native American, Asian Pacific Islander American, and Hispanic American students who have shown leadership promise but have demonstrated financial need" (Merkowitz, chapter 1, p. 2). These studies had a substantial impact on the achievement of this goal, at least for the first two cohorts of GMS recipients.

First, Trent et al. (chapter 3) found that high school curriculum made a difference for students who were successfully screened into the GMS programs—the applicants included in the GMS recipient and nonrecipient groups in the 2001 cohort. They found substantial differences in the high school attended by these students, compared to the average American high school. They suggest a standard of preparation for academic access:

> In addition to schools offering the opportunity to learn at high levels, as indicated by the number of advanced placement courses they offer, it is also important, based on these data, that schools maintain a climate of fairness as referenced by equitable rates of participation in gifted programs and parity in rates of

representation in special education and expulsion, across racial and ethnic groups. (chapter 3, p. 66)

Second, Walter Allen et al. (chapter 4), based on their empirical analysis of data on the 2001 cohort, concluded that "applicants for the prestigious and lucrative Gates Millennium Scholarships are among the nation's most accomplished graduating high school seniors" (p. 94). Further, based on interviews with 56 GMS recipients, they found "students acknowledged the many barriers to postsecondary opportunities, but they were resilient, knowing that the alternative to enrollment was continued economic and social hardship" (p. 95). They found that some students actually had to petition their schools to take advanced high school courses, an indicator that the opportunities to prepare did not come easily in spite of attending high schools that provided these opportunities to some of their students.

Third, the analyses of financial access (St. John & Chung, chapter 5) found that the receipt of GMS awards substantially improved the odds that recipients would enroll in four-year colleges and private colleges, as well as improved the odds of persistence, controlling for the type of college attended and other factors. Even among this highly successful group of students, the addition of financial support provided by the scholarship program was associated with higher odds of success. Clearly finances had a substantial direct effect on improving educational opportunity.

Fourth, Hurtado et al. (chapter 6) found that GMS recipients and nonrecipients differed along many dimensions related to academic success. GMS students worked fewer hours, were more engaged with faculty, and had lower debt than their peers. In spite of being from higher poverty families, GMS students had greater opportunity to engage academically. This paper illustrates that the benefits of having scholarships to support financial need are manifold, improving the chances of benefiting from the academic environment college provides.

Fifth, Sedlacek and Sheu (chapter 7) found further evidence of academic success associated with GMS funding. They found that scholars benefited from the program through improved self-concept, realistic self-appraisal, understanding and navigation of social systems, increased community service, and better grades.

When interpreted in light of Hurtado's findings (chapter 6), Sedlacek's findings reveal GMS students benefited personally and academically from the opportunity to be more involved.

In combination, these analyses reveal that financial aid made a difference in the academic success for students of color who had prepared academically. Not only did they have the opportunity to attend better colleges, with greater odds of persisting, but they were more involved, and they developed personally and academically as a consequence of this involvement.

Further, these findings were evident from statistical analyses that controlled for the role of parents' education and other factors related to college enrollment. Therefore there should be little doubt about the influence of the GMS awards on the opportunity to attend better colleges, to persist, and to be successful academically in college.

Potential Long-Term Effects

The GMS program was designed to promote college access and to encourage a new generation of leadership in minority communities in the U.S. The program aims to encourage leadership: a) by providing financial incentives for students to prepare to enter fields in which people of color are underrepresented and b) through leadership seminars that focus on social issues and civic responsibility. These initial studies of the GMS program provide early evidence related to these long-term goals.

First, the analyses of major choices by students in the 2000 cohort revealed that debt burden was associated with major choices in education and math/science (St. John & Chung, chapter 8). Controlling for other variables that influence major choice, there was not a strong association between GMS and major choices. For the 2000 freshman cohort, GMS was negatively associated with the choice of engineering majors, while continuing students in the 2000 cohort were modestly more likely to choose education majors. Thus, as a general pattern, students who received funding and those who did not had about the same odds of choosing the four majors encouraged by the program. If there were random assignment, we would expect to have little measurable effect of major choice because both groups of applicants would have similar initial preferences. Further, the modest findings on the effects of

GMS on choices of undergraduate majors were largely independent of GMS funding. However, it remains possible that the program will influence the choice of graduate programs.

This study did find an association between debt and major choice. The amount of debt students reported was negatively associated with majors in science/math and education (St. John & Chung, chapter 8). Both of these findings raise questions about the role of debt and the consequences of overemphasizing debt in the financing of higher education, an issue examined further below.

Second, Sedlacek and Sheu (chapter 9) found evidence of leadership activities among both GMS recipients and nonrecipients among the 2000 freshman cohort. There were significant differences in leadership across race/ethnic groups. In particular, Native Americans were less likely to have participated in leadership behaviors, a finding that could be related to culture and traditions. Taken together, these findings illustrate that there is a great deal of similarity among the people selected for the GMS awards. Further, they show there is little observable relationship between being involved in GMS and leadership behavior during college. Whether or not there will be long-term effects of the civic engagement of students in this cohort remains an open question to be determined by future events.

Summing Up

The students who applied for GMS exhibited similar characteristics with respect to the qualities of the high schools they attended and their predisposition toward academic success. In spite of attending relatively high-quality high schools, some of these students overcame barriers within their high schools to gain access to advanced courses. While random assignment was not used to make awards within this pool of talented applicants, recipients and nonrecipients were similar with respect to academic indicators of background. However, a larger percentage of recipients was from low-income families (i.e., Pell eligible).

There were differences in the aid packages for GMS students compared to other qualified students who applied for GMS and to similarly qualified Pell recipients. The award of GMS raised the level of grant awards and reduced the debt burdens, changes in aid that were linked to college choice and persistence. GMS recipients had improved odds of enrolling in four-year colleges and private colleges, as well as increased probability of persistence as a result of the additional scholarship aid.

There were differences in the academic opportunities available to recipients and nonrecipients. In spite of having low incomes, GMS students were less likely to enroll in two-year colleges and more likely to enroll in private colleges. They were more likely to be engaged in their learning environments and to persist in college. Thus, academic opportunities were expanded as a consequence of receiving GMS awards.

However, the direct effects of GMS were not evident with respect to long-term goals of the program. Even though debt burden was associated with major choices, GMS awards per se were not consistently associated with major choices. And leadership behaviors were evident among both recipients and nonrecipients, with more substantial differences being related to race/ethnicity.

Policy Implications

The research on GMS has implications for state and federal policy on student financial assistance and college admissions. Below, I outline these implications in relation to the three tasks presented in the introduction.

Task 1: Assess the Impact of Public Policies on Equal Educational Opportunity

First, it was evident from the analyses in this volume that there is a relatively large pool of college-qualified students of color and that there is not currently sufficient student financial aid available to many of these students. The GMS program is a last-dollar award, topping off student grants after other grant and scholarship aid. If colleges and universities meet financial need, then GMS awards would only cover the amount of work-study and debt included in aid packages. In focus group interviews with the students in the 2000 cohort, it was evident that a minority of students received grant aid equaling this amount, but most students had substantially greater unmet need (St. John, 2003a). In fact at the other extreme some continuing students indicated that they had been working to pay off unsubsidized loans before they received a GMS award, indicating that students fulfill parental obligations for aid through work. The average grant on GMS for the first two cohorts equaled about $8,000. Thus, from both quantitative and qualitative sources we know that the current aid award falls substantially below the level of need for qualified students of color enrolled in both two-year and four-year colleges.

Thus, the substantial impact of GMS on enrollment in four-year colleges, persistence, and other academic outcomes (Hurtado et al., chapter 6; St. John & Chung, chapter 8) indicates that there would be less inequality in educational attainment if there were adequate grant aid for low-income students. Low-income students who were well prepared would have great opportunity to enroll in four-year colleges and to persist. Indeed, this research supports the conclusion of the Advisory Committee on Student Financial Assistance ([ACSFA] 2002) and others (Lee, 2004; Fitzgerald, 2004; Heller, 2004a; St. John, 2003b) whose analyses of federal databases reveal that large numbers of academically prepared students have been denied the opportunity to enroll in four-year colleges due to inadequate public funding of student financial aid programs.

In addition, the studies in volume 20 of *Readings on Equal Education* provide further evidence that noncognitive variables can be used in the second stage of the selection processes for admissions as well as for scholarships. In particular, noncognitive variables (Sedlacek, 2004; Sedlacek & Sheu, chapter 7) can enable colleges and universities to select diverse students and students who appreciate diversity without explicitly considering race/ethnicity as part of the selection process.

If the U. S. is to move past the need for affirmative action in college admissions over the next quarter century or so, it will be necessary to do so through the use of new measures. It is crucial to understand that other variables in addition to achievement are important in predicting academic success. Appreciation of living in a diverse world is among the type of criteria that merits consideration in the final stages of admission and selection for scholarships, beyond a predefined set of admission criteria, such as grade point averages and test scores, can also be indexed for school contexts (Goggin, 1999; St. John, Simmons, & Musoba, 2002).

Task 2: Examine Effects of Public Policies on Excellence and Efficiency as well as Equity

Too often, equity considerations are juxtaposed as being in opposition to excellence. For example, Chester Finn (2001) has argued that adequate funding for student financial aid should be a lower priority than K-12 reform. Such arguments are based on valuing one policy goal (i.e., improvement in academic preparation) over others (i.e., equal access for students who are prepared) when setting priorities for public funding. To avoid this pitfall in public finance we need a balanced approach to policy analysis, one that considers equity, excellence, and efficiency, rather than pitting one or two of these aims against each other (St. John, 2003b). Three issues must be balanced when considering the role of public policy in promoting college access.

First, the GMS studies have substantial implications for the debate about academic preparation. NCES research has reported a high correlation between academic preparation—as measured by high school courses, grades, and test scores—and college enrollment and persistence (NCES, 1997a, 1997b,). Not only did these analyses overlook the role of student aid (ACSFA, 2003; St. John, 2003), but they overlooked a large number of qualified students who did not have the opportunity to enroll in college. This volume provides further evidence that there are college-qualified, low-income students, including students of color, who are denied the opportunity to enroll in four-year colleges and to persist in college due to inadequacies in federal, state, and institutional grant aid.

In addition to revealing limitations of the narrowly framed academic preparation argument, these studies of the GMS program reveal that finances have a direct effect on achievement and academic success. These studies clearly indicate that students become more involved in academic life and are more successful academically as a consequence of GMS funding (Allen et al., chapter 3; Hurtado et al., chapter 6; Sedlacek & Sheu, chapter 7; St. John & Chung, chapters 5 and 8). The evidence is substantial and overwhelming: student academic success in college results from having financial need met.

Second, these same results reveal that arguments against investing sufficiently in student financial aid promote a false efficiency, a reduction in costs that have high unintended costs (as defined by St. John, 1994). The failure of states and the federal government to invest sufficiently in student financial assistance is often rationalized based on other priorities such as academic preparation (e.g., Finn, 2001; Paige, 2003), but these arguments ignore the substantial effects of student aid on both academic success and equalizing opportunity for students who prepare. While it certainly costs less per student to use grants rather than loans (McPherson & Schapiro, 1997; St. John, 2003a), lower cost does not mean greater efficiency. Given the fact that adequate aid enables low-income students to attain the academic goals promoted by opponents of funding student grants, these arguments are based on false claims about the efficient and effective use of tax dollars.

If reductions in costs of education programs are a goal for conservatives, then they need to seek more efficient ways of reducing costs. If a finite amount of dollars is available for higher education, then the alternative of higher tuition and higher grants should be considered, along with higher loans (St. John, 2003b). If one quarter of the tax revenue saved by substituting tuition charges for tax dollars had be reinvested in student aid in the 1990s, much of the inequality in financial access would have been mitigated (St. John, Chung, Musoba, Simmons, Wooden, & Mendez, 2004).

Task 3: Rethink the Role of Policy When Considering Implications of Policy Research

Clearly it is critical that states and the federal government find better ways to finance higher education, approaches that ensure that financial need is met for the lowest income students. The evidence from the studies in this volume is compelling, if not overwhelming.

The average cost per student in GMS was about $7,000, but the gap in public grant funding may be less than this amount (Lee & Clery, chapter 8). Estimates of the shortfall in federal grant aid vary. Some groups have argued that it would be necessary to double the value of Pell grants to reach the purchasing power they had in the 1970s (ACSFA, 2002), which would mean Pell grants should be increased over their current levels by about $4,000 dollars. If we assume that self-help (the combination of work and loans) should fill about half of the gap, then the reasonable target for increase in need-based government grants would be about $4,000. If the target level was totally meeting need, or removing the use of the loans for the highest need students, then the target for increased aid would be about $8,000.

If about one-quarter of college students are eligible for the need-based grants, then an additional funding amount of between $1,000 per FTE would be needed if public sector tuition increased $4,000 to fund a similar increase in the maximum award for state grants. Similarly, additional funding of $2,000 per student would be necessary if there was an $8,000 increase in public tuition. If the only source of additional funding were tuition, assuming static state support per student of public colleges, then tuition would need to rise by $1,250 and $2,500 over current levels.[3] The questions are: Will more states seize the moral responsibility to meet this minimum equity standard in the public financing of higher education? And will the federal government integrate incentives into the Leveraging Educational Assistance Partnership (LEAP) program? These options have been proposed as an alternative to full federal funding of Pell grants (St. John, 2003b; St. John, Chung, et al., 2004), an option that seems extremely remote.

However, the funding for need-based grants should not be viewed as an obligation of colleges and universities. It is a public responsibility to ensure equal opportunity in the United States. When public colleges take on this responsibility for the state, they are imposing a system of taxation in a society that has chosen not to take the approach, a questionable practice. When colleges invest in grants and scholarships they usually choose to make strategic investments to improve the portfolio of students who enroll rather than commit to meeting financial need for all admitted students (McPherson & Schapiro, 1997). This approach is not consistent with the goal of equal educational opportunity that used to be central to education policy in the U.S. But the goal of equal educational opportunity is consistent with the U.S. and state constitutions, so these governments have legal responsibility for ensuring both equity and adequacy in education. While the nature of equitable and adequate public funding is being redefined in this period of growing privatization and accountability, it is possible to achieve greater equity and improved excellence (achievement outcomes) by adapting the systems of public finance, possibly in response to litigation aimed at ensuring equity in public finance policy.

This research on the GMS program has implications for the public financing of higher education. States and the federal government have the moral obligation—and may have the legal obligation[4]—to fund need-based grants at a minimally adequate level for residents within states, possibly with additional support from the federal government. While it may be feasible to litigate in states on inequalities created by state merit aid programs (Heller, 2004b; St. John & Chung, 2004), it is unlikely that such a legal strategy can be used to secure equity in state funding for higher education, a legal requirement that states equalize financial access to four-year state universities regardless of income. While such court decisions might reduce financial inequalities in educational opportunity, it is doubtful that there is sufficient legal basis for such litigation. However, policy studies, including this volume, illustrate that there is a definite inequality embedded in current public finance policies.

Conclusion

As a large-scale national experiment in providing adequate need-based aid, the GMS program provides compelling evidence of the inequalities that have resulted from inadequate state and federal funding of need-based grant programs. In combination, these studies document that subsidizing students to meet financial need substantially improves the odds that high-achieving, low-income students will have the opportunity to enroll and persist in four-year colleges, as well as have greater engagement and academic success during college. The recommitment to ensuring equal educational opportunity is within the financial means of states and the federal government, even given the tax revenue constraints (St. John, Chung, et al., 2004). Instead, the priority has been placed on having students pay a larger share of college costs without regard for the new inequalities created by these public finance polices.

Over the longer term, the GMS program may influence a new generation of leadership among people of color in the United

States, as well as facilitate entry of more minorities into professions in which they are underrepresented. It is too early to pass judgment on these long-term effects, but the early evidence suggests that the program could have substantial impact.

More generally, these studies illustrate that research on large natural experiments can inform public policy on education, including state and federal policy on the public financing of higher education. Given the large scale of public retreat from programs that ensure equal opportunity for low-income students in the U.S., it is crucial that foundations and other public interest groups engage in a new generation of philanthropic programs that demonstrate possible new pathways to improve education opportunity.

During the past two decades, education policy in the U.S. has emphasized academic excellence, but overlooked or even ignored the equal rights of low-income individuals who live up to the new educational standards. The research on GMS illustrates that highly qualified students are being left behind because they cannot afford to enroll in four-year colleges or to persist if they do enroll. This basic and fundamental inequality, a relatively recent development in the U. S., is not consistent with the legal and moral definitions of equal rights that evolved in the twentieth century. If this inequality is perpetuated, then future generations of Americans will be schooled in a country that makes a false promise to its citizens. The claim being made by education agencies in the U.S. that students who prepare for college will have the opportunity to attend is false in most states—a general finding (ACSFA, 2002, 2003; St. John, 2003b; St. John, Chung, et al., 2004) further confirmed by the studies in this volume. This basic and fundamental inequality will remain so, unless the basic rights to college access are recognized by states and the federal government and steps are taken to remedy the very substantial inequalities that are now so evident.

Notes

1. In addition to using the 2001 freshman cohort, Allen et al. (chapter 4) also included an analysis of focus group interviews.
2. The 2000 cohort was used in this analysis because the noncognitive criterion played a less direct role in selection given the staged approached used in the first year (see chapter 5).

3. These metrics applied the equity standard proposed by St. John, Chung, et al. (2004). Currently only four states meet or are very close to the equity standard.

4. *White v. Engler*, a case that calls into question the legality of merit scholarships in Michigan (St. John & Chung, in press), suggests the equity clauses may provide a basis for litigation aimed at ensuring equal opportunity in college access.

References

Advisory Committee on Student Financial Assistance. (2002). *Empty promises: The myth of college access in America.* Washington, DC: Author.

Finn, C. E., Jr. (2001, February 21). College isn't for everyone. *USA Today*, p. 14A.

Fitzgerald, B. (2004). Federal financial aid and college access. In E. P. St. John (Ed.), *Readings on equal education: Vol. 19, Public policy and college access: Investigating the federal and state roles in equalizing postsecondary opportunity* (pp. 1-28). New York: AMS Press.

Goggin, W. J. (1999, May). A "merit-aware" model for college admissions and affirmative action. *Postsecondary education opportunity newsletter* (pp. 6-12). The Mortenson Research Seminar on Public Policy Analysis of Opportunity for Postsecondary Education.

Heller, D. E. (2004). NCES research on college participation: A critical analysis. In E. P. St. John (Ed.), *Readings on equal education: Vol. 19, Public policy and college access: Investigating the federal and state roles in equalizing postsecondary opportunity* (pp. 29-64). New York: AMS Press.

Heller, D. E. (2004). State merit scholarship programs. In E. P. St. John (Ed.), *Readings on equal education: Vol. 19, Public policy and college access: Investigating the federal and state roles in equalizing postsecondary opportunity* (pp. 99-108). New York: AMS Press.

Lee, J. B. (2004). Access revisited: A preliminary reanalysis of NELS. In E.P. St. John, (Ed.), *Readings on equal education: Vol. 19, Public policy and college access: Investigating the federal and state roles in equalizing postsecondary opportunity* (pp. 87-96). New York: AMS Press.

McPherson, M. S., & Shapiro, M. O. (1997). *The student aid game: Meeting need and rewarding talent in American higher education.* Princeton, NJ: Princeton University Press.

National Center for Education Statistics. (1997a). *Access to higher postsecondary education for the 1992 high school graduates,* NCES 98-105, by Lutz Berkner & Lisa Chavez. Project Officer: C. Dennis Carroll. Washington, DC: Author.

National Center for Education Statistics. (1997b.) *Confronting the odds: Students at risk and the pipeline to higher education.* NCES 98-094, by Laura J. Horn. Project officer: C. Dennis Carroll. Washington, DC: Author.

Paige, R. (2003, Jan. 10). More spending is not the answer. Opposing view: Improving quality of schools calls for high standards, accountability. *USA Today,* p. 11A.

Sedlacek, W. E. (2004). *Beyond the big test: Noncognitive assessment in higher education.* San Francisco: Jossey-Bass.

St. John, E. P. (1994). *Prices, productivity and investment: Assessing financial strategies in higher education.* ASHE-ERIC Higher Education Report No. 3. Washington, DC: The George Washington University, School of Education and Human Development.

St. John, E. P. (2003a). *Diverse pathways: The roles of financial aid and student involvement in expanding educational opportunity.* Prepared for the Bill & Melinda Gates Foundation. Bloomington, IN: Author.

St. John, E. P. (2003b). *Refinancing the college dream: Access, equal opportunity, and justice for taxpayers.* Baltimore: Johns Hopkins University Press.

St. John, E. P., & Chung, C. G. (2004). Merit and equity: Rethinking award criteria in the Michigan scholarship program. In E. P. St. John & M. D. Parsons (Eds.), *Public funding of higher education: Changing contexts and new rationales.* Baltimore: Johns Hopkins University Press.

St. John, E. P., Chung, C. G., Musoba, G. D., Simmons, A. B., Wooden, O. S., & Mendez, J. (2004). *Expanding college access: The impact of state finance strategies.* Indianapolis: The Lumina Foundation for Education.

St. John, E. P., Simmons, A. B., & Musoba, G. D. (2002). Merit-aware admissions in public universities: Increasing diversity. *Thought & Action, 27* (2), 35-46.

White v. Engler, 188 F. Supp. 2d 730 (E.D. Mich. 2001).